1-TO-1 LEARNING

Laptop Programs That Work

SECOND EDITION

Pamela Livingston

International Society for Technology in Education
EUGENE, OREGON • WASHINGTON, DC

1-TO-1 LEARNING
Laptop Programs That Work
SECOND EDITION

Pamela Livingston

Director of Book Publishing
Courtney Burkholder

Acquisitions Editor
Jeff V. Bolkan

Production Editors
Lanier Brandau, Lynda Gansel

Production Coordinator
Rachel Bannister

Graphic Designer
Signe Landin

Copy Editor
Anna Raitt

Proofreader
Kathleen Hamman

Book and Cover Design
Kim McGovern

Book Production
Tracy Cozzens

Library of Congress Cataloging-in-Publication Data

Livingston, Pamela.
   1-to-1 learning : laptop programs that work / Pamela Livingston. — 2nd ed.
     p. cm.
   Includes bibliographical references.
   ISBN 978-1-56484-254-1
   1. Education—Data processing. 2. Educational technology. 3. Internet in education. 4. Laptop computers. I. Title. II. Title: One-to-one learning.
   LB1028.43.L58 2009
   371.33'4—dc22

2009001333

Second Edition
ISBN: 978-1-56484-254-1

Printed in the United States of America

International Society for Technology in Education (ISTE)
Washington, DC, Office:
   1710 Rhode Island Ave. NW, Suite 900, Washington, DC 20036-3132
Eugene, Oregon, Office:
   180 West 8th Ave., Suite 300, Eugene, OR 97401-2916
Order Desk: 1.800.336.5191
Order Fax: 1.541.302.3778
Customer Service: orders@iste.org
Book Publishing: books@iste.org
Book Sales and Marketing: booksmarketing@iste.org
Web: www.iste.org
Photo credits: iStock

ABOUT ISTE

The International Society for Technology in Education (ISTE) is the trusted source for professional development, knowledge generation, advocacy, and leadership for innovation. A nonprofit membership association, ISTE provides leadership and service to improve teaching, learning, and school leadership by advancing the effective use of technology in PK–12 and teacher education.

Home of the National Educational Technology Standards (NETS), the Center for Applied Research in Educational Technology (CARET), and ISTE's annual conference (formerly known as the National Educational Computing Conference, or NECC), ISTE represents more than 100,000 professionals worldwide. We support our members with information, networking opportunities, and guidance as they face the challenge of transforming education. To find out more about these and other ISTE initiatives, visit our website at **www.iste.org**.

As part of our mission, ISTE Book Publishing works with experienced educators to develop and produce practical resources for classroom teachers, teacher educators, and technology leaders. Every manuscript we select for publication is carefully peer-reviewed and professionally edited. We value your feedback on this book and other ISTE products. E-mail us at **books@iste.org**.

ABOUT THE AUTHOR

Pamela Livingston has held computer support positions at Pan American World Airways and Chemical Bank and served as a project leader at PC Magazine Labs and as technical editor for *PC Sources* magazine. Fifteen years ago, she moved to education technology and served as director of technology for several independent schools—leading information technology, academic, and administrative computing programs and teaching K–12 computer classes.

Currently, she is the educational technology analyst at the headquarters of EdisonLearning, Inc., furthering technology integration for EdisonLearning schools around the United States. Livingston is also an adjunct professor at Chestnut Hill College in Philadelphia, teaching a graduate course she designed on emerging technology in today's classrooms. A frequent presenter and keynote speaker at NECC, the Lausanne Collegiate Laptop Institute, and other venues, she has written for *PC Magazine, PC Sources* magazine, *Learning & Leading with Technology, Technology & Learning,* and *Digital Directions.* She also writes a monthly column for HotChalk. Livingston holds a BS in computer systems from the City University of New York and an MS in education and technology from Chestnut Hill College.

Acknowledgments

I want to thank the many educators nationwide and internationally who have given generously of their time, have written thoughtfully about 1-to-1, and have provided such important insights into the possibilities and challenges of 1-to-1 implementation. A full list would be very long; however, every single teacher, administrator, and leader mentioned in this book or who has written for this book has my utmost admiration and respect.

That said, I particularly would like to thank Dr. Dave Berque for writing an entire chapter on tablet PCs. I can think of no one so professionally qualified, knowledgeable, and dedicated to tablet PCs as Dr. Berque. It was an honor to have Dr. Berque write this chapter and a pleasure to work with him.

I would like to thank my employer, EdisonLearning, Inc., for its continued support of my writing and especially to acknowledge my supervisor, Mike Williams, for his solid support and insightful mentorship.

Additionally, I would like to repeat my appreciation of the administrators and teachers of The Peck School, my former employer, for their support, wisdom, and help.

Finally, I want to thank the International Society for Technology in Education for its support of this book.

Dedication

This new edition of *1-to-1 Learning* is dedicated to my daughter, Bryce—a phenomenal writer who inspires me always to take the high road.

CONTENTS

PREFACE

My Story

In May 2004, I graduated from Chestnut Hill College in Philadelphia with an MS in education and technology. My thesis project was a qualitative case study of the technology use and skills of seventh-grade students at The Peck School in Morristown, New Jersey, where I was head of technology. Truly a labor of love, this project allowed me to interview bright, articulate students to find out how they studied and learned with computers.

Seventh- and eighth-grade students at The Peck School have enjoyed 1-to-1 access to laptop computers since 1998. As I pursued my thesis research, I began to wonder what influence this ubiquitous access was having on students' studying and learning. I also wondered how having a powerful "digital assistant" of their very own might be affecting their learning. Might 1-to-1 access be enhancing the development of metacognitive thinking skills? By the end of my research, I was convinced that this was, indeed, the case for the small sample of students I interviewed.

As educators, we create and assess academic work and provide students with tools to do that work. My research brought home to me the paramount importance of those tools and the impact they can have on student performance. Why shouldn't we give students the best and most effective tools to do the work we want them to accomplish? Even more important, if we give students advanced tools and observe how they use them to organize and challenge themselves, what will this tell us about teaching and learning that we haven't even envisioned?

These are the insights and questions that led me to write *1-to-1 Learning: Laptop Programs That Work*. My experience writing this book and interviewing scores of people who have planned and implemented 1-to-1 programs across the country has only reinforced my convictions about the cognitive and educational values of ubiquitous access to technology. Putting a computer in the hands of every child—24 hours a day, 7 days a week—is key to meaningful, effective integration of technology in education.

INTRODUCTION TO
THE FIRST EDITION

AFTER YEARS SPENT REVIEWING COUNTLESS STUDIES and interviewing scores of education technologists from the United States, Canada, Europe, and Australia, I find myself returning to the same question all educators tend to ask when confronted with a new education technology or practice: Why?

Why write a book about laptop programs in K–12 schools? The answer comes back clear as a bell: because school laptop programs can make a difference in learning. It's because we—as educators, parents, and adult learners—can partner with children through technology to help them become better thinkers and problem solvers. If the front-end device used for information gathering and analysis can help streamline information processing, then it stands to reason that the vital back-end problem-solving and critical thinking can happen more quickly and easily.

Nearly every study I read showed that laptops can increase student motivation and engagement, and when motivation to learn increases, so does the retention of that learning. When we see our students immersed in a sea of technology—as they so clearly are in our 21st-century world—it's our duty as educators to help them navigate it smoothly, effectively, and purposefully. It's a responsibility we cannot avoid and a job that's made much easier when all students have their own "digital assistant."

What Is a Digital Assistant?

Throughout this book, I use the term *digital assistant* (or sometimes *learning assistant*) to refer to laptop and handheld computers used for learning. My reasons for doing so can be found in an article titled "Student Laptop Computers in Classrooms—Not Just a Tool" (Nair, 2000). In it, Prakash Nair states,

> I have started referring to computers in classrooms as 'digital teaching assistants,' . . . [my use of this term] is derived from what experts say and from my own personal observation of the way children interact with computers. It is also an accurate description of what computers do for children within and outside the classroom.

Nair goes on to describe how a tool can help with the completion of an activity but how an "assistant" can support thinking and learning in a much broader way than a tool can. A tool has a single, primary purpose. For example, a hammer is expressly designed for pounding nails. Computers, on the other hand, can serve myriad purposes: writing, reading, studying, learning, researching, organizing, making assumptions, solving problems, publishing, presenting, connecting ideas, and creating new ways of understanding. Thus, the importance and usefulness of laptop computers for learning goes far beyond the single purpose implied by those who would call them "just a tool."

A digital assistant can serve as a database for work and files, a sketchpad and planner for projects, a publisher for reports and papers, and a conduit for research that provides access to online resources. It's a communication facilitator for e-mail, instant messaging, and blogging; a calculator and what-if analyzer of data and information; and a digital processor for photos and video. It's a device that facilitates a student's thinking, analyzing, presenting, writing, reading, researching, revising, communicating, questioning, proposing, creating, surmising, and publishing.

A digital assistant offers much more functionality than any single tool, even a Swiss army knife. Students armed with digital assistants have an advantage over those students without them. They can expand on their studies, demonstrate and communicate their understanding and learning, retrieve and process data and information, communicate more precisely, and create presentations and products with greater substance and style.

Who Needs a Digital Assistant?

The world as a whole increasingly requires flexible, adaptable synthesizers of information who are discerning users of technology tools. Those who are fluent in the kinds of interconnected, collaborative work processes that these tools support and encourage have a distinct advantage in today's job market. There's a reason that terms such as *information technology* have gradually replaced the old term *data processing:* data is just raw numbers and facts, but information is what is needed to solve problems, connect ideas, make decisions, and create new products and services. Information is data that has been made useful and usable for whatever comes next.

We need to provide our children with the ability to transform raw data and facts into information that can be put to use. The generation of students—the so-called "millennials" born from 1982 to 2000—are already swimming daily in a sea of ubiquitous media and technology. So it only makes sense that we seek to use those same technologies to support that process.

Mike Muir, one of the architects of Maine's successful statewide laptop program, is among many experts who believe that students today are innately multitaskers. According to this view, the current generation of students finds it very natural to learn in an environment where they're constantly surrounded by multiple inputs and sources of information. Most teachers, on the other hand, are unitaskers. They view this kind of multimedia environment as being distracting and not conducive to learning. This difference, Dr. Muir says (personal communication, October 2, 2005), holds both sides back:

> Many of us (teachers) are unitaskers—we need to focus on one thing at a time and feel frustrated and anxious when we're being forced to do too many things at once. When we see our students working on more than one thing at a time, we worry that they aren't paying attention, or that they'll shut down because they have too much going on at one time. But many of our students are multitaskers, who comfortably work on multiple things at the

same time. The mistake we sometimes make, however, is thinking that we are helping them by having them focus on only one thing at a time, when in reality a multitasker can feel as frustrated and anxious when asked to focus on only one thing as a unitasker does when asked to perform multiple things at once.

Are we as adults trying to adapt today's children to a unitasking mode of learning that is unnatural for them to emulate? Outside of school, millennials are constantly using cell phones, texting their friends, listening to music, playing multiuser games online—in other words, accessing a broad range of media and information all at the same time. Can we hold them back and make them more like us? *Should* we hold them back and insist that they learn the way we've learned when multitasking clearly works well for them?

Some say today's multitasking millennials can share computers and still enjoy all the benefits computers have to offer. Banks of four or five computers have been installed in many classrooms around the country, and most schools have computer labs. So don't we already have enough computers for writing papers and getting projects done?

Here's the rub with that argument: because we've long known that students need to work at their own pace and in their own way, both at school and at home, no one expects students to stand in line or adhere to a schedule for using technologies such as books, pencils, or calculators. However, that's precisely what we're asking them to do when it comes to computers, the most powerful education technology of all. We provide (or require parents to provide) books and paper and writing utensils and expect each student to bring these tools to class and be ready to work. Since computers can do so much more than these tools to support learning, why have we been so slow to make them available to every student in every classroom? Yes, computers are costly, but is cost really the most important issue here? Or is our reluctance to embrace computers in the classroom a function of our generational inability to understand the needs and learning habits of the millennials?

If students are given access to computers only once or twice a week, in a separate room and without all the resources of the classroom, technology integration is simply not possible. If computers are something extra used occasionally for curricular enhancement and as rewards for good behavior, technology integration is not possible. Technology integration—not technology for technology's sake, but technology integration—isn't possible unless it's woven appropriately into everything a student or teacher does in the classroom. True technology integration requires 1-to-1 access—the same level of access to technology that most students take for granted outside of school and that our plugged-in world increasingly requires of all its citizens.

Ubiquitous Computing

Many experts believe that ubiquitous computing is the answer to our current generation of information-craving students. The term *ubiquitous computing* was coined in 1993 by the late Mark Weiser, who defined it as follows:

> Ubiquitous computing is the method of enhancing computer use by making many computers available throughout the physical environment, but making them effectively invisible to the user.

Weiser's initial vision involved the use of "tabs" that could be programmed to access information and help with school and home life, but this isn't exactly what has happened. We aren't waking up to view "electronic trails" from our neighbor's comings and goings (as Weiser described), nor do we look around our office for the visual tab displaying "fresh coffee." Weiser imagined multiple computing devices all around our environment that would be transparent and unobtrusive. He envisioned several stages, or "tiers," of this future, calling the final one "calm computing." Shortly before his death in 1999, he indicated that we were just beginning to move toward this final tier.

While we aren't there yet, most of us would agree that computers are a ubiquitous presence in our everyday lives. Students who learn how to use computers effectively when they're young are more successful when it comes to higher education or securing a job. Even now, it's difficult to find a position in the workforce that doesn't require some form of computer use.

Elisabeth Fraser, my predecessor as head of technology at The Peck School, relates (personal communication, August 6, 2005) that the graduate students she now hires are never more than five feet away from their computers, which they use for communication, thinking, analyzing, writing, and researching. This kind of ubiquitous use, and the comfort level and confidence in technology that it requires, doesn't just happen overnight. If we encourage our children to develop these skills early in their academic lives, think how much better prepared they'll be for every leg of their educational and occupational journeys.

The advantages of giving students a laptop computer for home and school use—24 hours a day, 7 days a week—are many. It means no more waiting in line for access, no more lab scheduling bottlenecks, no more need to move to another room or building to do a research project or Internet search. Dr. Muir described to me (personal communication, August 4, 2005) how one group of Maine students used their laptops to learn about Christopher Columbus' voyages to America. One student who wondered how big the ships were went online to find out, then showed the results to all the other students. They then went out to the hallway and mapped out the approximate size of the three ships. They were amazed at how small these three ships that carried over 90 people across the ocean really were and gained new insights into the communicable diseases suffered by the passengers during the voyage. This student-led teachable moment would not have been possible if the student had not had his own computer readily available in the classroom.

Most of the laptop programs described in this book allow students to take the computers home with them, though some schools and districts provide laptops only during the school day. In my opinion, however, the magic numbers are 1-to-1 and 24/7. When the laptop becomes a constant companion and a primary resource for information and communication, students become vested in caring for it and learning how to use it more effectively.

While not all the details of Weiser's vision have come to pass, few would argue that we have, indeed, entered into a ubiquitous computing age. Today, we can use the Internet to find information on nearly everything—and almost instantly. We can collaborate with colleagues in real time or asynchronously, view shared information on SmartBoards, and use wikis and blogs to communicate and co-create with people we haven't even met. Our cars and traffic lights can speak to us; all our banking can be done online; and we can access maps, books, and online shopping malls from coffee shops, airports, and hotel rooms. Ubiquitous computing is already here, and it's critical that we, as educators, respond to the changes it has made—and will continue to make—in the lives of our students.

Getting to the Thinking Faster

Educators want students to synthesize information, not just repeat it back. We want them to think, not just memorize facts and demonstrate skills. Since the typical school day is divided into fairly short segments of time, ranging from 35 minutes to one hour, helping students absorb facts more efficiently and encouraging more higher-order thinking in the classroom is a challenge teachers in all content areas face. Providing 1-to-1 access to computers can definitely help.

If it takes 40 minutes for an environmental science class to gather weather data from atlases and almanacs and turn it into pencil and paper charts, how much time is left to think about what the chart is saying? How much time is there to consider "what if" scenarios, such as, "What if the mean temperature rose by ten degrees?" Equipped with a laptop computer, access to the Internet, and a spreadsheet/graphing program, however, students can quickly find and analyze current data. They can plug that data into spreadsheet templates and prepare charts for half a dozen different "what if" scenarios in the same amount of time it would take to make a pencil and paper chart. Personal digital assistants allow students to get to the thinking faster.

This is an important idea because it helps answer critics who ask, "Why spend money on computers for students?" Supplying every student with a digital assistant provides a real, tangible benefit. Almost everyone will agree that a word-processed paper trumps a handwritten one, if only because it makes revisions so much easier. Think of the ol' days when students had to handwrite or type every paper for every course. Every time they wanted to make a change or correct an error, they had to start all over again if they wanted to present a clean copy to the teacher. Multiply that by every writing assignment or project a student worked on over the course of 12 years, and the result was hours and hours of tedious copying, most of it resulting in no appreciable new insights or learning.

With a computer, a student has immediate access to search engines, spreadsheets, online databases, and myriad other resources. Computers can help students gather and analyze information; synthesize, draft, and revise the response to it; and present the results in a clean, professional document that is much easier for teachers to read and evaluate. Computers help students become infinitely more productive, providing extra time for them to develop the higher order thinking skills that we all agree are crucial to success in higher education and beyond. Computers empower students to get to the thinking faster.

Who Should Read This Book?

1-to-1 Learning has been written for administrators, teachers, parents, researchers, and anyone whose school or school district is considering a laptop program. It can also serve the needs of educators who work in schools or districts that already have a laptop program but want to see what other schools have done and are doing. This book provides teachers with dozens of real-world stories describing how laptops have been used to transform teaching and learning. Parents can discover how students use laptops to deepen their learning and expand their horizons. Administrators will find the sections on planning, professional development, and logistics particularly useful as they steward their own laptop programs. Anyone considering a laptop program will find a host of anecdotes, ideas, lessons learned, and challenges overcome, each of which will be helpful as decisions are made.

Several research studies on the design and implementation of 1-to-1 laptop programs have been incorporated into the guidelines presented in this book. You'll find studies by Rockman *et al,* Maine's Learning Technology Initiative, the Laptops for Learning Task Force, the Laptop Initiative at Athens Academy in Georgia, Beaufort County (South Carolina) School District, EDC's Center for Children and Technology, Henrico County (Virginia) School District, and Michigan's Freedom to Learn. These studies are referenced in Appendix B. You can also find links to nearly every study by going to the Ubiquitous Computing Evaluation Consortium website at www.ubiqcomputing.org. It's a great, well-organized starting point that contains research, templates, and wisdom from laptop pioneers.

As with any new education initiative, many people work on the front lines, charged with coordinating the day-to-day effort that goes into providing ubiquitous access to students. I've conducted interviews with several dozen leaders whose generous and honest responses form the basis for most of the stories and examples in this book. The many different ways educators have planned and carried out laptop programs in schools both large and small is inspiring and rich with insights into the possibilities of 1-to-1.

Is 1-to-1 Right for You?

A laptop program is an expensive, complex undertaking, with no real end in sight once you commit to the journey. Most of us who have started down this road believe that the considerable time and energy we've put into our programs have been well worth it.

This doesn't necessarily mean that a laptop program is right for every school and every district. Only those with a firm grasp of a school's or district's mission, culture, and direction can determine if providing 1-to-1 access is the right thing for their students and teachers.

One thing you can count on, however: change will happen if you provide every student and teacher with a laptop. Learning from the mistakes and successes of educators who have gone before you is the surest way to guarantee that those changes will be for the better.

INTERVIEW WITH SEYMOUR PAPERT ON THE ONE LAPTOP PER CHILD INITIATIVE

Seymour Papert is considered the world's foremost expert on how technology can provide new ways to learn. He lives in Maine, where he has founded a small laboratory called the Learning Barn to develop methods of learning that are too far ahead of the times for large-scale implementation. He has been named distinguished professor by the University of Maine and is credited with inspiring the first initiative aimed at giving a personal computer to every student of a state. He spends a large part of his time working in the Maine Youth Center in Portland, the state's facility for teenagers convicted of serious offenses.

Q: How has Maine's 1-to-1 laptop program informed your thinking about one laptop per child, and how will that experience shape your influence on the $100 laptop program?

A: I got a unique general education in large-scale 1-to-1 from participating in all stages of the Maine program: initial conception, fierce political battles, implementation, disappointments. Numerous little lessons acquired from this will be useful, but I can mention a specific big one from each of the four stages: (1) start with visionary political leaders rather than with educators; (2) expect opposition and know that it can be beaten; (3) expect the toughest educational challenges to come not from opponents but from supporters of the idea, who tame and dilute its impact in order to make it work smoothly; (4) present from the outset the adoption of one per child as a multiyear ramp-up process.

I also learned that it's an illusion to make the transition easier by interpreting "per child" as "per seventh- or eighth-grader." For OLPC (One Laptop Per Child), child means child.

Q: Massachusetts is reportedly requesting 500,000 of the units. Are other states also interested; and if so, will the OLPC initiative grow to accommodate this?

A: OLPC's current model is based on partnerships with governments. Strategies for states, districts, individual schools, and so on are still developing but could take several shapes. Perhaps OLPC will expand the definition of government to include other entities; more likely it will cooperate with companies to make a commercial version. Another possibility is that the OLPC example will incite the independent development of different low-cost machines. If this happens, we'll say, "More power to them," rather than see them as competition. The goal of OLPC is not to dominate the market for hardware or software but to see computers get into the hands of the children of the world.

Q: What educational material will come with the laptops?

A: The OLPC is not trying to reinvent the curriculum for its partner countries. The machines will come with general-purpose tools designed to make it easy for each of them to find its own path to new forms of education. We will, however, exert a constructionist influence by providing a child-accessible programming system in the spirit of Logo and Squeak. We're also working hard to make the operating system and basic suite of applications far more intelligible and self-explanatory than, say, those of the currently used systems. We expect that as a result, the level of understanding, by students and teachers, of the computers and of computational thinking will be substantially higher than in any of the large-scale 1-to-1 projects in the so-called developed countries.

—Seymour Papert (Personal correspondence, December 20, 2005)

INTRODUCTION TO
THE SECOND EDITION

The first edition of this book was begun in 2004 and mostly written in 2005 and part of 2006. A reflection of the state of 1-to-1 at the time, the book reviewed several large-scale and smaller-scale programs, reflected a review of studies and research, and included the author's and others' experiences running 1-to-1 programs. It did not cover tablet PCs, because there were fewer installations at that time to consider.

What Has Changed Since 2006?

When it came time to write a second edition, two questions became clear: *What should be more fleshed out?* and *What has changed in 1-to-1?* The more fleshed-out ideas make up the bulk of three new chapters: "1-to-1 Leadership," largely written by esteemed 1-to-1 leaders Bruce Dixon, Leslie Wilson, Gary Stager, Milt Dougherty, and Ian Stuart; "1-to-1 Tablet PC Programs That Work," written by Dave Berque of DePauw University, the most qualified of anyone I know to write this chapter; and "The Shift (Web 2.0 and Beyond)," referring to the shift toward learner-centered environments.

Following are some of the things that have changed in 1-to-1 teaching and learning: first, some words about digital citizenship with input from Dean Ellerton and Doug Fodeman, followed by an interview with Tom Greaves describing the latest 1-to-1 results from the America's Digital Schools surveys; then Will Richardson on technology and his hopes for technology in education; and finally some closing thoughts.

DEAN ELLERTON ON DIGITAL CITIZENSHIP

We live in a time where the world's collective knowledge is literally in the palms of our hands with today's mobile technology and persistent and immediate access to the Internet. Thus, it is more important than ever to teach students to harness this power in an ethical, informed manner. A teacher that is still focusing on the memorization of large quantities of material is missing an opportunity to help guide students to use these powerful resources more effectively and more efficiently. In addition, the ease with which students can collaborate and communicate with any other connected individual is clearly an advantage that no other culture has enjoyed in our collective history. These powerful tools enable access to not only information, but also real-time thoughts, conversations, and ideas of experts, peers, colleagues, leaders, and even enemies in a way that has never been available to scholars before. This, I believe, is what sets the current climate for a modern education far ahead of anything we have seen before. Consequently, I believe that it is the responsibility of schools and teachers to finds ways to help children to learn these skills before they enter the workplace.

—Dean Ellerton, CIO, Information Technology Department, Brooks School, 2007

Smaller Devices

This book does not survey the smaller devices available for 1-to-1, but it is obvious that, beginning with OLPC (One Laptop Per Child) and the XO, smaller computing devices, many with the ability to write on the screen, all with wireless connectivity, and most with nearly full functionality, are being rapidly developed and manufactured. These devices include the XO, Fourier's Nova devices and other products, the ASUS Eee PC, and HP's Classmate. There are others available and more in the chain, but it seems that smaller and less expensive devices are the growing trend. Whether they all offer the functionality of full-sized tablets or laptops is the question, and the jury is still out.

Personal Learning Networks

While not precisely a 1-to-1 development, the concept of your Personal Learning Network (PLN) is a growing factor for educators everywhere. Your PLN is how you keep learning and from whom, the people and resources that help you and to whom you offer help, and the way to stay current. But who is in your network, how do you keep up with trends and what's happening in terms of 1-to-1, and how do you keep yourself informed?

Finding fellow educators and leaders to follow and to share with and to query is at the root of formulating your PLN. My PLN involves Twitter (follow me at www.twitter.com/plivings); RSS feeds of various edu-blogs; a number of Nings including www.classroom20.com; attending conferences including NECC, the Lausanne Laptop Institute, and k12onlineconference.org; listservs; magazines online and in print; and e-mail. Others also use Diigo, Delicious, Plurk, and other applications. The goal is to have a wealth of people and resources to further your own learning and sharing. Additionally, your PLN can help respond to questions like, "What's Plurk again, and why might I want to use it?"

How's Your Scaffold?

Let's step back a bit here to consider the idea of scaffolding. Scaffolding learning assumes there is a scaffold in place so the learning can "stick"—the scaffold being existing knowledge (long-term memory) that has a relationship to the new learning so that the new ideas can find a place with the existing ideas. During a recent EdTech Live, some of us were talking about teaching adults, the assumptions we'd made, and how at times our assumptions about the scaffolds in place were incorrect. If it is not clear what Twitter is and how it can be used, and you haven't seen it used effectively, jumping right in to try to use it may cause more frustration than value. Easing in and watching and reading might be a better start.

In general, you may want to check your own scaffold in terms of technology to see where there are gaps, because every one of us has them. If you are in the position of teaching other adults, you may want to consider the scaffolds in place for your adult learners and find kind ways to help everyone to identify and work on what is needed, so we can all take on the important business of integrating 1-to-1 in our classrooms with our students.

**AN INTERVIEW WITH DOUG FODEMAN
ON BALANCING SECURITY AND THE OUTSIDE WORLD**

Q: How do you recommend schools balance keeping their networks safe and allowing teachers the tools—some of them quite new—that they need to bring the outside world and resources into their classrooms?

A: The easy answer, from a simple network point of view, is that schools have to be extremely vigilant and use firewalls, antispam, and antispyware. Schools are seen as easy targets for outside threats because they *were* easy at one point. There are also threats from the inside. Savvy children might install keyloggers, install their own servers, networks, and RS chatting, or install gaming software. Keeping networks safe is a full-time job.

You can keep your network safe and still allow conferencing, blogging, and access to the Internet. The hard part is that with these new telecommunication applications and new technologies come unforeseen and unpredictable issues. For example, Marje Monroe, a colleague, reported that a student wrote her an e-mail and signed it "see you later, babe." Marje confronted the student, asking why the student addressed her that way in an e-mail when he would never address her that way face-to-face. The student said, "Everyone talks that way in e-mail." This became a teaching moment for explaining to the student about appropriate boundaries.

In another case, a teacher wanted to create a Facebook class page to further educational conversation. My colleague Marje and I were against it. Here's why: On Facebook, depending on your settings, you may have no control of what is posted. It's a social network for the outside world. Facebook is not like the controlled classroom at all. It is an entirely different environment. On the other hand there are blogs, for

---

(continued)

(continued)

> example, that require passwords, moderated comments, and are not available for just anyone to participate in. This type of social networking might be more appropriate for a classroom.
>
> We need to be thoughtful and mindful in how we use newer technologies, including being mindful of the downside. Our experience is that few people consider the downside. The anonymity associated with the Internet is a huge draw. People do and say what they would never do or say in person.
>
> We need to build upon good practices, to teach responsible web use. It needs to be added to the list of what all students learn, just like sex and drug education.
>
> —Doug Fodeman, 2007, www.childrenonline.org

Virtual Schools, Online Learning, Distance Learning, LMSs

As of the writing of this section, 42 states have some type of online, distance, or virtual learning in place. Estimates for the future are that 50% of all high school courses will have an online component in the next ten years. This is a large trend and only getting larger. 1-to-1 will continue to be a primary vehicle for online and virtual learning. Along with this and hand-in-hand with this trend is the proliferation of LMSs (Learning Management Systems), which are portals or systems to manage learning that often include student information as well. Many companies are getting into online learning and LMSs (including [full disclosure] my current employer, EdisonLearning, Inc.).

Web 2.0

It would be a major oversight not to mention web 2.0. It is also discussed in Chapter 11 ("The Shift"). In the first edition, blogs, wikis, and podcasts were defined and briefly mentioned. But the educational use of web 2.0 applications for education has spread into classrooms all around the United States and overseas, adding possibilities along with complexity to teaching and learning. No longer is the web a passive vehicle for viewing links. No longer is the web master the omniscient creator (or gatekeeper) of all information. Anyone can add to the knowledge (or misinformation) available to anyone with an Internet connection.

What this means in the classroom is complex and layered with wonder, thrills, and caveats. Others have written more deeply about web 2.0, including Gwen Solomon, who, along with Lynne Schrum, wrote the best-selling and highly recommended *Web 2.0: New Schools, New Tools,* and who kindly contributes to Chapter 11. Web 2.0 has opened up potential for 1-to-1 classrooms everywhere in terms of the creating and publication of new, student-generated ideas.

Information Literacy ▶ Information Fluency ▶ Information Synthesis

In the early days of the web we talked about information literacy: understanding how to find and evaluate information. We then moved to information fluency: how to be fluent with the use of information so that we could fluidly choose and use it. It seems now that information needs to be synthesized and created, not just understood and evaluated, and that educators should help their students grapple with the fact that any one of them can create new information quickly and easily and publish it just as quickly. As far as our students are concerned, learning is no longer just about other people's information. It's about all of us taking information from others, morphing and synthesizing it, and creating something entirely new and unique.

Still Not Enough Solid Research

This item concerns me. I have not yet found metastudies of 1-to-1 implementations, meaning comparisons of large numbers of 1-to-1 implementations have not been undertaken to measure what's happening and why scientifically. The closest I'm aware of follows in the form of *America's Digital Schools* and is a worthy effort. Still, I am hopeful that a university or consortium of universities will band together to study what 1-to-1 is doing in our schools and not just in the United States. If this is happening, please contact me at livingstonp@mac.com so it can be described in a future edition.

AN INTERVIEW WITH TOM GREAVES ON *AMERICA'S DIGITAL SCHOOLS*

At NECC 2008, I asked Tom Greaves about his latest research, called *America's Digital Schools 2008* (www.ads2008.org). The first version of *America's Digital Schools* detailed responses from the top 2,500 U.S. school districts with more than 4,000 students and 100 questions on 100 topics. This time, the survey polled the same schools on six topics:

- ▶ 1-to-1 computing
- ▶ Learning management systems (LMSs)
- ▶ Online assessment
- ▶ Computing devices
- ▶ Interactive whiteboards
- ▶ Bandwidth

One thing of interest is that some of the topics like online assessment and LMSs are becoming very important to 1-to-1. As we have eliminated many of the big barriers, schools are finding out you need a learning management system to best integrate and use 1-to-1 programs. Some create this as a portal, some will use their LMSs to deliver teacher professional development, some LMSs are full online learning courses. But if every student has a computer, assignments, assessment, and teaching can change; and this change needs to be managed.

One possible disaster story of 1-to-1 happens when no one calculates bandwidth—the actual KB per second per student out to the network has not been really considered. Even highly regarded chief technology officers don't always understand the scale and numbers when multiple students are involved. A single T1 is not enough out to the network when

---

(continued)

(continued)

there are so many computing devices. 1-to-1 therefore becomes a huge bandwidth driver. Give every child a computer, and they really start to use it.

One of the things we learned since the first survey was that the number of schools using 1-to-1 went up slightly, and the net number of students using 1-to-1 increased. This means some districts dropped out and some districts started anew. With a slight difference within sampling error, there was about a 2% overall increase.

The average number of students in a 1-to-1 implementation also increased. Ten years ago it might have been 200 students using 1-to-1 per district, perhaps in a few pilot classrooms. The average implementation now is 1,631 students using 1-to-1 per district. Logic would say this started at zero in 1990 and has been climbing ever since. Now the survey says we have 3% of the school districts polled with 20,000 or more students with 1-to-1. Clearly we are past the pilot stage. No longer are districts just introducing 1-to-1 for a single grade or class.

The number of teachers who have computing devices showed a spectacular increase: 57.8% of the districts polled say 100% of teachers have a computing device (not necessarily a laptop, but probably many are laptops). Five years ago, less than 30% had a computing device. It seems to be expected for many districts that every teacher have a computing device.

The report shows significant academic improvement attributed to 1-to-1. The statistic previously reported as 17% has now has moved to 33%. What's clear is that the schools have gotten a lot better at handling infrastructure and logistical issues. We don't hear about every computer failing. We are hearing less about issues around training the teachers. Schools seem to be more comfortable defining an effective 1-to-1 implementation. Vendors are finding better ways to approach hardware issues. Battery life is a lot longer and will continue to improve.

Prior planning prevents poor performance. Too often schools and districts take on 1-to-1 with too little planning. Another consideration is the concept of interlocking dependencies. Everything brought into a school has dependencies; the more things brought onboard, the more dependencies. If a school brings in online testing, for instance, they often don't stop to think about what makes online testing successful. They may have enough computers for the students and think they have enough bandwidth. But they don't realize that someone else is using bandwidth. The most frequent reason why first-year implementations are not successful is not considering all the factors and dependencies.

It's unclear when (or if) tablet PCs may tip. When tablet prices fall and ruggedness increases, they may become a more widespread factor. Also, Apple is not yet in the tablet market. People are saying that cell phones are taking over, but you can't name a school with over 5,000 students that has purchased a cell phone for each student.

Some things that are coming up include answers to battery issues. We'll be moving toward lower powered processors resulting in several hours more battery life with the same performance. A year from now it will be very easy to find computers that run six, seven, nine, ten hours. Another issue to be solved is connectivity. Schools are not using digital curriculum everywhere until students can use their laptops wherever they are. They need connectivity at the orthodontist, at grandma's house, at the ball field. They need always-on connectivity.

Individual educators can get the entire *America's Digital Schools* study from www.ads2008.org/ads/OrderRequest/.

AN INTERVIEW WITH WILL RICHARDSON

Q: What have you seen or experienced that gives you hope for education and education technology and why?

A: What's given me hope recently is that I am finally seeing more and more people beginning to understand the magnitude of the shifts that are occurring and at least beginning to contemplate what that means for education. But I've become more and more convinced that significant change is only going to happen when we have a critical mass of educators at all levels who understand these shifts in their own personal practice. I think we are still years away from that happening; and unfortunately, I don't see a lot of potential leadership on the issue coming from the national level.

Q: What challenges/hurdles/blockages to meaningful learning do you see as vital for schools to address in the short- and long-term and why? Do you have suggestions for solutions?

A: I think we have to get over the fear factor that is associated with the web, and I'm not just talking about the safety issue. We're scared of bad information and that children will plagiarize and cheat and that people out there will lead them astray, and so our reaction is to "protect" them from all of it by blocking it. That doesn't protect them at all. It makes them less safe and more ignorant. We have to be willing to give them opportunities to "fail safely" (not my phrase) by sitting next to them and teaching them how to make good decisions about the content and the interactions they are having online. But in order to do that, we have to get it for ourselves. And that is, at the end of the day, the only "solution" I see out there is for educators to begin to embed these tools and connections into their own practice. But to do that, we need to really rethink how we deliver professional development around these technologies. If we can't find ways to provide long-term, job-embedded training that really immerses teachers into networked learning environments, we're not going to really help them get down that road very far.

Q: What one change is essential for schools to become a place you want your own children to attend?

A: That their teachers have to own the uses of these connective tools and technologies in their own practice and that they can model those tools at every turn. My children may not be cognitively ready to use a lot of this, but all children are ready to see their teachers employing a safe, ethical, and effective learning practice and sharing that practice and process in their classrooms. Right now, my own children, and most children their age, are given no other context for learning except what happens in the text, behind the desk, from 9–3 each day. That has to change.

—Will Richardson (Personal correspondence, December 11, 2007)

How This Book Is Organized

The book has three parts and can be sampled or read from start to finish.

Part 1 describes what a 1-to-1 laptop program can mean for students, teachers, and schools. It begins with an overview of the laptop program at The Peck School. It then looks at similar programs at The Denver School of Science and Technology; The Urban School in San Francisco; and Whitfield School in St. Louis, Missouri. Next, it surveys three large-scale laptop programs—Maine's, Michigan's, and Virginia's Henrico County School District's—and ends with a review of research on the effects of 1-to-1 access on teaching and learning in K–12 schools.

Part 2 delves into the nuts and bolts of planning and implementing laptop programs and the individual components that can make them or break them. Included is an all-new chapter on 1-to-1 leadership.

Part 3 looks at how laptops can change the teaching and learning environment and how teachers and administrators can effectively manage the 1-to-1 classroom and make the most of ubiquitous access. Included are all-new chapters on tablet PCs and the successful programs that use them and on "The Shift"—how 1-to-1 programs and web 2.0 resources facilitate the movement toward learner-centered educational environments.

A number of useful resources are gathered in the appendixes. These include a model acceptable use policy (AUP), a laptop-specific AUP, an assessment sheet for laptops, a list of professional resources for laptop programs, a glossary of terms and acronyms, a chart mapping web 2.0 resources to various subject areas, and ISTE's National Educational Technology Standards (NETS).

Summary

It has been an interesting journey for 1-to-1 over the past several years. Providing a digital assistant to every child for his or her use 24/7, in school or at home, can truly transform the classroom. But what does that transformation mean, and what form does it take? It's still an experiment in process but one that many of us still believe can work with effort, guidance, planning, thought, commitment, and visionary educators at the helm.

Part One

1-TO-1 PROGRAMS THAT WORK

AMAZING AND POWERFUL THINGS happen when students have digital assistants at their fingertips to help them learn. Giving every student a laptop computer opens up an entirely new set of opportunities for both collaborative and self-directed learning. The educational paradigm shift that proponents of technology have long promised can become a reality when students have 1-to-1 access. The chapters in Part 1 reveal the possibilities of that paradigm shift by looking at successful 1-to-1 programs from around the country.

We're a species of storytellers and story listeners, and some of our best learning comes from hearing what others have experienced, especially the challenges they've faced and the lessons they've learned. So the stories that follow can teach us much about the possibilities of 1-to-1 laptops. Each story reflects the unique factors—pedagogy, mission, demographics, teaching philosophies, and funding—that determined the particular implementation strategies these pioneering programs adopted. We're fortunate to be able to learn from so many thoughtful educators who have started down the 1-to-1 road before us.

One of the most important things I've learned while working on this book is how the same basic hardware—laptop computers—can serve equally well the needs of schools and districts with very different goals and demographics. For instance, the Forney (Texas) Independent School District is one of the fastest growing districts in the country and faces a huge challenge each year when it comes to ordering textbooks. Books must be ordered in the spring for the following fall, but when September rolls around, the number of children attending a particular school may have doubled. How then to provide enough textbooks for all the students without having them wait months for reordered books to arrive?

Forney's answer has been to provide its fifth- and sixth-graders with e-textbooks that can be accessed with school-issued laptops. Once the school district has obtained the e-book license, it's a simple matter to update the license count and burn as many CDs as needed. Forney is even pushing the envelope a little bit and negotiating directly with publishers who don't yet offer e-books. Plus, by encouraging laptop use in the classroom, Forney has set the stage for teachers to try new approaches and integrate technology more effectively into their curriculum.

Maine was motivated to institute a first-of-its-kind statewide laptop program for a whole different set of reasons. Angus King, former governor of Maine, wanted to produce a more technologically literate populace to help the state compete for new jobs in the information age (Peterson, 2000). Once educators took over the project that he started, these two goals morphed into specific teaching and learning goals. Both sets of goals have been reached with the help of 1-to-1 access. Maine is now producing more tech-savvy graduates, and the classroom experience in Maine has undergone a sea change.

Meanwhile, St. Thomas Episcopal School in Tampa, Florida, had the goal of implementing more differentiated learning for its students. Teachers believed they could serve their students better if they grouped them according to learning styles and pace. Teachers were given considerable professional development and instruction on the philosophy and implementation of differentiated learning. They also were given laptops. Soon they began creating projects that allowed students to work on different aspects of a single, overarching activity, grouped according to the individual students' abilities and development levels.

1-to-1 laptops made this move to differentiated learning possible. In a traditional setting, resources are spread thinly when several groups are working on the same project. If, for instance, the library has ten copies of a particular book, it is almost inevitable that 11 or more students will need that same book. Add to that the different abilities and development levels of students, and a teacher's ability to provide every student with the resources needed to research, analyze, and present on a given topic is often quite limited.

When each student in each group is equipped with a laptop, in contrast, student-directed projects can be taken to a new level. The need to share limited resources is no longer an issue, and every student can present and publish at a developmentally appropriate level. Students get to the thinking levels faster when they have their own digital assistants to help them.

Previewing the Chapters

The first chapter tells the story of The Peck School. A traditional, independent school that's been in operation for more than 100 years, Peck has administered for the past eight years a 1-to-1 laptop program for its seventh- and eighth-grade students. The Peck School embarked early on this trend toward ubiquitous access, forming stakeholder partnerships and learning lessons along the way.

Chapter 2, "Individual School Programs," looks at several school and classroom laptop programs. The first school surveyed is The Urban School in San Francisco. Student-centered and progressive, Urban has achieved great success and curricular vitality through laptops. Whitfield School in St. Louis and its unique process-oriented approach to technology is profiled next. The Denver School of Science and Technology, which has provided laptops for all of its teachers and students from the moment it opened its doors, is the final school profiled.

Chapter 3, "District-Wide and Statewide Programs," describes some larger-scale laptop programs, such as those running in Maine, Michigan, and Henrico County (Virginia) Public Schools. These stories offer rich insights into the challenges of implementing a district-wide or statewide 1-to-1 program.

Chapter 4, "What 1-to-1 Can Mean for Students, Teachers, and Schools," presents current research on the effectiveness of 1-to-1 programs and summarizes what these studies reveal about teaching and learning with ubiquitous technology. Studies from Maine, the Beaufort County School District in South Carolina, and the Athens Academy in Athens, Georgia (among others) provide quantitative and qualitative data on how laptops can change schools.

A Framework for 1-to-1 Success: EPC

As I reviewed the principles and strategies employed by the many different laptop programs profiled in this book, it became clear to me that three traits above all others seemed to separate the successful programs from those that encountered more challenges. I've tried to capture those traits in a conceptual framework that goes by the acronym **EPC**.

The **E** in EPC is for **Educators**. For a laptop program to be successful, **Educators** must be at the helm, whether they be education professors, K–12 teachers, or school administrators. Educators need to be on the front lines in the classroom, of course, but they should also take the lead in the strategy and implementation meetings in which a laptop program is planned, steered, assessed, and renewed year after year. Without the **E**, the program won't get off the ground properly, and the tremendous potential of 1-to-1 won't be effectively realized.

The **P** is for **Planning**, which is often the area given shortest shrift. Considerable planning needs to happen before a single laptop is purchased. Jumping on the laptop bandwagon without a clear idea of where that wagon is heading will result in frustration at the very least, and total chaos and failure if you're really unlucky.

C represents **Commitment**. Educators need to be committed to the success of the overall program and do their part to make it happen. This commitment means believing in the results even though challenges will arise and time-honored habits and traditions will change. To be successful, all stakeholders must be equally committed to providing their piece of the laptop puzzle: hardware, software, network infrastructure, logistics, professional development, and classroom implementation.

Schools and districts moving ahead with a laptop initiative should consider how they're structuring their programs to facilitate each of these crucial elements. If, for instance, your school's technology plan is full of technical acronyms and provides little focus on pedagogy or the curriculum, it's time to add some more **E** (Educators) to the mix. If you're pressured to start up with laptops right away, make sure you don't overlook the importance of **P** (Planning), so that you can get it right the first time. While there's no set formula for how much planning should be done, "as much as possible" is always a good yardstick. Finally, it's crucial to keep your focus during the difficult months of planning, setup, and initial roll-out so that you don't let contingency dilute your vision along the way. Inevitably, what separates the successful programs from the less successful is the **C** (Commitment) of leaders. Effective use of technology requires continual planning, ongoing professional development, frequent assessment, and the commitment of resources, including dollars and staff.

Chapter 1
THE PECK SCHOOL

Introduction

WALK THROUGH THE DOUBLE DOORS of the main entrance of The Peck School, and you'll find yourself surrounded by beautiful wood paneling decorated with carved moldings from an earlier age. Gaze upward and your eyes will follow an ornate staircase leading to a landing backed by a multicolored, lead-paned, stained glass window. It's the source of the many-hued light that floods the open area below.

To your right is a striking fireplace, with a large painting above it. In fact, paintings hang on every wall, because Peck uses its lobby as an art gallery and displays works by different artists on a rotating basis.

If you walk forward a few steps, you'll notice a small window to your left with a switch next to it. Turn this switch on, bend down to look through the window, and you'll see a scene that looks similar to the room you're standing in. It's filled with tiny furniture. Peer inside and you'll see a miniature knight clad in full armor. You're in an institution that combines tradition and academics with a love of students, a self-termed "family school."

Suddenly, it's 8 a.m., and you hear the opening bell. Boys and girls dressed in uniforms enter through the double doors, rolling or carrying backpacks. There's something different about many of the older students, however. They carry silver briefcases rather than the standard backpack. These are Peck's seventh- and eighth-graders, who are given laptops to use 24/7 for all their schoolwork. Just a few minutes ago, many of them were in the "before school" program—laptops open—studying, printing, and listening to music.

Look around the walls of Peck, and you might spot a wireless access device, blinking intermittently, sending a signal for faculty and student laptops. These access points provide a little 21st-century razzle-dazzle to the staid, 19th-century wood paneling.

Figure 1.1
Two students work on their wireless laptops at The Peck School.

TIMELINE
THE PECK SCHOOL'S LAPTOP PROGRAM

1982	Peck chooses the Apple II as a hardware platform for its wealth of educational software.
September 1984	Elisabeth Fraser becomes Peck's first technology chair.
September 1985	Technology teacher hired for the Lower School. Apple computers are used to teach Logo.
October 1993	2020 Vision document represents a first draft of The Peck School Technology Plan.
May 1994	20 student laptops are purchased to equip one classroom.
September 1994	Leslie Maguire hired to be Upper School technology coordinator.
	Board presentation on funding needs for a new seventh- and eighth-grade school building with an infrastructure to support laptops.
	Faculty workshops on word processing and network use.
January 1995	Board considers whether to require students to purchase their own laptops.
	A Finance Committee report recommends a fund-raising effort to provide students with laptops, targeting Grades 5–8.
	Professional Development plan for technology instituted.
May 1995	First school-wide technology showcase.
September 1995	New building for Grades 7 and 8 opens for classes.
February 1996	Updated technology plan refers to "school-owned laptops" or "student-owned laptops."
September 1996	Eight teacher laptops are purchased to support technology and communications classes.
September 1997	Upper School academic faculty provided with school-owned laptops, a gift from the Parents Association.
	A technical support specialist is hired.

Founded in 1893, The Peck School is a coed K–8 independent school in Morristown, New Jersey. Known for its academic rigor, Peck attracts students from 37 zip codes. They attend an accelerated educational program that stresses academics, personal responsibility, hard work, athletics, the arts, and technology.

The 2009–2010 school year marks the 11th year that laptops have been provided to every seventh- and eighth-grade student at Peck. All faculty members were given laptops 12 years ago. My predecessor as head of technology at Peck, Elisabeth Fraser, was the visionary and steward for this successful program from its inception in 1998 until I took over in June 2002.

Why Laptops? Why Peck?

The initial goal of the laptop program, Fraser remembers, was to encourage more seamless integration of technology into all aspects of the curriculum. Having tapped into the wisdom of her husband (a scientist and researcher at Bell Labs), Fraser believed that everyone, everywhere, would soon be using laptops. The earlier Peck School students got comfortable with this technology, the better it would be for their educational and career prospects.

Peck had already made significant strides with computers, integrating them into the math curriculum in the 1980s. Two computer labs were outfitted in the early '90s, permitting regular computer classes to be offered. Even with these resources, however, disparities remained between home and school in terms of software and hardware. Peck decided to address this issue by purchasing home and school licenses for AppleWorks, a software suite that can run on both PCs and Macs.

This helped, but it still wasn't enough to ensure uniform and problem-free transportation of work from home to school and back again. Some students didn't have ready access to computers at home. Some had computers or printers in need of repair. In addition, many students who participated in sports often traveled on weekends and were unable to use the family computer to complete assignments. Students whose parents were divorced often split their time between two residences that didn't have the same computer resources. This typically resulted in 10,000 student excuses at homework-collection time, and frustration ensued for the entire staff and faculty.

Enter the portable, affordable laptop. If every student were given an identical laptop computer, the home-to-school connection would be facilitated, travel problems would be mitigated, and homework could be uniformly processed. In addition, technology skill-building could be integrated into the curriculum in a much more consistent and enduring way than was possible before, when students had to travel once or twice a week to the computer lab.

Why did a school steeped in more than 100 years of tradition become one of the earliest to institute a 1-to-1 laptop program? Elisabeth Fraser's leadership was certainly critical, but it also may have to do with the fact that educators at The Peck School tend to be early adopters by nature. A favorable mention of computers is made as early as 1976 in *Because They Cared* (Morrison, 1992), a history of the first 100 years of The Peck School. A student quote from the 1976 yearbook reads: "During the Spring Term, we took a computer course at the Newark Institute of Technology. We learned a lot about how to program a computer and look at problems from different angles" (Morrison, 1992, p. 81). Even at this early date, educators at Peck recognized the value of computers in the classroom and took the time to send students to a computer institution.

In 1980, four TRS-80 computers were donated by the school's Mother's Association. That same year, computer study was made an official part of the seventh-grade math curriculum. Seven brand-new Apple IIe computers followed for K–8 classes. In 1984, the first computer lab was completed in the Lower School, and a different space was designated for Upper School computers. These computers were used for Logo programming and word processing.

Along with this affinity for computer technology, The Peck School also has a tradition of regularly assessing its curriculum and approach to learning. This is done every five years or so in part to prepare for the Middle States and other accreditations, but also because Peck's leaders are committed to pursuing more effective teaching and learning.

TIMELINE
THE PECK SCHOOL'S LAPTOP PROGRAM

September 1998 ▶ All faculty members are provided with school-owned laptops.

A stipend is paid to six teachers to be TAG (Technically Adept Gurus) Team members to support faculty and staff.

Board members visit classrooms to see and participate in laptop learning.

July 1999 ▶ Tech support specialist leaves, new person hired as a systems administrator.

September 1999 ▶ All seventh- and eighth-grade students are provided with school-owned laptops.

January 2000 ▶ Music Department uses 20 old laptops for MIDI lab and music production.

October 2001 ▶ Tech support person hired to run the laptop program.

June 2002 ▶ Pamela Livingston takes over for retiring Elizabeth Fraser as head of technology.

Peck's laptop program is evaluated by technology directors from Choate Rosemary Hall and Dwight-Englewood School.

June 2005 ▶ Construction begins on Academic Link building and new gym, both fully wireless.

September 2005 ▶ Laptops are provided to every sixth-grader but must stay in school on a cart. Laptops are also provided to fifth graders (2-to-1) on a cart.

New schedule begins. Seventh- and eighth-graders no longer have formal technology classes. Laptops are used throughout classes instead. Fifth- and sixth-graders continue to take technology classes once every six days, with teachers using laptops as part of regular class instruction.

P Is for Planning

Planning a major initiative at The Peck School always involves the Board of Trustees, a group of volunteers—educators, business leaders, and parents—who are mandated to oversee the school's fiscal health and steer the school into the future. The board hires and evaluates the Head of School and provides stewardship over the school's future, ensuring its continuance for future generations.

Peck School is fortunate to have a strong and committed board whose members bring a variety of skills and professional expertise to the table. When Fraser first proposed the idea of a 1-to-1 laptop program, the board was ready to role up its collective sleeves and work with Peck's faculty to make things happen. Cathy Walsh, a Peck board member for nine years and a member of the board's Executive Committee, recalls that the first crucial step was to get everyone on the board up to speed on the unique capabilities of laptops: "I think we knew right away that we had to keep educating everybody. When I joined the board, we found that we had to educate the board before we could educate parents, teachers, or anyone" (personal communication, August 30, 2000).

First, board members visited a technology-infused corporation to see how 1-to-1 access to computers was being managed in a corporate environment and what impact this access was having on employee productivity and interoffice communication. They took a virtual tour of the building and realized how 1-to-1 access could be used in the classroom for, say, halving a sphere to understand its volume. Since many board members came from corporations and industry and because few 1-to-1 school programs existed at that time, they also toured a high tech company. These visits gave them a better idea of how technology skill development could benefit Peck School students.

Not everyone was immediately convinced that putting laptops into the hands of every seventh- and eighth-grade student made sense for the school educationally, philosophically, or fiscally. But once board members were able to see 1-to-1 in action and it was no longer just a concept in their minds, things started to happen.

First, the board nominated one of its members to co-chair the Technology Committee with Walsh. Together, the two co-chairs devised a strategy of reaching out to all stakeholders to solicit their buy-in (**E** for educators), asking them to contribute ideas and assess current capacity and progress (**P** for planning). Through their efforts, the 1-to-1 laptop initiative stayed alive and fresh in the minds of faculty and staff, encouraging their active support (**C** for commitment).

Their approach to consensus-building is an exemplar of how to get multiple stakeholders educated, informed, and on board. A number of presentations featuring laptops were arranged, and faculty and staff members were regularly asked to share their feelings and concerns. Teachers and administrators formed groups and committees to reflect on the potential and challenges of implementing a laptop program. They discussed the educational and logistical pros and cons and imagined what could be done in the future. Educators (**E**) were centrally involved in the entire process.

Information about the initiative's ongoing progress was shared with the entire school community through official communications from Peck's Head of School, David Frothingham; Elisabeth Fraser's internal communiqués; the *Peck Tech News* newsletter (filled with articles from students, parents, administrators, teachers, and board members);

letters home to parents; and the publication of a thoroughly revised and detailed technology plan for the school. No one could feel that details weren't forthcoming or that people weren't working hard to inform them. The education of stakeholders was vital, ongoing, and varied in its delivery.

Peck also sought out exemplars to help in planning (**P**) its program. Committee members researched the Anytime, Anywhere Learning (AAL) program and its group of 52 schools, as well as Cincinnati Country Day School's formalized laptop institute for schools. The AAL program was the focus of a three-year study by the independent research group Rockman *et al*, which provided invaluable information on the benefits and challenges these early adopter schools encountered. Cincinnati Country Day School provided ideas on planning, implementing, managing, and sustaining a laptop program, and they hosted a visit by several Peck faculty and board members.

Paying for It

Independent schools such as Peck rely on tuition, donations, and grants to run the school. Adding a major program to the school's budget isn't done without considerable thought and planning. Walsh remembers that funding was an issue that generated a lot of discussion during the planning stages. One early funding suggestion was the institution of a dedicated technology fee or laptop fee. However, Peck had never before levied any separate book or athletic fees, relying instead on a single yearly tuition fee to cover the majority of costs. With that as a precedent, the board decided to raise tuition to cover the first-year cost of laptops. That higher tuition rate has been retained in subsequent years, sustaining the program year after year.

While this raise in tuition was used to pay for laptops, the board decided to pay for other, related costs—primarily to upgrade the school's network and infrastructure—by inaugurating a small capital campaign. Typically, capital campaigns at independent schools are fundraisers for specific improvements or programs. This campaign was called Challenge 2000, and a target of $650,000 was set. A committee went to work to ask for contributions from board members, parents, alumni, faculty, and others affiliated with the school. A special effort was made to solicit those parents whose children were scheduled to get the laptops in the first and second years, because they would receive the most immediate benefits. In the end, enough money was raised to pay for the laptops and the infrastructural improvements needed to support them, and a laptop program was born.

Staffing

The talent and expertise of the computer coordinators at Peck—Leslie Maguire for the Upper School (Grades 5–8) and Theresa Deehan for the Lower School (Grades K–4)—have from the beginning been critical to the planning and implementation of the laptop program. Visitors to Peck School often remark on the school's commitment (**C**) to technology in general and the laptop program in particular, and much of the credit goes to these technology professionals.

Peck also decided to hire another full-time technology support person for the laptop program. The school realized that if laptops were to be truly integrated into everyday learning tasks, they would have to be maintained and repaired on a timely basis so that teachers and students could rely on them. Any sustained downtime could lead to potentially devastating effects on the seventh- and eighth-grade curriculum. So having a dedicated tech support staff to handle setup, configuration, distribution, and maintenance was deemed critical to the long-term success of the program.

During my time at Peck, the school had two excellent, service-oriented tech support people on staff: Kevin Grieshaber, network manager, and Nirav Patel, technical support specialist. Both hold multiple technical certifications in hardware, software, and network administration, and both are genuinely kind and helpful. When the person who comes to fix a teacher's misbehaving laptop is pleasant, efficient, competent, and never condescending, teachers are more likely to have a positive view of the role technology can play in their classrooms.

A First Step Toward 24/7—Rolling Carts

Having your own laptop to use 24/7 is a serious responsibility, one that 12-year-old students aren't always ready to handle. Consequently, laptops are provided to fifth- and sixth-graders on rolling carts and are to be used in classrooms only. Fifth-graders share laptops 2-to-1: two students are assigned one laptop that can be used for teacher-directed activities. The rolling carts at Peck are "wet carts," meaning they're wired to provide electrical charging for the laptops.

Figure 1.2
Laptops plugged into a rolling cart.

Because Peck has only two homerooms per grade, asking two students to share a laptop doesn't cause much contention. Classes for all subjects are split into groups of 18 students, so fifth-grade teachers arrange their use of laptops around class meeting times. Usually, when one homeroom needs the laptops, the other homeroom doesn't. In addition, technology classes that teach technology skills using content from the academic subjects are held regularly. These classes also emphasize laptop care and use.

Starting in 2005, all sixth-grade students were given 1-to-1 access to laptops on a rolling cart for use on teacher-directed projects and activities. Formal technology classes for sixth-graders reinforce basic technology skills, including the care and use of laptops. As in fifth grade, sixth-grade technology classes incorporate content from academic subjects.

Laptops are used frequently to support the curriculum for fifth- and sixth-grade English, history, math, science, and language arts. In addition, several new "short course" offerings—such as iMovie, PowerPoint and public speaking, Adobe Photoshop Elements, and Earthquake Research—make regular use of laptops. Fifth- and sixth-grade students can check their homework assignments online using FirstClass software and participate in regular homework conferences on every subject that they can access from school or at home. Parents can check their children's homework in this way as well.

Tech Support

Peck leaders who planned the laptop program realized their commitment (**C**) to success would require a full-time tech support specialist to help the network manager manage the new hardware.

A major part of the specialist's job is care of the laptops and first-line support to students and teachers who have computer issues. Students bring their laptop issues to the tech support area during recess, before and after school, and sometimes during school. Problems include logic board failures, screen problems, lost or forgotten power cords, and setup issues related to different networking configurations at home and at school.

Figure 1.3
Tools of the trade at Peck: spare and loaner parts.

Peck keeps a ready supply of extra power cords and batteries and helps students with their dial-up, DSL, or cable modem connections so that they can access their home Internet accounts. The school has arranged with Apple Computer to help with timely repair and replacement of defective or damaged laptops. Apple determines if the iBook needs repair because of normal wear and tear, hardware failure (covered by an extended warranty), or user damage. If the problem is due to damage, Peck shares the cost of repairing the unit with the student's parents.

Thanks to the technical support staff's skills and their genuine desire to help, the school has had relatively little difficulty integrating laptops into the daily routine. Tech staff members are always available via walkie-talkies and are quick to come to the aid of teachers and students when failures or problems occur.

Tech staffers have also helped resolve bigger issues, such as the difficulties experienced in 2002 when a wireless network was installed. The initial placement of wireless access points around the school wasn't always the best; there were dead zones in some areas and signal interference in others. Tech support resolved these issues by walking around the school with laptops and redesigning access point placement. The network coverage is now solid. As part of new building construction, the school also upgraded some of the older wireless access points to Cisco equipment and hired a systems integrator to plan a wireless infrastructure for the entire campus.

Network Infrastructure

As with many schools, Peck's original network was installed in the early '90s. It was an Ethernet network, with cabling designed to support desktop computers in classrooms and computer labs. For the most part, this meant small hubs able to accommodate several computers in a single classroom location. Computers had to be placed close enough to the hubs to connect their network cards to the hub port. Some of these hubs are still in place in Peck's Lower School, where laptops aren't used.

Lessons Learned

Wireless Networking and Hindsight

Planning for a 1-to-1 laptop program in today's schools means planning for wireless access. You need enough electrical outlets and access points around the school to provide wireless network coverage for everyone. Wireless access still requires an Ethernet backbone, however, because behind every wireless access station is an Ethernet port and cable. Wireless works from the wall outward, but cables still need to be pulled through the walls and ceilings. Electricity still needs to be provided at access points unless power is fed to them directly by the network switches.

Peck benefited from having a parent who worked for the Lucent Corporation, which provided network hardware and wiring at a reduced cost. The network hardware was originally leased for three years to allow the technology department to replace it with better, faster equipment when it became available. Much of that equipment has since been replaced, but the item that cost the most—wiring—was still in use years later.

All computer networks need continual maintenance and updating, and the network that supports Peck's laptop program has changed considerably since the laptops were first introduced. Among other things, Cisco switches have replaced older, unmanaged ones. Also, an SMTP gateway with web filtering has been brought online, and industrial-strength antivirus and firewall capabilities have been installed on a new server that replaced the original Unix box. As an extension of new construction completed in September 2006, Peck performed a wireless access evaluation.

Networks are continually morphing entities. Once state-of-the-art 10 Mbps Ethernet networks first gave way to 100 Mbps Ethernet and then to gigabit Ethernet. T1 lines have given way to T3 lines. Switches and connections need periodic upgrading, as do firewalls, packet shaping devices…; the list goes on and on. At The Peck School, the best defense has been a network manager who has stayed on top of developments and vendors who have taken the time to understand the plans and ideas for growth.

See Chapters 5 and 8 for ways to keep your network running smoothly, even with the demands placed on it by a 1-to-1 program.

Building Design

The timing of the 1-to-1 laptop initiative was very fortunate because it coincided with the design and construction of a new building at The Peck School. The best time to install network cables is before walls are completed, so that you don't have to cut through drywall or other materials. Similarly, the best time to institute a laptop program is during the construction of a new building, when planners are designing classrooms, storage for students, network cabling, and so forth. For Peck, this meant that all electrical and network connections were planned, purchased, and installed with the needs of the laptop program in mind. Many districts and schools face the challenge of retrofitting their buildings for laptops, but Peck could literally begin from the ground up and design a building around and for laptops.

There did turn out to be one need for retrofitting, however. The building was finished and in use when the technology department realized the soft-sided cases originally purchased for the laptops were providing too little protection. Rather than install lockers, which are too narrow for laptops and hard-sided cases, Peck decided to build open, square cubbies with anchor bolts for long, looping cables. At the ends of each cable are loops through which a regular Master combination lock can be threaded.

Students lock their laptops in these cubbies by threading the cables through the handles of the hard-sided cases and closing the combination lock (see Figure 1.4). In this way, laptops can be secured when not in use. Teachers check the laptops frequently to be sure they're all locked in place; if not, they're "kidnapped" and brought to the Upper School office. Students face disciplinary action if they fail to secure their laptops properly. Cubbies have been such an effective addition to the seventh- and eighth-grade building that Peck's Academic Link building was designed to have cubbies as well.

Figure 1.4
Peck School's cubbies accommodate laptops locked in place.

Even though the CT building for seventh- and eighth-graders was designed for laptops, it wasn't originally designed for a wireless network. In fact, although some of the design features made sense when the building was constructed, they aren't used much anymore. For instance, in the multipurpose room, pull-down electrical outlets were installed in the ceiling so that students could plug in their laptops. These are rarely used now, because iBook batteries last longer. In the new Academic Link building, this design feature has been replaced by floor boxes housing both electrical and data outlets.

The long tables with hard-wired Ethernet drops in place that were purchased especially for the CT building are another example. Students originally used Ethernet cables to plug their laptops into the tables, which also had electrical outlets. These tables have since been moved to storage because network access is fully wireless and most students arrive at school with fully charged batteries.

While a few overhead projectors were included in the original design, Peck has added several more. The school is planning to install overhead projectors in every classroom in the new buildings as well. Some in the new building will be wireless, and some will have hard-wired connections for laptops or desktops.

Protective Cases

Peck initially purchased soft-sided, briefcase-like cases for its laptops. Within the first year, however, many laptops suffered major damage, particularly to their screens. The cost to repair them was often greater than the cost of a new computer. These cases just weren't standing up to the wear and tear that seventh- and eighth-graders were putting their laptops through while transporting them to and from school in the back of a car. They were no doubt surrounded by hockey equipment, tennis rackets, backpacks full of books, and maybe a golden retriever or two.

After investigating other options, Peck decided to purchase Zero Halliburton cases, which are exceedingly sturdy. These have proved to be equal to everything that Peck School seventh- and eighth-graders have (quite literally) thrown at them. There's even a tale,

Cautionary Tale

Laptop Cases

Peck initially used soft-sided laptop cases and experienced major damage, particularly to screens. Moving to hard-sided cases cut damage costs by more than half. Samsonite makes an aluminum case with a combination lock that works perfectly for Peck's needs, especially as a local luggage company was willing to customize the cases' interior foam padding to fit the iBook laptops that Peck students were using.

which fortunately has neither been confirmed nor repeated, about an SUV running over a case without damaging the laptop inside. In 2003, Peck contracted with a local luggage store to purchase hard-sided Samsonite cases that were nearly as durable but cost much less. The store customized the cases by cutting the interior foam padding in the shape of an iBook. These cases, which cost $165 apiece, have worked extremely well to protect the school's investment in technology. So far, the only damage that has occurred has happened when the laptops were outside of their cases.

The school has also looked at various "always-on" protective case options, such as those from InfoCase, and Peck may go in that direction in the future. However, because the cases open easily and the laptop could slip out, these cases may not fit so easily into Peck's cubbie and cable-lock system. The school will revisit this issue annually as more cases and options become available.

Insurance

For the first several years of the laptop program, insurance was purchased from a company that specialized in insuring laptops for schools. The premium was high, about $12,000 per year for the 80 laptops. This policy covered all damages over and above Apple's extended warranty, less a $100 deductible. If the damage occurred because of neglect or abuse, the school submitted the bill to the insurance company, received a check, and billed the parents for the deductible. This worked well, especially before more durable cases were purchased for each laptop.

Once the school purchased hard-shell protective cases, however, damage to the laptops began to occur much less frequently. Administrators reviewed the insurance policy and realized that for Peck's annual $12,000 payment, the school was receiving less than $2,000 back for damaged equipment. Most problems were being covered by Apple's extended warranty, and damage wasn't excessive. By 2006, fortunately, there was no incidence of theft. Consequently, the decision was made to become self-insured and cover the cost of laptop damage directly.

When Apple determines damage is over and above the warranty plan in place, Peck School splits the cost of the damage with parents of students who incur the damage. Generally, the most costly damage is to laptop screens, which can cost $900 to repair or replace. So far, it's been cheaper to self-insure, as generally only three or four such incidents occur per year.

The Peck School laptop program is small enough for this plan to work. Other schools and districts will have to consider whether this plan makes sense for them. Every year, Peck looks at these costs and determines how much they're impacting the budget, and so far the decision to self-insure has proved cost-effective.

Professional Development and Teacher Support

Peck knew that for technology to be integrated successfully into the classroom, teachers had to be on board with the program first. To facilitate this, teachers were given laptops a full year before students. In addition, several professional development initiatives were begun to support teachers' use of the laptops in their everyday teaching and preparation.

One initiative was known as the TAG Team approach. Technology-Adept Gurus—faculty members who already had an affinity for computers and were willing to be trained a bit more—were identified to provide peer-level technical support to other teachers. A special stipend was given to these TAG teachers. This initiative was based on the premise that it's often less intimidating to ask a colleague for help than it is to call technical support.

Figure 1.5
Inspiration created by Peck School's Leslie Maguire, Upper School technology coordinator, showing how teachers were brought on board with the laptop program.

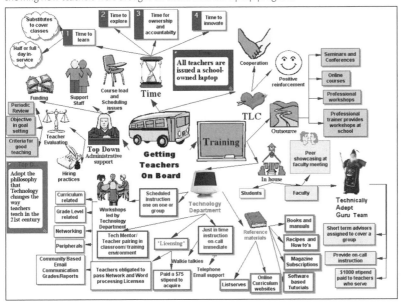

Another initiative was "licensing" teachers for their demonstrated ability to use the network and productivity software. Teachers who attended a series of classes and passed a battery of skills tests earned a license when they were finished. It carried a small stipend as well as a certificate of completion.

These classes were conducted using differentiated instruction principles. Three types of training were offered. The first involved a tech-trainer-led computer lab, where teachers followed instructions step-by-step to familiarize themselves with a particular program or process. A second type brought teachers together to learn with a self-guided handout, with the tech trainer circulating to answer questions and fix glitches. The third approach was entirely do-it-yourself. These different training methods were supplemented and reinforced at regular faculty meetings. Teacher projects and technology successes were showcased, and teachers were able to ask questions and learn from one another.

A commitment to just-in-time learning and just-in-time technical support was part of the plan from the beginning. When teachers need to learn or use something new, they know the technology department will respond quickly to phone or e-mail requests, arriving within minutes to get them out of a jam. This technical support helps feed professional development, since Peck's network manager and tech support specialist always discuss with teachers what they're doing to fix the problem. Then, they show them how to do it the next time themselves.

One Teacher Tells His Story: Don Diebold

Without educators (**E**) in the classroom who truly believe in the potential of laptops to transform the learning environment, and without their commitment (**C**) and willingness to change their teaching approaches to embrace this new technology, the laptop program at The Peck School would not have flourished as it has.

Figure 1.6
Don Diebold is committed to improving teaching processes through the use of technology.

One of these committed teachers and leaders, Don Diebold, typifies the experience many teachers have gone through over the years while adopting and embracing computer technology.

Diebold has taught at Peck for more than 30 years. He's Peck's athletic director and teaches all seventh- and eighth-grade science classes. When he came to Peck in 1973, he was immediately impressed with how the administration promoted creativity in the classroom, not just in the curriculum but also in the mode of instructional delivery. When computer technology started to take hold in the corporate world, he paid close attention, knowing instinctively that the same technology would eventually find its way to the classroom.

Diebold saw how technology was helping corporations accomplish tasks more efficiently, so he began using technology to automate the athletic department. He remembers first using word processing and spreadsheet programs to inventory equipment and uniforms. Previously, as changes occurred, schedules and inventories had to be typed, crossed out, and retyped many times. The advantages of doing this work on a computer, including instant access to information and the ability to change details easily, were immediately apparent to him as an administrator.

Seeing how computers could facilitate the running of the athletic department, Diebold began using them to generate tests and lesson plans. However, there wasn't much in the way of digital teaching materials for a number of years. When the world wide web got off the ground in the early '90s and software and hardware options for science teaching and laboratory work became more widely available, he realized it would just be a matter of time until these professional science applications began to filter into the classroom.

Next came laptops on a rolling cart. Diebold requested and received special hardware and software to collect data for seventh- and eighth-grade science labs. The result was higher quality lab reports, which took less time for students to complete and teachers to assess.

Whereas 90% of lab time had formerly been spent on mechanics and paperwork and only 10% on working with students to deepen their conceptual approach to assignments, Diebold now found he could spend "a bigger percentage of time on teaching students how to think like scientists and less time on the mechanics of the process" (personal interview, October 6, 2005).

What he describes is exactly what an outside evaluator picked up on very quickly when he visited Diebold's class in December 2002. Joel Backon, director of information technology at another independent school, Choate Rosemary Hall, visited Peck that year in response to Peck's request for an outside evaluation of its laptop program. In his report, Backon singled out Diebold's use of laptops in the science lab for particular praise:

> In your science program, Mr. Diebold's observations that the use of laptops and probes for scientific investigation has improved the quality of lab reports and increased the number and complexity of labs is evidence that technology integration is working. Many high school teachers find these notions counterintuitive. Because you are integrating rather than simply using technology, you have captured additional class time rather than sacrificing it.

As technology has gotten better, Diebold's classes have become more integrated. He's been able to find more and better teaching resources, and laptops have become faster, more reliable, and easier to use. The Internet has provided him with useful professional contacts: for example, a professor at the University of Virginia who had developed dissection software was willing to work with Diebold to give him a better understanding of how it worked and its benefits.

The web also provides numerous learning opportunities for his seventh- and eighth-grade students. Diebold reports: "I have websites for every concept I teach. Some are simple sites that are easy to understand, others are more complex ones that I use just for the graphics." The value of the web for him is how rapidly it responds to changing ideas about science.

Before Peck School started its laptop program, Diebold says,

> There was a lot of debate between the board, the administration, and the faculty as to whether [laptop use] was appropriate. The users of laptops did presentations to the board on numerous occasions to show how laptops could be used. It worked because of the vision of administration, trustees, and the head of technology at that time, as well as some of us in the faculty who believed technology was crucial to education in the future.

While cautioning that "traditional methods are still needed—nothing replaces the teacher," Diebold believes that technology can help teachers communicate their passion for learning to a new generation of students more comfortable with computers and the Internet than with thick reference books.

Diebold tries to incorporate laptops into everything he does in class. He e-mails lesson plans to his students ahead of time to inform them before the class meets. Student assignments are returned by e-mail so that an electronic backup copy of all student work exists. Diebold is enthusiastic about the changes to his teaching process that the laptops have helped bring about, particularly in their ability to support differentiated instruction. He says:

> I cover the same concepts that I did prior to the laptops but I do so in probably 200% greater depth than I did before. The laptops enable me to conduct a class where I guide the

students, spend more time with those having difficulty with fundamental concepts or skills, and allow other students to move forward with enrichment work related to what we are studying. I can reach every student in the classroom. The laptops have allowed me to do that without doing double the work.... We need to find as many different ways as possible to say the same things. That is what a master teacher can do with technology: show concepts in many different ways, and be ready with a mode of delivery that works for every student, no matter where they are developmentally.

The relative strengths of every student can be encouraged with a laptop, Diebold believes. The creative student may create a poster or a PowerPoint presentation to explain a scientific concept with artistic flair, while the analytical student may feel more comfortable explaining the same concept with a chart generated from a spreadsheet program. The fact that laptops can support both students' strengths inspires their passion for learning.

Diebold believes that teachers need to act now to embrace technology, because that increasingly is the language students speak: "Technology is their language. It's a huge part of their lives, of the world they are living in today. If you don't talk their language you are not going to reach them" (ibid.). He is committed (**C**) to Peck's laptop program because it puts students first and gives them the best tools available to organize and personalize their learning. This is why it works.

Acceptable Use and Parent Buy-In

After much discussion and nearly going another direction, Peck decided to raise its tuition and provide laptops to all seventh- and eight-grade students as part of the tuition cost. This was in lieu of charging an extra laptop fee or asking parents to buy the laptops on their own.

It's true that Peck has a graduated tuition, with parents of seventh- and eighth-graders paying higher tuition. But when the tuition increase for the laptop program was instituted, it was decided to make it an across-the-board increase that would be shared by all constituents. The idea was that younger students will eventually benefit from the laptops and that Peck's overall technology program builds from kindergarten right up to the eighth grade, providing a solid base for effective laptop use.

This approach answered the concern of many parents about having to pay extra money. It also allowed Peck to retain ownership of the computers, simplifying software compatibility, maintenance, and other issues. Still, there was then, as there is now, a need to reach out to parents to solicit their buy-in and support for the 1-to-1 laptop program. As a consequence, parental outreach and education are crucial to the program's ongoing success.

Every year, parents are sent information about the program, and all seventh-grade parents purchase a case for the laptop. The parent handbook has a special section on laptop use and maintenance, which is updated every summer (see Appendix A). In addition, the Peck School Acceptable Use Policy (also in Appendix A) must be signed every year by the parent(s) or guardian(s), as well as by the student. Finally, parents must also sign a laptop assessment sheet every year that details the serial number and the condition of the laptop. This document contains a statement that outlines parental responsibility for the costs of any damages not covered by the laptop warranty.

Since Peck wants students to use their laptops in meaningful and appropriate ways, the Peck School Acceptable Use Policy has a student summary requiring that all use of computers be **LARK**.

The **L** stands for **legal**, which covers plagiarism issues as well as the downloading of unpurchased music and software. Recently, in a "themes" class for seventh-graders, teachers divided classes in half and asked each half to investigate Napster vs. Metallica, a file-sharing case of several years back. The students themselves came to the conclusion that copying music onto a CD and distributing it to friends is illegal.

The **A** is for **appropriate**. Seventh-graders are told that this refers not only to the sophisticated 13-year-old's view of whether material is appropriate, but also to what the student's grandmother, 4-year old sister, and Peck School teachers and administrators would consider appropriate. This approach works better for students and helps them step outside their own norms.

R stands for **responsible**. Responsible care and use includes not having a can of Coca-Cola next to the computer and not balancing the laptop precariously on one's knees while sitting on a cement sidewalk.

Finally, **K** is for **kind**. Peck is committed to being a community of people who are caring and kind to one another, and this must be exhibited in computer use as well. Every use of computers needs to be kind, from e-mail messages, to pictures and images chosen for display, to respect for passwords and personal files.

Cautionary Tale

Having LARK Is Not Enough

Having LARK as your acceptable use policy doesn't preclude correction, discipline, and monitoring. Students at Peck are told that their laptops, e-mail accounts, and network use are not private but subject to oversight and inspection. However, student infractions are generally handled as teachable moments. They're considered opportunities for students to reflect on their actions, both in light of LARK and in terms of their own reputations and membership in a community of learners.

Overall, these methods have worked very smoothly. According to Cathy Walsh, during the first year of the program one parent said she didn't want her child to receive a laptop. Walsh solved that by telling her she'd already paid for it and described how tuition includes a laptop. Today, most parents sending their children to Peck know all about its technology program, and Peck's admissions director makes sure that prospective parents tour classrooms with laptops and learn about the school's plan to go to a fully wireless campus. The laptop program has become a major factor in encouraging parents to consider The Peck School.

Laptop Integration

Peck's goal from the very beginning of the 1-to-1 laptop program has been to integrate these digital assistants as much as possible into daily classroom activities. Wherever appropriate, laptops have become a part of seventh- and eighth-grade teaching, learning, communicating, thinking, and problem solving. This process of integration is repeated day in and day out, and teachers, students, and parents have learned to accept the process that this integration requires.

Lessons Learned

Permission Forms

Sending a student home with a shiny new laptop computer and a set of forms for the student and parent to sign doesn't mean the forms will necessarily come back the next day. Or the day after. Or even the next month! To combat this problem, The Peck School requires that both the forms and the computer be returned the next day. If the forms haven't been signed, the student doesn't get the shiny new laptop back, and instead gets an old, slow, ugly loaner computer to use. Since every student naturally wants the beautiful, fast iBook and will do whatever it takes to keep it, few forget to bring their signed forms back on a timely basis.

It isn't always easy.

It requires that educators commit to evaluating laptop use in their classrooms continually. Every day, teachers must address the management challenges presented by classrooms of laptop-enabled adolescents. They must regularly check out new online textbooks and resources and stay current with education technology developments and approaches.

It requires an administration willing to invest the resources and time needed to make sure the program continues and flourishes. In Peck's case, this has meant continuous investment in cabling, wireless access points, server rooms, air conditioners, and other infrastructure needs—not just in existing buildings but in every building planned for the future.

It also requires a board of trustees that understands the fiscal responsibility of maintaining an adequate technology budget, approving new technology infrastructure purchases, and staffing the school with experienced technology administrators and tech-savvy teachers.

Integration requires the coordination of all these different pieces, but where it finally plays out is in the classroom, with the integration of the technology into the seventh- and eighth-grade curriculum. Curricular integration requires that teachers help their students get up to speed fast on the hardware features and software applications they'll use the most to get their schoolwork done.

Since the laptop program's inception, Peck has continually addressed the "chicken or egg" debate over whether it's best to teach technology skills as a discrete subject or implicitly, by means of projects. In the next two chapters, you'll read about some schools that have chosen the projects approach, believing that students learn technology skills best in the context of real work.

Peck, however, feels that basic technology skills are very important. Peck has revamped some of the curriculum to ensure that students spend time learning typing skills (Mavis Beacon, Typing Tutor, Type to Learn) and such basic tasks as printing documents and saving and backing up files to the network. Students also receive training in productivity software (Microsoft Word and Excel), concept mapping software (Inspiration), presentation software (Microsoft PowerPoint, TimeLiner), digital editing software (Adobe Photoshop, iMovie), and subject-specific software, such as Geometer's Sketchpad. As much as possible, these skills classes use content from the existing academic curriculum.

Program Evaluation

Peck has a long history of evaluating its various programs, and technology is always part of that evaluation. Self-assessment studies are conducted every five to seven years, to prepare for formal accreditation review and to evaluate the education that students are receiving.

Other evaluations are periodically undertaken as well. In 2003, Peck conducted an "Outcomes" evaluation during which Peck graduates, former parents, and former faculty were polled on how well they felt Peck's education measured up after several years.

In December 2002, I requested through my membership in edACCESS (Educational Administrative and Campus Computing Environment at Small Schools, an organization for technology in small independent K–12 schools and colleges) that a team of technology professionals come to Peck to evaluate our laptop program. I was asked by edACCESS to specify a few questions and particular areas for evaluation. The organization sent two evaluators, who spent a day with our seventh- and eighth-grade students and teachers. Their subsequent evaluation report was interesting and affirming.

To the question *"Does our technology curriculum and laptop use prepare our students for the ninth grade at rigorous schools?"* Joel Backon, director of information technology at Choate Rosemary Hall, replied (personal communication, June 21, 2003):

> Quantity of content has not traditionally fit well with technology integration…[however,] you have developed an enlightened approach to teaching and learning…[and] your best students could not be more prepared for the most rigorous schools. They will have received an excellent middle school education supplemented by a rich technology experience and the responsibility of managing their studies with a laptop computer—an impressive set of skills and talents for any rising ninth-grader.

Backon also challenged us to move ahead (ibid.), and this became a piece that we added to our "Outcomes" evaluation:

> Think more about outcomes; what you observe and what you expect. How is technology impacting those outcomes? Are you able to develop metrics that will "prove" that you are graduating better students than you graduated ten years ago? Are you able to show that Peck students are more prepared for high school than students at your peer schools?

In 2006, Peck completed a curriculum review following publication of the first edition of this book. These evaluations, along with student and teacher surveys conducted every few years, have helped to keep Peck grounded and committed to growth and renewal. Suggestions from evaluators often lead directly to improvements in programs and processes. For instance, one reviewer mentioned how frustrated students were with the laptop loaners given out to students who had lost or damaged their iBook. The Technology Department subsequently found that it could provide a slighter better loaner model for basically the same price. This still provided the disincentive of not being as cool and fast as the standard iBooks, without causing as much student frustration.

Conclusion

The Peck School has learned that an academically rigorous and traditional school with an accelerated program can successfully integrate technology into teaching and learning, benefiting both students and teachers alike. Often people think that 1-to-1 is all about replacing traditional pedagogy and rigor with project-based learning and other constructivist practices. While 1-to-1 certainly *can* support this move to more progressive approaches, it can also sustain a traditional program such as Peck's. When students are empowered by 24/7 access to a digital assistant, all the learning they do, at school and at home, is enhanced.

The next two chapters profile other schools and districts that have implemented 1-to-1 programs. Several of these programs feature a more progressive approach to education. Regardless of the pedagogical philosophy of these different schools, however, what has determined their level of success has been the same: informed educators (**E**) who have taken the time to plan (**P**) their program carefully and have worked through the implementation challenges and processes with commitment (**C**) and passion.

Figure 1.7
Components of successful laptop programs.

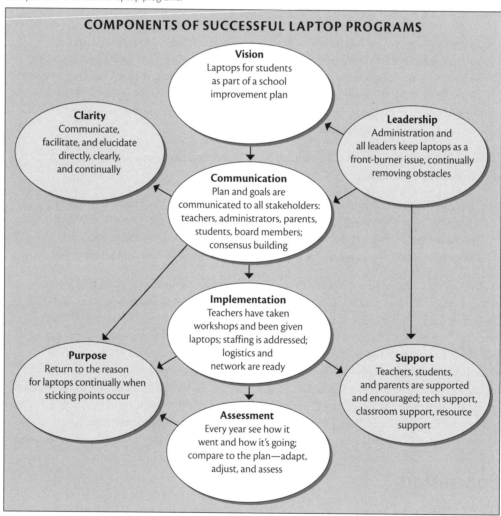

Chapter 2
INDIVIDUAL SCHOOL PROGRAMS

Introduction

REGARDLESS OF A SCHOOL'S SIZE, population, or technology infrastructure, starting a 1-to-1 program is a major undertaking. In the previous chapter, we looked at the development of The Peck School's laptop program from its earliest planning stages to its current, evolving state. It's a development process made possible by educators' commitments to plan, fund, evaluate, and improve the program year by year. A 1-to-1 program is never a "do it once and you're done" proposition.

Figure 2.1
A normal day in a normal classroom at The Urban School.

For Peck, the commitment to 1-to-1 has had a lot to do with academics: the need to support and sustain students' work at school and at home, as well as the desire to integrate technology across all disciplines. All schools considering a laptop initiative will go through similar processes, even though the reasons, contexts, and outcomes may differ depending on the school's composition, mission, and instructional philosophy. In this chapter, we'll look at three other schools that have implemented a 1-to-1 program and see how the same basic ingredients have created distinct but equally successful programs.

The Urban School (www.urbanschool.org) is a high school in San Francisco that's added 1-to-1 laptops to its student-centered learning environment, greatly benefiting students and teachers alike. The school has used laptops to help its students reach out and interact with the community at large, especially with its Telling Their Stories digital storytelling project. Laptops are fully integrated into the curriculum at The Urban School, where computer skills are honed through content-based activities and projects rather than separate computer skills classes. Howard Levin, director of technology, gave generously of his time to contribute to this profile of Urban's award-winning laptop program.

Whitfield School, an independent school in St. Louis that only recently instituted a 1-to-1 program, has found a great deal of immediate success with laptops. Whitfield espouses a process-oriented instructional philosophy, in which the process of learning and not just the content being learned is a primary focus. Alex Inman, Whitfield's technology directory, came to St. Louis a couple of years ago after successfully leading laptop implementation at University Lake School in Milwaukee. He found a ready and willing constituency at Whitfield School, where educators were already committed to teaching in a student-centered way that is perfectly complemented by ubiquitous computer access.

The Denver School of Science and Technology (DSST) sprang up as a charter school, formed and funded with the help of Colorado governor Bill Owens and Microsoft cofounder and chairman Bill Gates. As a brand-new school, DSST was built from the ground up with wireless laptops in mind. Unlike Peck, Urban, and Whitfield, there's been no need to retrofit the curriculum or school infrastructure—or to solicit buy-in from teachers and staff—to make 1-to-1 work at DSST. When technology is such a primary focus of a school's mission and approach that it's included in the school's name, educators know that integrating technology into everything they do is a mandate, not simply a goal.

FUNDING OPTIONS FOR 1-TO-1 PROGRAMS

All 1-to-1 programs are different, taking their particular forms from the populations they serve and the instructional philosophies they embrace. The approaches to funding those programs can be even more distinctive. There's no perfect or tried-and-true formula for funding a laptop program.

At The Peck School, startup costs were funded by a capital campaign to raise dollars specifically for technology. The program has been sustained in the years since by an across-the-board tuition increase.

At The Urban School, on the other hand, a survey taken of all current and prospective parents showed that most had already planned to buy a laptop for their children. So Urban sold those parents on the idea of paying the school to purchase laptops instead, thereby reaping the economy-of-scale benefits of a bulk purchase and support package.

Whitfield has phased in its laptop program gradually, limiting it initially to certain grades and providing laptops to teachers first to give them time to create curricular plans. Consequently, Whitfield is now funding its programs from existing dollars.

The Denver School of Science and Technology, a charter school, has received grants and funding from many sources to run its state-of-the-art wireless laptop program.

The Urban School, San Francisco

The Urban School in San Francisco is an independent coed high school with approximately 265 students in Grades 9 through 12. Administrators plan to grow the school to about 320 students in the next few years and add a building in response to the increasing competition in San Francisco for private school space.

The Urban School prides itself on its student-centered philosophy and has received awards for its student-generated digital storytelling program titled Telling Their Stories: An Oral History Archive (www.tellingstories.org). With compelling interviews and profiles of Holocaust survivors, as well as concentration camp liberators and Japanese-American internees, this excellent program is an exemplary model of project-based learning that integrates technology and speaks to audiences far beyond the classroom.

Director of Technology Howard Levin relates that some of the biggest successes of Urban's laptop program—in place since 2000—have come in the most surprising areas. For example, teachers in the language arts program were among the most hesitant and unconvinced of faculty members when the program began, but they're now among its strongest supporters. This difference in attitude, Levin says, is the result of those teachers "finding [laptop] tools that enhanced their ability to engage students in serious discussion."

Teachers at The Urban School were first given laptops in 2000, and laptops for students were provided on mobile carts. This didn't prove to be the best for students, however, and Levin now believes that students should have been given their own laptops from the beginning. The biggest initial challenge was simply getting the program started. At first, faculty members didn't express a lot of interest; the majority of teachers seemed rather ambivalent about the laptop program, seeing it as more of a nuisance than a benefit. Fortunately, most went along with it without too much resistance. The few individuals who strongly opposed the program did not, in the end, stand in the way of implementation.

Today, faculty members are nearly unanimous in their strong approval of the laptop program, and Urban's biggest challenge is simply keeping up with laptop maintenance issues. When laptops are totally integrated into a school curriculum, all school assignments involve them, and timely repair and maintenance become crucial to learning outcomes. "If [students] lose the laptop for 15 minutes," Levin says, "that can be devastating." Managing the human resources needed to support the program has become Levin's number-one job.

GETTING TEACHERS ON BOARD

It took three or four years for Urban School to go from the initial laptop program proposal to final implementation. It was first announced in 1998 as a single line in the school's strategic plan. Head of School Mark Salkind wanted to institute the laptop program, and he hired Levin to help pull it off. To pave the way among faculty members, Levin led a series of technology workshops offered over several summers. These workshops were meant to build both teachers' computer skills and their interest in the program. Teachers could choose what to study, and instruction focused on skills and resources that could be immediately applied in the classroom.

At the time, many teachers were interested in learning PowerPoint. Students were hired as tutors and paired with teachers, shadowing them and helping them complete projects. The only thing these student tutors were told, says Levin, was "don't touch the keyboard or the mouse, just be the guide." These weeklong workshops proved to be very successful. They encouraged technology integration efforts in subsequent school years and helped prepare teachers to take on the challenges that the 1-to-1 laptop program presented when it was first rolled out.

While teachers' instructional methods overall may not have changed drastically since the laptop program began, Levin sees indisputable evidence that teaching practices are evolving due to the many different things made possible when students and teachers have 24/7 access to a laptop computer. Urban has always encouraged a student-centered, project-based learning environment, and laptops have enabled teachers to take that approach to the next level. The digital storytelling project Telling Their Stories is a perfect example of this: without laptops and ubiquitous access to the Internet and video editing software, this project would not have been so successful.

GETTING ADMINISTRATORS AND PARENTS ON BOARD

Salkind was on board with the concept of 1-to-1 laptops from the beginning, as evidenced by his hiring of Levin to help implement and evangelize the program. Salkind's support was crucial, Levin says, and because of it, convincing other administrators of the merits of the program wasn't a problem. Convincing the Board of Trustees proved to be a little more difficult, however. Salkind and Levin moved slowly and carefully with the board, since there were few laptop programs in the Bay Area to point to for success stories and comparisons.

Initially, figuring out how to pay for the laptop program was also a big challenge. Today, student laptops are purchased with a parent-user fee that equals the three-year leased value of the computer. Parents are given the necessary information in print, and there's no opt-out option. Many other schools couldn't do this, Levin admits, but it works at Urban because Urban parents have such a high degree of trust in the head of school and the Board of Trustees. Consequently, getting the parents on board really was a matter of getting the Board of Trustees firmly on board first.

To increase the board's awareness of the potential of laptops in education, a technology task force was formed, comprising several board members as well as Salkind and Levin. Urban sent this team to the Dalton School in New York City and to Cincinnati Country Day School in Ohio to view their programs. The team then developed a laptop implementation plan for The Urban School and brought this proposal to the rest of the board.

A key selling point was the task force's assertion that a laptop program wouldn't cost the school a significant amount of money. This was important because a survey of Urban families showed that 78% to 80% of them already had a computer or were planning to buy one. A school-mandated but parent-funded laptop program, then, would simply redirect funds that were being spent anyway so that everyone could benefit. In the end, there was very little disagreement about what was anticipated to be the biggest problem: cost was really a nonissue. The laptop proposal received unanimous board approval.

PROGRAM SUCCESSES

Levin says that increased collaboration and sharing of information is "the number-one positive change universally felt by everyone" involved in the laptop program. Urban uses FirstClass, an e-mail program installed at many schools. According to Levin, this communication tool is "the cornerstone of what we do." Teachers appreciate how easy it now is to share information with other teachers, students, and parents and how that can lead to better integration and organization of curriculum across all content areas.

Another big success of the program has been the dramatic increase in the use of computer technology by everyone at the school. This was both an overt and covert priority, says Levin: "We didn't talk much about it…[but] it was one of my objectives from the start. Knowing technology gives kids an enormous advantage." While students at The Urban School don't consider themselves to be particularly tech-savvy because they don't take technology classes, their proficiency with computers is actually quite high, Levin says. Simply by using laptops to do all their schoolwork, they quickly become comfortable with the hardware and software, to the point students are increasingly doing their own tech support and helping each other fix problems.

HOW LAPTOPS ARE USED AT URBAN

Levin says that "communication, organization, information and production" have been enhanced by laptops at The Urban School (personal communication, November 23, 2004). He points to the example of Urban science department chair Algis Sodonis. Sodonis posts online solutions to difficult problems and maintains an archive of Help Files and exemplary student work.

In keeping with Urban's constructivist philosophy, collaborative work and project-based learning are major elements of the curriculum, requiring students to plan and organize their workloads independently. Levin says that surveys of Urban students confirm that enhancing their ability to stay organized and keep track of projects is seen as a primary benefit of having laptops 24/7: "When asked about the best school-related use of their laptop, 63% of student narrative responses dealt with organization" (ibid.). Laptops give Urban students access to specialized resources: students in the constitutional law class use the web resource FindLaw (www.findlaw.com) to research laws in ways that were previously possible only by visiting a law library. Teachers use their laptops to hold online conferences with writing groups to encourage student collaboration on projects.

Levin concludes that Urban's laptop program "is smoothly making the transition from its earlier experimental phase to one where use is becoming more truly seamless, ubiquitous and normal. The reported advantages are also helping to support a truly dynamic curriculum filled with a sense of new possibilities" (ibid.).

Whitfield School, St. Louis

Whitfield School is an independent, non-parochial school in St. Louis, Missouri, that enrolls approximately 475 boys and girls in Grades 6–12. Director of Technology Alex Inman, who previously developed a 1-to-1 initiative at a school in Wisconsin, is drawing on that experience to plan and implement Whitfield's laptop program. Inman's plan is to roll out the 1-to-1 laptop program for all Whitfield School students over the course of four years.

The program was launched in the 2004–2005 school year, when laptops were provided to all Whitfield teachers and a limited number of students. During this first year, there were two carts of laptops that could be rolled from class to class and three pilot classrooms.

Initial funding was obtained through a self-funded grant competition called UTSUT (Uber-Teachers Seeking Ubiquity with Technology). Eight or nine Whitfield teachers applied. They agreed to be the program's "indentured servants" for at least three years, working with the laptops in their own classrooms the first year and then teaching others how to use them effectively over the next two. It was tough to determine the grant recipients, says Inman, because many qualified teachers applied: "We picked people who were good at professional development."

Whitfield took this "gradual rollout" approach both to create a manageable experience set within the school and for financial reasons. Gradual rollout enables teachers and administrators to better manage the changes in learning environment and teaching practice that ubiquitous computing entails. It also creates a committed cadre of experts who can help colleagues figure out how to integrate laptops into their classrooms with as little disruption as possible. Whitfield's gradual approach has also allowed it to absorb the cost of the program in more digestible and sustainable chunks.

Rather than funding laptops as a one-time capital expense, Whitfield has chosen a "phased lease" approach that helps to create a defined timeframe for the laptops and permits more predictable annual budget planning. By implementing the program gradually, the school's been able to fund not only the initial cost of the laptops themselves but also the operational and network costs associated with their introduction. Inman says a similar approach will be used to build in upgrades to the hardware as the program continues to grow in the years ahead: the newest laptop models will go to faculty and seniors, the year-old models will go to 10th- and 11th-graders, the two-year-old models will go to 8th- and 9th-graders, and so forth. This way, as students become older and more sophisticated users, they'll get newer and more powerful computers to use.

Together, this phased lease approach and the gradual rollout has allowed Whitfield to roll the cost of the laptop program into each student's tuition fees. Because tuition is the main source of funding for instructional programs at Whitfield, administrators were concerned that they not raise tuition too precipitously to fund the laptop program. By going with the gradual rollout and the four-year leasing arrangement, Inman says, the school was able to limit the technology-related tuition hike to about $150 per year per student.

GETTING THE PROGRAM STARTED

Whitfield School follows a process-oriented instructional philosophy, focusing more time and energy on the overall learning process than on any particular academic discipline's content. Grade-level teams meet once a week so that teachers can coordinate curricula and collaboratively implement cross-curricular projects.

When Inman first came to visit the school at the invitation of Whitfield President Mark Anderson, he was immediately inspired by this student-centered approach. He remembers his first impression of the school (personal communication, December 15, 2004):

> [President Anderson] gave me three hours and said, "Go where you want and wander around." In that time, I saw only one teacher standing at a board. Every other class had students working in groups. This school really espoused a student-centered model of teaching. I was sold!

Inman responded so readily to Whitfield's process-oriented instruction because he believes that while teaching content is fine, a lot of that content eventually becomes obsolete. What's more important, he thinks, is to teach students how to "garner, gather and synthesize information so that students are prepared to learn and create new knowledge in the future." Whitfield's instructional approach is perfect for making that happen on a daily basis: "All of the tools and approaches I have brought in here have found a home almost immediately" (Inman, 2004).

When Inman came on board at Whitfield, school president Anderson accompanied him on a tour of six laptop-using schools in the area (**P** for planning). In their subsequent report to Whitfield's Board of Trustees, they indicated that much of what they'd seen in these programs was disappointing. The technology was simply being used to automate the same teacher-centered modes of instruction that had been in place before. Many of these schools had pointed excitedly to their use of electronic SmartBoards, some funded by the Missouri eMints program. However, Inman and Anderson felt the SmartBoards were only facilitating and automating the "sage on the stage" teaching methods that Whitfield wanted to avoid. Inman says (2004):

> Though we saw some great things, we saw too many teachers making the technology fit an existing model of teaching rather than letting the technology be a more transparent tool.... SmartBoards and projectors are great tools, but if they only further entrench the teacher's power in the front of the room rather than help students facilitate their own learning, the school is not getting the full educational value for their investment in laptops.

Inman and Salkind worked on creating a laptop program that would reflect Whitfield's process-oriented philosophy and make learning a student-centered activity. Seeing how other schools in the area were using technology helped Whitfield design its own program.

IMPLEMENTING THE PROGRAM

In 2006, Whitfield was in the second year of its four-year gradual rollout. Even now, much remains to be done before administrators and teachers will be able to evaluate confidently the laptop program's overall effects on Whitfield's learning environment. Major pedagogical changes of all types typically take three to five years to take effect, so Inman believes Whitfield's laptop initiative is on the right timetable.

Having led a similar program at University Lake School, Inman has the advantage of experience. He recalls one student there (a relative of one of the school's founders) who, when laptops were first handed out during his sophomore year, called them "$1,600 paperweights" that would quickly become "$1,600 music storage systems." Two years later, Inman taught him in one of his senior classes and noticed that the laptop never left his side. Inman asked the student what he thought of his paperweight now. He responded that he could no longer imagine living without it: his research and writing were much improved, and he was so much more organized than before. He'd devised a number of ways to use the laptop to help him with his studies. Rather than using index cards to organize the 50 resources needed for a history project, for example, he'd developed an Access database with hyperlinks. His database model was so useful, the history teacher had been using it on other projects ever since. "The kid did it," Inman remembers. "He understood the goal and context, understood the tool, and brought it to the next level" (2004).

Similar things are continually happening at Whitfield School. In 11th-grade English classes, for example, students are required to identify a truth that's important to them or their generation and design a book cover that depicts both the truth and their perspective on it. The project is intended to help students learn to communicate in an increasingly visual world. After students have designed their covers, the covers are displayed and a jury of peers tries to intuit the truth depicted as well as the designer's perspective on that truth.

Before Whitfield 11th-graders had laptops, most students created their book covers by cutting out images from magazines and making a collage. When laptops became available, however, students asked for and received permission to use digital tools for the project. They looked for images on the Internet, took their own digital photos or scanned and manipulated existing images, and assembled their covers using Adobe Photoshop.

The English teacher in charge reports that students seemed considerably more involved in the project when using digital tools, and their designs communicated their intended message to the student juries 90% of the time. When covers were designed using the old magazine cutout method, student juries were typically able to identify the truth depicted only 50% of the time. Inman says (personal communication, December 10, 2004) this is precisely the kind of anecdotal evidence that is most persuasive to him.

> This project was done during the pilot phase of a laptop rollout plan. We believe deeply in a notion of a community of learners in which teachers have just as much to learn from the students as the students do from the teachers. I believe this understanding is critical for the success of a laptop program.... Many of our teachers speak "technology" only as a second language whereas many students speak "technology" as a fluid part of their day-to-day lives. This teacher created an environment in which students felt comfortable challenging the design of the assignment, and the teacher was comfortable being challenged. What resulted was a more appropriate and more challenging lesson.

1-to-1 access to laptops gave these Whitfield students the ability to communicate more precisely using digital images and tools. By giving them a chance to select, manipulate, and own their own digital designs, the entire project had more meaning for them. This is an exemplar of what can happen when teachers and administrators are open to process-oriented curricular design facilitated by laptops.

The laptop rollout has not been without its problems and challenges, of course. Inman mentions two in particular: hardware maintenance and teacher training. He cautions schools considering a laptop program to plan carefully for the challenges of keeping hundreds of laptops up and running while simultaneously maintaining the viability and security of the school network: "This is hard but has to be done" (Inman, 2004).

With regard to training teachers to use laptops more effectively in the classroom, Inman says what's most important is to teach them to enhance their existing curriculum by using the standard features of their computers creatively rather than relying on canned digital material. "[Laptops] can be a sweet catalyst to get teachers to think about curriculum, and think differently," says Inman, leading to more dynamic, process-oriented teaching practices (2004).

HOW LAPTOPS ARE USED AT WHITFIELD

During the 2005–2006 school year, all 11th- and 12th- graders at Whitfield were given laptops for the first time. Inman was immediately impressed with how well they were integrated into the classroom. The 12th-grade history class at Whitfield quickly became paperless. Laptops enabled students to work on the NAIS Challenge 20/20 project—a global schools initiative created by the National Association of Independent Schools—and interact with students at a school in Germany by means of an online web portal.

"Laptops [are] used nearly daily for research, writing, electronic communication, and presentations," Inman says. Individual projects include the use of Photoshop in 11th-grade history classes to create stamp designs that "represent a decade within the context of a single event or person" (2004). Twelfth-grade math classes use laptops to graph solutions and take online quizzes. In both 11th- and 12th-grade science, students work in online virtual labs and use probes that can be attached to the laptops to measure force and temperature. Inman says (personal communication, December 28, 2005):

> In foreign language classes, the free audio-editing program Audacity is used to record and play back conversations so that students can hear and improve their pronunciation. Students are asked to do impromptu research on a regular basis: "When a conversation or discussion in class yields an interesting question, the teacher takes advantage of that teachable moment to assign students to do a little instant online research and find different perspectives or answers to that question."

The Denver School of Science and Technology

While the other schools profiled in this chapter had their own institutional histories of earlier school reforms and improvements to draw on when they implemented their laptop programs, this was not the case for The Denver School of Science and Technology (DSST). Whereas both The Urban School and Whitfield School carefully considered how to adapt their existing structures to accommodate a laptop program that would support and further their school mission, DSST gave all of its teachers and students laptops from the moment it first opened its doors in 2004. Founded and funded by grants from the Bill and Melinda Gates Foundation and other benefactors, it's the first public school in Colorado to provide laptops to all students.

On the school website (www.scienceandtech.org), the founding of the school is described as the result of a conversation between Bill Gates and Colorado governor Bill Owens about educating students more thoroughly in math and science.

Mark Inglis, director of technology at DSST, describes the school's approach to technology integration in this way (personal communication, July 28, 2005):

> We seek to enable and support transformative uses of technology.... If technology is simply used to do things that students could do in other ways—if it is used only to enhance rather than transform what they are learning—then it is not worthwhile.

DSST provides laptops to all of its students to engage them and motivate them to experience learning in ways that would be impossible without laptops. These include direct communication with researchers in the field; collaboration using wikis, blogs, and other tools; computer-enhanced student-to-student, teacher-to-student, and school-to-parent interactions; and so forth.

When asked about the challenges of launching the DSST laptop program, Inglis emphasized the importance of transparency. Making technology transparent for all users and getting everything to work from day one is difficult but doable with good planning, he says. Funding and staffing are crucial issues: Inglis himself runs the school network and provides tech support, and a half-time full-time equivalent (.5 FTE) staff member is dedicated to working with faculty and students on technology integration. He says administrators must carefully consider the workload of teachers who must learn how to teach effectively with technology: "Nearly all teachers are overworked to begin with, and when they have to learn some new technology and how to teach with it, it takes time on their part. Finding the energy and resources for teachers is significant work" (Inglis, 2005).

Laptop cases were another start-up challenge. Initially, the school provided laptop cases for every student. However, finding cost-effective cases that would stand up to the rigors of student use proved difficult. Consequently, they now require students either to buy a backpack built especially for the laptop or purchase a used case from the school. Most choose the former. Inglis has also looked into the always-on cases available from such vendors as InfoCase and now believes they're the better option. In the future, he plans to offer this option to families.

No retrofitting was needed for wireless access as the brand new school building was outfitted with numerous wireless access points. Lockers weren't part of the original design, but they've since been added. "We originally had laptop 'pigeonholes' throughout the building that could be secured with a cable," Inglis says, "but since we found that students were having a hard time remembering their AC adapters, we thought the same might happen with the cables and keys" (2005). Consequently, laptop-friendly lockers have been installed for those rare times when the laptops are out of students' hands.

Despite DSST's short history, the school has already succeeded in ways that differentiate it from other, more traditional schools. "If I were to pick one [success]," Inglis says, "it would be in communication. Between all parties. Students, staff, teacher to student … everyone communicates far more and far better because everyone is connected wirelessly all the time" (2005). Inglis echoes other educators at laptop-using schools by saying that students at DSST seem far more engaged when using technology, and attendance problems have been virtually nonexistent (see http://scienceandtech.org/results.html for school academic results).

GETTING TEACHERS ON BOARD

Teachers knew what they were getting into when they applied for jobs at DSST: "Everyone knew students would have laptops and teachers would be expected to use them," Inglis says (2005). Still, there were some initial challenges getting these teachers to integrate the technology into their normal teaching practices. This figured into the school's decision to go with tablet PCs rather than laptops in the second year of the program. Tablets were a natural for math, but not every teacher was immediately comfortable with them.

As the school's first year came to a close and teachers received their performance reviews, specific issues were addressed, and professional development needs were identified. Teachers who felt confident in their technology skills were dispatched to help those colleagues who felt less comfortable. "It's impossible to do as much [teacher professional development] as I'd like," Inglis says. "We do some [workshops] every year before school starts, and we would like to do more ongoing sessions on an intentional, not reactionary, basis" (2005).

"I think you can't overdo professional development, and the more exhaustive workshops you do, the better off you'll be," Inglis says (2005). He recommends that school or district administrators who want to improve their professional development program in support of laptop integration should look for ideas from colleagues who have "been there, done that." Inglis himself contacted the Cincinnati Country Day School and the Henrico County School District in Virginia, and both were very helpful in the planning process at DSST. Good planning and flexibility, along with establishing a solid infrastructure from the beginning, are all key components for program success. When it comes to student technology training, on the other hand, he recommends (2005) that it always be contextualized as part of a project or curricular activities.

> We don't have any formal, ongoing student training. Our philosophy is that in order for this [technology] to be transformative, the training needs to be in the context of learning. As [students] are writing research papers, or working in Geometer's Sketchpad, they are learning the technology. We have instituted a mandatory 'seminar' class that teaches introductory skills and a few pieces of software (e.g., Dreamweaver) required for more independent projects such as our Digital Portfolio. (Inglis, 2005)

CO-OPTING TECH-SAVVY STUDENTS

DSST has found that a good way to empower students and encourage their active involvement in school is to use them as technical support specialists. "Our tech support crew is about 20 or 25 students," says Inglis. Students work to keep the laptops' software and operating system up-to-date and operational. DSST typically re-clones its computers during the school year to ensure they have the latest updates and are running optimally: "First we tell students to make sure they have all of their files backed up. Then we have the student tech support crew gather and clone all of the computers." Using students for tech support increases productivity and reduces the down time when laptops are out of student hands. "Last year, we took two-and-a-half days to re-clone all the laptops. This year, we did it in a day and a half. We expect it to take no more than a day next year" (Inglis, 2005).

Membership in the tech support crew is open to any DSST student but requires recommendations from an advisor, a teacher, a non-tech crew student, and a sponsoring member of the current tech crew. An extensive training and observation process takes place, after which students become full-fledged members and are allowed to use the local admin password to work on all laptops. Two-thirds of the tech crew are tenth-graders, and the rest are ninth-graders. Their contribution is essential to keeping laptops up and running.

One of the great benefits of this program is that it tends to co-opt the most tech-savvy (and potentially most trouble-making) students and encourages them to use their skills to good purpose. With the tech crew's emphasis on integrity and responsibility, combined with a reasonable dose of power, this program provides an incentive for fledgling hackers to work toward a positive goal.

HOW LAPTOPS ARE USED AT DSST

Students at DSST take their laptops with them everywhere they go: "They're used almost every moment of the day, except for gym class," says Inglis (2005). While some of this constant usage undoubtedly involves web games and social communication, a lot of homework's being done. In fact, the vast majority of assignments at DSST are delivered via computer. Some teachers notify students of assignments by creating Outlook calendar appointments and sending them to a distribution group. This puts the assignment and all its details directly onto the students' calendars and takes advantage of Outlook's automatic reminder feature. In this way, assignments can be accessed by students anytime and anywhere they have an Internet connection. Students can see the assignments, plan their work, and keep track of their progress, all in one location.

At school, the file server provides a drop box and class resource folder for teachers and students to share work back and forth. Students can access their own individual network folders, but no one else's. Teachers can retrieve homework assignments from the class drop box and return them directly to individual students' folders.

Last year, DSST introduced tablet PCs to all their sophomores. According to Inglis, "Virtually all of our tenth-grade teachers now use tablets on a daily basis, because it allows students to take notes in their own handwriting" (2005). Tablet PCs have built-in microphones that teachers have used to do student interviews, while language teachers have used the same capabilities to record language lessons and speaking practice. Presentation software is commonly used by both teachers and students.

DSST students are also required to create and post materials and work samples in a digital portfolio, a series of webpages used for goal-setting and assessment. According to the DSST website, "The Digital Portfolio (DP) will be a core academic assessment tool accessible to the entire school community … [and] will include a student's resume and a statement about his/her learning goals and achievements. Samples of a student's best work will be showcased and archived through the digital portfolios."

Other interesting software tools being used at DSST include SynchronEyes, a program designed for student computer management and control, and Microsoft OneNote, a collaborative document creation program that allows teachers and students to work together on brainstorming sessions, collective composition, and peer editing for written assignments. Recently, DSST teachers have begun to use Exam View, a network-based testing program that allows the creation of classroom tests that can be tied, question-by-question, to Colorado's state content area standards.

Chapter 3
DISTRICT-WIDE AND STATEWIDE PROGRAMS

Introduction

IT'S ONE THING TO DEPLOY a few hundred laptops in a single school building. It's something else again when laptop numbers run to five figures and the deployment is across an entire school district or state. The planning, logistics, politics, and infrastructure issues—not to mention the media attention likely to follow—can be quite daunting. Fortunately, for those of us watching and learning, a number of school districts across the country as well as a few states have taken a leap of faith and inaugurated large-scale laptop programs.

Figure 3.1
Teaching 1-to-1 becomes a reality when the student has a laptop computer.

This chapter profiles laptop programs instituted by Henrico County, Virginia; Maine; and Michigan. All three programs were kind enough to allow me to interview key planners and administrators. I've distilled their firsthand experiences in the descriptions that follow. Each of these programs has also received considerable media scrutiny, some of which is referenced here.

Henrico County, Virginia

Lloyd Brown, director of technology at Henrico County School District in Virgina, spoke to me about the district's laptop program. One of the first large-scale laptop initiatives in the United States, Henrico is in the fifth year of its district-wide program. Henrico found itself growing rapidly at the end of the '90s and struggling to keep up with changes in education technology, wondering how best to outfit its existing and new classrooms. The district's commitment (**C**) to graduating students with solid, transferable computer skills was strong, but it had old buildings and not enough computer labs. The usual solutions seemed inadequate to the district's needs.

Fortunately, Henrico County's leaders were ready and willing to consider all options and were unafraid to take some risks. Their commitment to providing students with the best technology tools possible encouraged them to take an aggressive approach to addressing the district's technology needs.

The district didn't want to start converting classrooms into computer labs and displacing students because most schools simply didn't have enough space or electrical capacity for this kind of expansion. Nor, with enrollment rising, did the district have the capital resources necessary to replace the old schools with expensive, high-tech buildings. District administrators looked briefly at a plan to install six or so computers per classroom, but the same issue—lack of space and electrical capacity—made this plan untenable.

Consequently, Henrico formed a committee of district and site administrators to look at other ways to provide technology to their students (**P** for planning). The conversation soon moved to laptops, as these machines were getting smaller and more durable. Once they began considering different ways they could deploy laptops throughout the district, a consensus emerged in favor of a 1-to-1 initiative.

Brown took part in this planning right from the beginning, undertaking a "total cost of ownership" study to consider laptops for every student in the district. It quickly became apparent to him that buying hardware and putting it in place for six or seven years wouldn't further the district's overall goal of giving students the opportunity to use and learn the newest technologies. Eventually, the antiquated hardware would become unusable, and the software that ran on it would no longer be transferable to the business world. Brown decided that leasing laptops made the most sense for the district, since that meant the hardware would be renewed every four years.

Henrico aggressively negotiated the leasing arrangement to lower costs enough to provide 18,000 laptops the first year of the program (2000–2001). Today, that number's up to 41,620, enough laptops to outfit every teacher in the district as well as all middle and high school students. Additionally, the 48 elementary schools now receive five laptops per classroom plus three carts per school (25 laptops to a cart.)

Knowing that getting buy-in from teachers (**E** for educators) was key, Henrico invested a lot of time and professional development dollars getting faculty comfortable and ready for the new program. Teachers were shown how the new laptops could be used to build a stronger school-to-home bridge and increase communication and accountability with parents and students. Increased teacher productivity was also addressed by implementing an electronic grading system. The goal of these professional development efforts, Brown says, was to encourage teachers to believe that "technology should work for me, not the other way around."

These outreach efforts quickly paid off, as teachers warmed to the benefits of 1-to-1 computing. But starting up such a program—one that had to be implemented at several different sites simultaneously—was not without its challenges. Brown initially felt it would take five years to get the

Cautionary Tale

Dealing with Inappropriate Downloads

One of the things we can learn from Henrico is flexibility. Things you don't expect to happen will happen. It's how you respond that counts. During the first year of the Henrico laptop program, some students were found downloading music and pornography to their laptops. This caused a few naysayers to jump on the ever popular "we told you so" bandwagon. Henrico responded by recalling the computers, reformatting them, upping their memory and security, and closing network loopholes. Inappropriate downloads haven't been a major problem since.

program fully off the ground, given the huge pedagogical and cultural changes that needed to take place across the district.

However, Henrico's School Board remained firm in its support and gave the district Technology Department the time it needed to work out all of the initial bugs. After piloting the program in 2000–2001, Brown and his team spent the summer planning (**P**) how to provide wireless networking for every laptop in every building. They carefully calculated bandwidth needs so that all would be able to connect to the Internet from their laptops. By the third year of the program, most teachers were comfortable with it, and more professional development training was scheduled to help teachers integrate computers into their classrooms.

HOW LAPTOPS ARE USED IN HENRICO COUNTY SCHOOLS

With more than 40,000 laptops in the program today, Henrico has the purchasing power to negotiate good prices for the software and peripherals included with the laptops. Tech planners have taken advantage of this to provide teachers and students with a wide variety of learning programs and productivity software. Among the most popular programs used by Henrico teachers are the following:

▶ Beyond Books offers online curriculum that extends in-class exercises with web links, worksheets, organizers, and self-assessing features.

▶ Explore Learning offers interactive math and science simulations called Gizmos.

▶ Larson's Pre-Algebra helps math teachers customize their curriculum and testing.

▶ Apex Learning provides accelerated activities and assessment tools optimized for advanced placement students.

▶ Quia offers web-based tools for creating interactive games, flashcards, word searches, and other reinforcement applications.

Another popular application available to students and teachers in the district is Virtual Share, a file-sharing program that allows teachers to upload assignments and documents to the school's server. It also allows students to send homework from home or school to the teacher's drop box (Henrico County Public Schools website, http://staffdev.henrico. k12.va.us/parents/index.html, retrieved January 1, 2006).

From the beginning, one of the primary goals of Henrico County's laptop program has been to encourage innovative teaching:

> We wanted ... fewer lectures and more engaged, active learning using dynamic, current content.... Today, in many of our classrooms, there is a new sense of discovery and the feel of a research laboratory. Every student has access to a universe of online libraries. A class exploring Italian Renaissance artists, for example, reaches a depth and breadth of study well beyond what they would have been exposed to previously. (eSchool news, 2006)

Lessons Learned

Henrico's Kid-Friendly Laptop Support Page

Henrico has put together a very kid-friendly area of its website. It provides useful information about using and caring for a laptop computer. With its colorful locker room entrance, playful fonts, and concise and simple information, this site is well worth your look. The site even has an Apple-to-Dell comparison to help high school students make the transition to new laptops. Go to http://staffdev. henrico.k12.va.us/students/index. html.

Along with these new instructional methodologies have come improvements in test scores:

> After 2 years of a laptop initiative in Henrico County, high school score results increased on all 11 of the Virginia Standards of Learning tests. In 2000, only 60% of Henrico's regular schools were accredited according to Virginia Standards of Learning criteria. By 2003, 100% of Henrico's regular schools were accredited. This includes 40 elementary schools, 11 middle schools, and 9 high schools. (Barrios, 2004, p. 22)

Another important lesson to be learned from Henrico's experience is the role laptops can play in making the home-to-school transition seamless and fluid. As Henrico subsidizes low-cost Internet access for students and teachers who don't have access in their homes (www.henrico.k12.va.us/laptopinitiative/, retrieved January 1, 2006), the transfer of homework, assignments, evaluations, and communications with teachers becomes ubiquitous and easy. Laptops have made it easier for educators to determine if students are learning and for students to demonstrate that they've learned.

Brown allows that there's always more to be done. Public school education has changed drastically in the 25 years he's worked as an educator, and instructional approaches and learning resources continue to evolve and improve. He believes, however, that Henrico's laptop program has placed the district in a better position to respond to those changes quickly and effectively. The program has given its teachers and students access to the tools they'll need to succeed in the 21st century.

As far as sustainability is concerned, Brown says Henrico is committed to maintaining the current size of the program for at least four more years. The district recently signed a four-year lease agreement with Dell after severing a similar lease with Apple.

Henrico is also committed to studying the effects of 1-to-1 computing on student achievement and behavior. Several researchers are planning studies. Brown cautions, however, that it will be difficult to tie the results of these studies directly to scores on state-mandated standardized tests, because of the way those tests are administered and because what the tests are measuring are not necessarily influenced by technology.

Cautionary Tale

Repairs, Recycling, and Media Attention

In August 2005, Henrico decided to switch from the Apple laptops it began its program with to Dell. The district decided to sell its used iBooks for $50 each. After first offering them to district staff, the district advertised the laptops to county residents, holding the sale at a local racetrack. If you're still unsure of the popularity of and demand for laptops, just go to the following website and read the *Washington Post* article regarding the melee that followed: www.washingtonpost.com/wp-dyn/content/article/2005/08/16/AR2005081600738.html.

The State of Maine

The story of Maine's statewide laptop program is fascinating. In December 1999, faced with something every state governor wants—a budgetary surplus—then-Governor Angus King realized there was enough money available to make a significant difference in education in his state. He began to cast around for ideas (Kim, 2002).

Dr. Seymour Papert, a Maine resident and researcher at MIT, where he co-developed the educational programming language Logo and published numerous influential books on computers, learning, and artificial intelligence, was called in to meet with the governor. The governor asked Papert what he thought would happen if the state government equipped every school in Maine with enough computers to lower the student-to-computer ratio to 3-to-1 or even 2-to-1. To the governor's surprise, the MIT scientist said, in effect, nothing much: "It only turns magic when it's 1-to-1" (Apple Learning Exchange). To his great credit as a leader, King took this advice and ran with it. In March 2000, he announced his plan to provide every seventh-grader in Maine with a laptop computer.

Dr. Mike Muir, director of the Maine Center for Meaningful Engaged Learning (www. mcmel.org), spoke to me at length about the founding of this program and the challenges he and others faced in turning this lunchtime conversation into a reality. In August 2001, Muir and other representatives of the University of Maine system were brought in to help with the planning stages (**P**) of this ambitious program. A committee was formed called the Design Team for Curriculum and Professional Development, and Bette Manchester, an award-winning principal and Distinguished Educator in Maine, was appointed its leader. I had the pleasure of interviewing Manchester at a recent 1-to-1 symposium, and her comments also inform this profile of Maine's laptop program.

The Maine Learning Technology Initiative (MLTI) was formally established in the winter of 2002, with the stated goal of providing "the tools and training necessary to ensure that Maine's students become the most technologically savvy students in the world" (www. state.me.us/mlti/). The Design Team worked in the summer of 2001 to bring together teachers, administrators, and university professors to set goals and establish the groundwork for the MLTI. According to Muir, a formal request for proposal (RFP) process was in place by the end of that summer, and a hardware vendor (Apple Computer) was selected by the committee in the winter of 2001–2002 (personal communication, August 4, 2005).

Around the same time, Muir was given a half-release from his university teaching load to direct a federal Preparing Tomorrow's Teachers to Use Technology (PT[3]) Program technology grant. While it was still not clear what the state was planning to do with the laptops, he saw obvious and useful connections between this state laptop initiative and his PT[3] grant, so he looked for ways to get involved in the administrative end of the project.

Manchester made it clear from the outset that MLTI needed to reach out to teachers directly and involve them (**E** for Educators). She believes there's too often a disconnect between the promises made by education technology visionaries and the actual implementation of technology in schools. That disconnect, she says, comes from a lack of empowered, knowledgeable teachers and technology leaders in individual school districts.

The vision and driving force behind the Maine laptop program may have come initially from the governor's office, but Manchester knew that a purely political mandate would not be enough to make this program successful. She sought ways to empower teachers and technology leaders to take active roles in the planning and implementation process. Consequently, teacher leaders, principals, and technology coordinators from every district and middle school in the state were identified, and an e-mail database was created to facilitate communication.

According to Manchester (personal communication, November 23, 2005), this collaborative method of planning has been instrumental in the program's success:

> This is about shared leadership and shared ownership.... [We wanted to] pay attention to the transition, pay attention to the changes that stakeholders were going through, their fear factors, [so as to] develop and sustain a sense of a learning community.

In taking this approach, the leaders of the MLTI were intentionally modeling what they wanted to happen in 1-to-1 laptop classrooms. They've sustained this learning community by continuing to convene regular face-to-face meetings with stakeholders. Manchester says:

> Our meetings with principals, technology personnel, and teacher leaders are held within each of the nine superintendent regions in Maine. Thirty building leadership groups meet within each region. During the first two years of the project, we met three or four times a year along with a two-and-a-half-day retreat for the teacher leaders and two-day workshops for the leadership team regarding the change process, embedding technology in the curriculum, and data driven decision making. We continue to meet twice a year during the school year in each region of the state, convening 30 schools at a time in the fall and spring. We also hold workshops each year at the principals' conference.

Daylong staff development meetings are held with teachers in each of the nine regions twice a year, offering training in literacy, math, science, information literacy, and project-based learning. Altogether, there were seven full days of professional development available to all content area teachers in every region during the 2005–2006 school year. This was in addition to summer institutes and workshops held throughout the state during the summer months. In previous years, there were as many as ten days of professional development. Manchester adds (personal communication, January 2, 2006), "We also go and work with teachers at school sites, upon request. Twice a year, workshops are held for those who are the technology integrators in the schools. Apple and MLTI do workshops for all tech directors as well."

While Maine wasn't the first educational body to provide laptops to students and teachers, it was the first state to do so on a massive scale. More than 37,000 laptops were deployed in 239 middle schools (Muir, Manchester, & Moulton, 2005, p. 1). Initially, keeping everyone informed of the program's progress was a major challenge, Muir recalls (personal communication, August 4, 2005):

> By February of 2002, teacher leaders, technology staff, and principals were all coming to us saying "Why didn't we get this information?" The fact is, we were giving them information, as soon as we got it ourselves. They just thought we already had [more information], when we didn't.

In response to this overwhelming demand for more information, Muir formed a team to make a half-hour documentary on the laptop initiative that was distributed to schools to inform teachers and principals and ease concerns. Funding for this documentary was provided through Muir's PT^3 grant.

When asked what she might do differently if given the chance to start the program over, Manchester says she would make sure "that the same people working on the laptop project have the funds to prepare building principals and superintendents." She mentions a particular grant from the Bill and Melinda Gates Foundation that was awarded in

November 2000 to Maine's Department of Education to improve administrators' use of technology (Maine.gov website www.state.me.us/newsletter/backissues/nov2000/leading_to_change.htm, retrieved January 2, 2006). She wishes now that she could have used that money to prepare principals and superintendents for the laptop initiative.

Instead of teaching technical skills, Manchester says (personal communication, November 23, 2005), this training should have tackled leadership issues:

> Working on leadership with principals and superintendents needs to be cyclical and systematic.... People in leadership roles cycle in and out of Maine. Perhaps they are new to their position; others are new to technology. There should be a way to formalize and make systemic the teaching of technology leadership, especially [for a program that] is this important.

Muir says that everyone involved in the early stages of the MLTI knew they needed to start collecting data immediately on how the use of laptops was affecting teaching and learning. The sheer size and complexity of the project, however, delayed this evaluation. The Maine Education Policy Research Institute (MEPRI) was charged with evaluating how students' learning styles were responding to the ubiquitous presence of laptops. Additional research was conducted by the Mitchell Institute, the Maine Learning with Laptop Studies (Mike Muir, Gerald Knezek, and Rhonda Christensen), and Gail Gartwaite.

The MEPRI studies constitute an excellent and comprehensive body of research. Anyone considering a laptop program would do well to spend some time with these reports (www.usm.maine.edu/cepare/mlti.htm). These studies show that students with laptops are more engaged in their learning and have a greater ability to explore, analyze, and communicate, while teachers in laptop classrooms are varying their lessons and using newer resources (Muir, Manchester, & Moulton, 2005, Summer).

PROGRAM GOALS, OFFICIAL AND OTHERWISE

The original goal of the MLTI was, in part, to improve the economy of Maine. Governor King realized that Maine wouldn't remain economically competitive for long if the state didn't try something new and ambitious with its educational programs. While this economic goal remains at the heart of MLTI, the program, from the start, had other, less official, goals.

The Design Team's unofficial goals included improved learning and teaching in Maine middle schools. To realize this goal, the team believed it was important for the program to focus on instruction and professional development rather than on hardware and software. This caused some disagreement along the way. Muir recalls (personal communication, August 4, 2005):

> Although some wanted straight technology training, the Design Team recommended doing training in the context of teaching with technology. Instead of doing workshops on spreadsheets, for example, we wanted to teach teachers to analyze data *using* spreadsheets.

While Muir believes the program's professional development goals have largely been realized, he cautions that it's difficult to draw connections between this professional development focus and student achievement under the MLTI. While there's a lot of anecdotal evidence that teachers are teaching differently with laptops and that Maine middle school students are now more engaged in their learning and have better attendance and fewer behavioral referrals, Muir admits that these outcomes could simply be evidence of a Hawthorne effect.

Muir believes the state has been "hit hard by NCLB" and its ideas about highly qualified teachers and local assessments. Still, professional development must be an ongoing effort: "Resistant or cautious teachers making professional advancements need to be nurtured and supported" (2005).

While most stories collected by evaluators of the MLTI have been success stories, stories about teachers having a hard time and not integrating laptops into their teaching have also been told. Manchester emphasizes the importance of establishing and sustaining a professional development network for teachers and administrators involved in the 1-to-1 program: "Your network has to be both face-to-face and virtual. There has to be a place to put resources, including web presences—a place for teachers to collaborate and share material." In Maine, that place is www.mainelearns.org.

HIGH SCHOOLS—THE NEXT STEP

While the initial plan was to provide laptops to all seventh- and eighth-graders as they moved through the system, Maine officials began to strategize how best to extend the program into high schools as well. Thirty-nine high schools have subsequently acquired laptops through the 1-to-1 state contract, and other high schools have found ways to fund equipment purchases on their own.

A lot of the high schools have invested heavily in mobile carts. Muir explains (2005) that state financial challenges have forced Maine to delay expanding the program to high schools:

> Although carts are a good first step toward 1-to-1, there are significant differences between the two, with benefits of 1-to-1 which aren't realized with a cart program.

1-TO-1 ADVICE

Muir's advice to other schools or districts considering a 1-to-1 program is unequivocal: "You have to do it! I think [a laptop program] better meets the needs of this generation of students. Do it 1-to-1, not on carts" (2005). He's not a believer in mobile laptop carts because they tend to become just another form of computer lab. With laptop carts, there's no chance for spontaneous or serendipitous learning because the computers need to be scheduled in advance.

Other lessons cited by Muir include the following:

- ▸ Pay attention to teaching and learning first (**E** for educators *and* education).

- ▸ Leadership is vital. Leaders need to set a vision for teaching and learning. Appropriate polices need to be created.

- ▸ Find sustainable funding systems. This includes good partnerships, educational organizations, grants, and so forth.

- ▸ Be sure to support your teachers. Every school needs to have a technology integrator, someone who focuses solely on integrating technology into the classroom.

▶ Professional development is an ongoing process, not a one-shot deal. It needs to be adapted in response to the successes and challenges experienced by teachers and the institution as a whole.

▶ Students and teachers need complete, 24/7 access to technology. It needs to work when they need it to work.

▶ Infrastructure, logistics, insurance, acceptable use policies—all must be addressed in the planning process.

▶ Laptops need to be at home and not just at school.

Manchester offers similar advice (personal communication, November 23, 2005):

> Definitely talk to people who have been involved in [similar laptop] projects. Don't just take the RFP [and buy hardware]—go and visit, and be clear about why you want to establish a laptop program. Set a purpose. Purpose drives what happens.

Manchester cautions (2005), however, that vision and purpose must also be discussed at the building level. Successful implementation of any program depends on the community in which it takes place, so each community must establish its purpose first. These communities are not just internal:

> Another example of [community] inclusion is the Digital Media Group—an organization of content providers in Maine that includes Public Broadcasting, the Maine Historical Society, Northeast Historic Film, the Portland Museum of Art, Maine libraries, and other organizations.

In Maine, these learning communities operate for students as well. Student tech teams called iTeams help teachers with technical support and lend a student voice to the project. One group has even developed a video to help educate other student tech teams. Once a year, these teams gather for an annual conference to share and plan, just as teachers gather regularly to share and plan: "Students are at the heart of this project. It's the same [model] for students, [finding out] what works and what doesn't work," Manchester says (2005).

Both Muir and Manchester believe strongly that educators today have a moral obligation to provide their students with access to digital educational tools because their learning styles and needs are fundamentally different from those of earlier generations. While for most adults the standard medium of instruction and information sharing is text, the natural learning medium of the millennials is video. Adults are uni-taskers, but millennials are natural multitaskers and shouldn't be forced to adopt the learning behaviors of their teachers. If educators ignore these fundamental differences, they risk irrelevancy in the minds of the students they are hoping to teach. As Papert says (2003), students don't mind hard, they mind boring. Motivated and engaged learners are not bored, and the experience of the MLTI tells us that providing students with laptops can be a key to better engagement.

The State of Michigan

Like Maine, the driving force for Michigan's laptop initiative was a visionary politician. In 2002, Rick Johnson, speaker of the house in Michigan's legislature, was invited to visit Microsoft's and Apple Computer's corporate campuses. He also visited both Maine and Henrico County, Virginia, to learn more about their 1-to-1 programs.

Johnson was motivated to make these trips out of concern that Michigan wasn't doing enough to help those students who needed it most. He was looking for answers in education technology. He was particularly impressed that Henrico County students often congregated in their high school parking lot on Saturdays to access their wireless network. He saw the potential benefits for students in his own state and went to work to find funding for a pilot program called Learning Without Limits.

Working with fellow state legislators, Johnson pieced together a program with $3.5 million in state funding and $6 million in federal funding (Wireless Developer Network, www.wirelessdevnet.com/newswire-less/aug302002.html, retrieved January 2, 2006). David Seitz, one of the authors of the No Child Left Behind legislation, also got involved in the early stages. He used his contacts with industry and the Bush administration to help get this initiative off the ground. At the time, Seitz was serving as deputy director and policy development coordinator for the Michigan House Republican Policy Office. The initial project was tied to NCLB and offered laptops to low-income districts that had at least one school on the NCLB school improvement list.

Bruce Montgomery was subsequently hired to be executive director of an expanded program, renamed the Freedom to Learn Program. Montgomery graciously agreed to be interviewed about the planning and execution of Michigan's laptop program, and his answers form the basis of this profile.

The program began with a demonstration phase in which eight different 1-to-1 programs were funded. Participating schools were allowed to choose either laptops or handhelds, but the devices had to be wireless. A total of 8,000 students participated in these eight programs, and about half were using handhelds. All the major hardware vendors were represented, including IBM, Gateway, Apple, Hewlett-Packard, Palm, and Dell. The focus of this demonstration phase, however, was not on the vendors but on the devices themselves. In the end, laptops were preferred by both teachers and students because they better supported the types of things students and teachers wanted to accomplish and learn.

Montgomery was then faced with the challenge of turning these pilot programs into something that would be scalable for the entire state. Rather than allowing each district to select a provider and then trying to manage this at the state level, Montgomery felt it would be best if the state could identify and choose a single vendor that would offer a single solution package. This kind of large-scale procurement is also something the state does on a regular basis for other resources. Consequently, Montgomery and the state legislature proposed a laptop procurement program with three key stipulations:

1. The state would authorize the funds to do this as a laptop program and nothing else.

2. The state would set aside a full 25% of the total funding for professional development for teachers.

3. The state would choose a single solution provider to handle the entire program.

The media got wind of this proposal and initially projected that Michigan would either choose Dell or Apple. Instead, after reviewing all proposals, Michigan selected Hewlett-Packard based on the selection criteria in the state's RFP, which included the quality of the laptop device, support for wireless networking, the maintenance and warranty agreement, support services to schools, content and curriculum resources, and professional development. Michigan's procurement decision was based on the delivery and maintenance of a complete education package for less than $275 per student per year, a total of $1,100 per student for the program's initial four years (Montgomery, personal communication, January 4, 2006).

THE ADVISORY COUNCIL (P FOR PLANNING)

Michigan put together an advisory council in 2003. The first year, the advisory council included representatives from every major hardware manufacturer. These early meetings proved frustrating and unhelpful, however, because they were more about overt and covert sales pitches than about moving the program forward. Each vendor wanted to direct the program its own way, and this proved untenable.

The makeup of the advisory council was subsequently changed in the second year to refocus the discussion on education rather than hardware. Meetings included technology coordinators, curriculum specialists, and educational association representatives, such as the Michigan Association of Computer Users in Learning. The Michigan State Department of Education was also at the table.

Montgomery felt it was important to have representatives from all three areas—education, industry, and government—to ensure that no perspective was being overlooked. As the Freedom to Learn Program was taking resources and Title II funds that individual districts would otherwise have had free control over, Montgomery wanted to make sure that the program represented a broad-based consensus on what would really work and what could be implemented consistently throughout the state. The advisory council continues to receive feedback today, Montgomery says, from "a cross-section of organizations, especially the Michigan Department of Education, Hewlett-Packard and its partners, and the participating school districts" (Montgomery, 2006).

PROGRAM GOALS

The Freedom to Learn Program's principal goal is to help individuals develop into self-sustaining, self-directed learners. Montgomery emphasizes, however, that this goal doesn't mean to disparage the role of teachers. Instead, the program seeks to give teachers the tools they need to reach their students more effectively. Once they get some experience teaching with laptops, he says, teachers realize they no longer have to be the dictator

Cautionary Tale

Cobb County, Georgia

Cobb County, Georgia, announced a major laptop initiative in May 2005, but it was stopped by a court order just before rollout in July 2005 (www.macworld.com/news/2005/07/29/cobbcounty/index.php, retrieved January 2, 2006). At issue was how public money was being spent and how the vendor contract had been awarded. The Superior Court judge in Cobb County decided district administrators hadn't adequately informed taxpayers how sales tax money was to be used for the program. Cobb County's superintendent resigned, multiple subpoenas were served, and a grand jury has been impaneled for a full investigation to see if any laws were broken. That investigation is ongoing, but what's certain at this point is that Cobb County doesn't have laptops for its 63,000 students as planned. The moral of the story: always communicate thoroughly with all your constituents.

of all learning in the classroom. When they get beyond the fear of losing power over what and how students learn, they find that laptops free them up to be learning facilitators and student advocates rather than the dreaded (and thus often ignored) authority figure typified by the "sage on the stage" archetype. Montgomery says (personal communication, August 9, 2005):

> We don't wave a flag around, but we are not shy about what we hope [to achieve]—we are hoping that this works so well that all educators will begin to ask for [laptops] and schools will figure out how to integrate them at many levels. It's not just a fad.

Like Maine's, Michigan's laptop program was motivated in part by economic self-interest, with leaders desiring to produce highly computer-literate graduates who would be attractive to high-tech employers. However, improving student achievement has always been a primary goal as well. This is no easy task, as Montgomery points out (personal communication, January 4, 2006):

> If you are just measuring the effectiveness of the programs based on standardized tests, what educators fear is that the whole notion of critical thinking, independent learning, and the construction of new understanding will be ignored. These progressive goals have to be accommodated even while schools and districts hew to the accountability line. Schools must look to improve student achievement on standardized tests, but they also must keep students engaged. I am of the mind that you can do both with a 1-to-1 teaching and learning program that is student-centered. That's what we have to do to move these programs forward— show that they can lead to improved student performance while at the same time supporting project-based, constructivist learning activities.

HOW LAPTOPS ARE USED IN MICHIGAN SCHOOLS

Michigan evaluated its Freedom to Learn Program in March 2005 and published an internal progress report that looks at the early impact of the Freedom to Learn Program on student learning and engagement. The report notes statistically significant improvements in standardized test scores, including improved reading and math scores at Bendle Middle School and Bear Lake Schools. The study also reports fewer discipline issues and increased attendance in school.

The report also includes anecdotal stories describing how teachers are using laptops to encourage collaborative and group work. Teachers and students are using the laptops to enhance writing assignments, perform virtual science labs, analyze data with spreadsheets, research on the web, and create more professional PowerPoint presentations. In all content areas, laptops are being used to support higher order thinking, collaborative and cooperative learning, and student inquiry.

The teachers quoted in the report describe richer and deeper projects, more engaged students, and opportunities to work in ways that would not be possible without computers. One teacher says laptops have had a transformative effect on her classroom: "Because of our laptops, my students were able to do all of their research, writing, and publishing right here in our classroom.… No one had to wait for a computer, everyone was on task, no one was disruptive, and everyone participated" (2005).

LOOKING AT THE PROGRAM TODAY AND PLANNING FOR TOMORROW

In 2006, Michigan had 22,000 students using laptops. The state has been monitoring the program in conjunction with site-based monitors. Individual districts have different policies on whether or not students are allowed to take their computers home. In areas with higher crime rates, this can be dangerous. Hewlett-Packard and Microsoft have stepped in to help with the school-to-home issue by setting up a centralized server, so that Freedom to Learn participants can use any Internet connection to access their school files and applications. Thus, they don't have to take their laptops home with them.

For professional development, Michigan has constructed a number of demonstration and advisory sites. The people involved with these sites are "the practitioners that I listen to now," says Montgomery. Michigan manages the program like a business, with planning tools, timeframes, and assessments: "We use both formative (ongoing) and summative evaluation tools to measure success in the classroom and across the state. Our classroom assessment tools allow us to measure our progress school by school and student by student" (2005).

As for sustaining the program into the future, the Freedom to Learn Program must go back to the state each year to renew funding. So far, both houses of the state government have voted to continue funding the program. Montgomery says the program will continue with or without the funding. However, he also says the plan is to build a model for school-based funding that would enable individual schools to fund their own laptop programs using money from a combination of sources. This will require total-cost-of-ownership studies, which are underway. Montgomery doesn't think it's reasonable to expect the state to fund the entire program year after year; the combination of funding sources will always vary. In the future, the state may match title funds with Freedom to Learn funds, thus combining state and federal sources. He hopes Michigan's program will eventually lead to a national 1-to-1 movement that will have broad-ranging support. He says (2005):

> Recently the program received start-up private funding to initiate an institute to help other states and large school districts plan and prepare their own 1-to-1 programs. It is inevitable that technology will someday be in the hands of every student on an anytime, anywhere basis. With our partners from Maine, Texas, Virginia, and other locations, we would like to help school districts—especially high need urban schools—get ready to efficiently and effectively plan and launch successful 1-to-1 programs. We have learned a lot over the past few years and want to help others avoid repeating our mistakes while making use of our lessons learned and best practices. Sustainability will continue to be an issue until businesses, educational stakeholders, parents, and taxpayers see the value of this program. That is the challenge.

Chapter 4

WHAT 1-TO-1 CAN MEAN FOR STUDENTS, TEACHERS, AND SCHOOLS

Introduction

THE SCHOOLS, DISTRICTS, AND STATES profiled in the first three chapters provide plenty of anecdotal evidence about the benefits 1-to-1 laptops can bring to students and teachers alike. But what about formal evidence: what quantitative or qualitative research has been done on the benefits of 1-to-1 computing?

While formal research is still scanty and fragmentary—largely because 1-to-1 programs are so new—some compelling studies have been published recently that suggest 1-to-1 can have a strongly beneficial impact on a variety of measures of student performance. This chapter will summarize the most pertinent findings from these studies as well as the lessons learned and insights gleaned by experts who have pioneered laptop initiatives.

Figure 4.1
Beaufort County students create mutimedia projects using their laptops.

What 1-to-1 Can Mean for Students

At the end of the day, the success of a 1-to-1 program must be measured by the ways and extent to which it improves student learning. Disregarding for the moment the politically charged debate over how best to measure student performance, we must keep in mind that if students don't gain something important from ubiquitous access to their own digital assistants, then a lot of time, energy, and money will have been wasted. In the end, all education reforms must be about students—how they learn and what they learn. This section summarizes the most important benefits to students when digital assistants are part of the learning mix.

1-to-1 helps students improve their technology and information processing skills, preparing students for higher education and jobs in the technology-driven global economy.

Students are natural explorers, unafraid to point and click and figure things out. But it's by getting students to go beyond familiar tasks and the easy-to-discover secrets of a particular program or web resource that the true promise of technology can be realized. We must challenge them to tackle more advanced activities that require active collaboration and higher order thinking skills.

I once observed a student type the following search string into Google: "Vietnam War supplies Ho Chi Min Trail difficulty of getting." When he hit enter, he received a long list of unrelated documents on the Vietnam War: office supplies, Ho Chi Min City biking trails, and so forth. Wading through all these hits was clearly going to be a time-consuming—and possibly useless—task, so the student promptly pronounced to me that there was "nothing out there" on his topic.

This example reveals that no matter how quick and accessible the best technology tools are, technology users still need to learn how to use them effectively and thoughtfully if they're to support critical thinking and problem solving. This kind of learning can only take place over time and through frequent use. It will not happen if students get only 15 minutes on a computer every other week or so.

Laptops enable students to take their digital assistants everywhere and use them for all kinds of learning activities: writing, sorting, organizing, experimenting, linking, making mistakes that no one sees, and so on. Computer labs—and even laptops on carts—cannot give students the 24/7 access they need to become operationally adept with digital resources.

Having a digital assistant at one's fingertips means increased opportunities to hone crucial technology skills. Howard Levin observes (personal communication, December 22, 2004) that student technology skills improved significantly across the board when laptops were introduced at The Urban School in San Francisco:

> One of the overwhelming successes [of the laptop program] is that it has dramatically increased computer technology confidence among everyone.... This provides an enormous advantage because it enables students to be far ahead of other students who are not as tech savvy. [These laptop-using] kids don't even think they're especially tech savvy because it is such a normal part of their lives.

Independent educational research firm Rockman *et al* (2000, p. iv) compared students who have laptops with those who don't and found laptop-using students were far more fluid users of technology:

> Laptop students consistently show deeper and more flexible uses of technology than their Non-Laptop matched groups.

Administrators at the Athens (Georgia) Academy report (Hill & Reeves, 2004, p. 43) that students with laptops were far more productive and efficient in their use of common applications:

> The data indicates that there is an increased use of e-mail, web browsers, Word, PowerPoint and Excel for productivity for both teachers and learners. Further, the data indicates that

teachers and learners have realized that the laptops make getting schoolwork completed easier and more efficient.

The students have also reported growth in their perceptions of personal abilities with technology.... This was not the case in Year One when many Middle School girls reported feeling like their peers knew more than they did. (Hill & Reeves, 2004, p. 16)

Barbara Catenaci, the education technology development specialist at Beaufort County (South Carolina) School District, also marvels at how much more productive students become when they regularly use a laptop to complete schoolwork (personal communication, November 15, 2004):

They use the computers less as the years [go] on. It's because they [are] better at it. If you ask how much time they are spending at a computer, you will see it. The first time they did an Excel spreadsheet it took a lot longer.

1-to-1 provides crucial support for constructivist instructional practices and motivates students to become self-directed learners.

With a digital assistant for use at school and home, real time is available for students to go beyond teacher- or textbook-generated lessons and activities and seek out their own sources of information and learning. Laptops are a great enabling tool for project-based learning and other constructivist practices. Administrators of Project Hiller—a laptop program for ninth-graders in Union City, New Jersey—point to this as a major benefit of 1-to-1 access:

In one example, a ninth-grade [laptop user]... was involved in a class project to do field research and write about the impact of different inventions on society. On his own, he and his partner—who were studying the impact of the automobile—distributed surveys over the Internet to contacts in Miami and rural Tennessee so that they could compare trends.... The teacher was pleased not only with the initiative but that the duo asked if they could exceed the ten-page limit for their report. (Light, McDermott, & Honey, 2002, p. 24)

Alex Inman was impressed with how quickly students at Whitfield School in St. Louis developed into active, self-directed learners when provided with laptops (personal communication, December 15, 2004):

It was great seeing students go from fumbling kids who could not use the tool to becoming curriculum designers, asking what is it that you want to accomplish, and fitting what they did to the overall goal.

A seventh-grade parent in Maine reports that her son's whole approach to learning has changed since he was given a laptop:

Simply put, my seventh-grade son is loving his laptop.... [He's] done virtually *all* of his homework since November on this machine, and in general enjoyed every discovery he's made.... He feels good about his accomplishments in a way I haven't seen for the past seven years. He's learning more material, and he's learning it faster. He's excited about learning. Bravo!!! (Lane, 2003, p. 18)

A student participant in Project Hiller describes quite succinctly the changes she noted in herself:

> I can do whatever I want and teach myself... before, I was clueless. (Light, McDermott, & Honey, 2002, p. 23)

Teachers know what a difference student motivation can make in the classroom. 1-to-1 empowers students and gives them a more active role in choosing what and how they study, resulting in better study behavior and improved learning outcomes. As researcher Mel Levine points out in his book *A Mind at a Time* (2002, p. 263):

> Success nourishes motivation and motivation makes further success more likely.... The neurodevelopmental systems require constant exercise if they are to stay in good shape. Such persistent use is partly dependent upon motivation to learn, that is, a willingness to absorb and endure the risks that go with new and ever more demanding brain challenges.

1-to-1 helps students stay organized and on track with their schoolwork.

Anytime access to all learning materials and assignments helps students stay organized and study more efficiently. These benefits go beyond preventing lost homework and keeping track of grades: students can use their computers to customize their personal learning environment, making connections and organizing the parts and processes in a way that makes the most sense to them. This is one of the most powerful educational benefits of a personal digital assistant: everything is easily accessible, personally organized, and instantly available—anytime and anywhere.

In their study of laptop programs, Rockman *et al* (2000, p. 61) found that laptop-using students almost universally felt that they were more organized and kept track of their schoolwork better with the help of their digital assistants:

> **Organization:** Laptop students felt that computers helped them keep their work organized; they felt they didn't lose their work when it was all on their own computers.

Having everything they're studying and learning in one place, organized in a way that makes sense to them, is powerful and motivating for students. Bill Ivey describes (personal communication, February 8, 2005) what a difference this has made at Stoneleigh-Burnham School in Greenfield, Massachusetts, the all-girls' school where he works:

> I think maybe the greatest success has been the ability to allow kids to be working at their own level, always moving forward, using their time differently depending on their own learning styles and needs, staying organized and on topic in a way that would be much more difficult without the laptops.

A Peck School seventh-grader typifies the reaction of many laptop-using students who compare 1-to-1 favorably with the hassles of sharing a computer at school and at home:

> Last year, I found it much more difficult to do my computer-related homework, because I would have to go to a whole other computer and put in my password, search frantically for history papers, and English essays that had gotten lost in all the other materials. This year, I just turn my laptop on, and everything I need is right in front of me. (Livingston, 2004, p. 78)

Another Peck School student elaborated on his method for keeping track of notes, class materials, software, and other electronic information:

> My homework, class notes are on the laptop. I take all the old work from those chapters and put them in a folder for Chapter 1, 2, and so on. All of the schedules I have to have, the syllabus for science... I have a folder for extra stuff that I need to keep but can't categorize, another folder for software.... It's just easier for me. (Livingston, 2004, p. 76)

What 1-to-1 Can Mean for Teachers

A teacher's work extends far beyond the dismissal bell each day. Some of it involves staying in the classroom after students have left, and some of it's done from home on nights, weekends, holidays, vacations, and over the summer. Just as students can organize their work, customize it according to their own learning styles, and complete it with more depth and better resources, so, too, is the vital work of teachers made easier and better when they have ubiquitous access to a digital assistant. A laptop can help a teacher with myriad needs: planning, instructing, communicating, revising, researching, analyzing, reflecting, writing, presenting, publishing, recording, calculating, and a lot more.

Teachers are professionals charged with the life-altering mission of educating our youth. Providing laptops to teachers is not just about having them become more comfortable with computers and technology. It's about giving them the best tools available to succeed in their socially critical work with our country's next generation.

1-to-1 can help teachers become more adept and confident in using education technology for planning, teaching, and communication.

Surveys of laptop-using teachers and interviews with laptop leaders indicate that teachers become more comfortable with technology and more adept at its use when they're provided a laptop computer and teach in a laptop environment.

Rockman *et al* (2004, pp. 24, 36, 43) spent three years studying laptop schools that were part of the Microsoft/Toshiba Anytime Anywhere Learning initiative. When comparing data they compiled on teachers who used laptops versus those who didn't, they found big differences in each group's overall use of education technology:

> Laptop teachers use computers far more often in a wider variety of learning activities than non-laptop peers. Their students use computers more often for data analysis (77% vs. 5%), presentations (59% vs. 16%), writing (72% vs. 21%) and research (85% vs. 35%).... Laptop teachers also have greater confidence in using technology tools like word processing, e-mail, and the Internet.

Researchers at WestEd (2002, p. 2) are similarly categorical about how regular use of computers can help teachers become more effective at integrating technology into the classroom:

> For technology to become a core component of teachers' instructional repertoire, they not only need familiarity with equipment, but—more important—they need to see and practice the most productive ways of using it to support learning.

Administrators at Athens Academy found (Hill & Reeves, 2004, p. 32) that teachers' use of technology expanded significantly when they were provided with a laptop:

> Another area of change has occurred in teachers' and learners' perspectives related to their individual abilities with the technology. The data indicate significant growth in use of tools by both teachers and learners in the Middle and Upper School. Teachers reported higher degrees of confidence in their technological abilities. Further, many teachers have expanded the tools they are using and are exploring how other tools might impact their classroom practices.

1-to-1 can provide teachers with ready access to a whole world of curricular resources that encourage and support the development of richer lessons.

The enrichment of resources available to students is something all good teachers want. When I was in school, I loved getting a shiny new textbook and would peruse its pages with awe, wondering what worlds it would help me explore. That same excitement and enthusiasm can be multiplied many times over when students gain access to the endless supply of well-designed learning resources and authentic materials available online.

Administrators at the Athens Academy found (Hill & Reeves, 2004, p. 43) laptops encouraged teachers to incorporate online resources more readily into their classrooms:

> The data show teachers are increasing use of the laptops to enable them to bring real resources into their classrooms easily and in a "right on time" fashion.

Likewise, evaluators of Maine's statewide laptop program report that teachers readily expand their curricular horizons when given a laptop to use in the classroom:

> Teachers feel the laptops are very helpful in developing integrated lessons and extending learning. In many teacher interviews, teachers have described how they have been able to locate materials and information to use in developing interdisciplinary units—to help students see connections between different pieces of information and knowledge.... [Typical comments from teachers include the following:] "The laptop is such an integral part of all my management routines that I can't imagine life without it. I use the web to find rich teaching resources." (Sargent, 2003, p. 11)

> Teachers are seeing the greatest impact of the MLTI [Maine Learning Technology Initiative] on their work in planning and presenting lessons, creating integrated lessons, and creating assignments. Teachers reported that having the laptop as a tool enables them, in many cases, to expand their own knowledge and increase their efficiency. (Silvernail & Harris, 2003, p. 10)

Beaufort School District (Stevenson, 1999, p. ii) reports that finding classroom resources is one of the primary uses that district-supplied laptops are put to:

> Teachers personally used the computers most often for lesson planning or research.

1-to-1 can help teachers communicate more frequently and effectively with students, parents, and colleagues.

So much of learning is about communication. Teachers continually check for understanding in a variety of ways: directly querying their students, giving tests and quizzes, assigning reports, asking students to present their findings. All are modes of communication through which new learning and understanding take place.

Providing teachers and students with 24/7 access to computers expands and reinforces their ability to communicate. Questions and ideas can be composed, reviewed, revised, revisited, and submitted more easily and frequently, expanding the opportunities for learning.

Research from Maine (Sargent, 2003, p. 7) points to how teachers have increased their communication with one another now that they all have laptops:

> One of the most frequent uses of the laptops by teachers is in communicating with colleagues. Approximately 55% of the teachers surveyed reported that they use their laptop to communicate with colleagues at least a few times a week.

Administrators at the Athens Academy also noted an increase in the ease and frequency of communication among their laptop-using faculty and students (Hill & Reeves, 2004, p. 42, 52):

> Teachers and learners are using the laptops for enhanced communication between themselves and others. Teachers reported that working with teammates and colleagues in general has been enhanced with the ease in communication brought about by Internet tools, especially e-mail.... Teachers also indicated an increase in the use of e-mail for communicating with parents and students.

Howard Levin reports (personal communication, November 15, 2004) that a Spanish teacher at The Urban School found having a laptop made a huge difference in his ability to provide students with appropriate language input outside the normal boundaries of the classroom and class assignments:

> The key, the catalyst, was he has been able to extend oral and aural language practice through e-mail. This demonstrated a real way to extended language discussion with students beyond the classroom.

What 1-to-1 Can Mean for Schools

In 2002, at the National Educational Computing Conference in Seattle, I gave a presentation about Peck School's laptop program. Just before my presentation, I listened to one about Maine's laptop initiative. I was eager to learn what they'd experienced in their program's first year. The speaker told us the major benefit was improved school attendance. After the session, several in the room expressed disappointment in that limited result: "Is that it? Just better attendance?"

Evidence has mounted for a variety of other instructional and student performance benefits in the years since—in Maine as well as in other 1-to-1 programs. However, we should not discount the importance of this very simple but profound improvement: when students are given their own laptops, their school attendance invariably improves. Clearly, this means that laptop-using students want to come to school more. In the long run, this is bound to lead to increases in student performance as measured by standardized test scores, graduation rates, and career success outside of school.

1-to-1 can improve both student attendance and school enrollment.

Solid evidence has emerged from multiple sources that students given laptops tend to be more involved and interested in what they learn and are thus less likely to stay home (Lane, 2003, p. 2). Since that first year, Maine has continued to see a significant increase in attendance rates:

> Preliminary findings suggest that since the implementation of the laptop program, student engagement and attendance has increased and the classroom atmosphere has shifted, including more student/teacher and student/student collaboration.

Fewer absences have also been reported in Manatee County (Florida), which has a laptop program in 22 classrooms from elementary through high school (Barrios, 2004, p. 2):

> Absences have declined nearly 40% among students with laptops.

Administrators of Project Hiller report not only an improvement in student attendance, but also an increase in the number of high-achieving students enrolling in public schools (Light, McDermott, & Honey, 2002, p. 2):

> The possibility of participation in Project Hiller encouraged high performing eighth-grade students to stay in the public school system. In the year prior to Project Hiller (1997–98), Union Hill enrolled just 38 ninth-grade honors students, while in 1998–99, the first year of the program, Union Hill drew 44 freshman students into its honors program. In the second and third year of the project, Union Hill admitted 59 and 55 students into the ninth-grade honors program respectively, representing a 25% increase from 1998 in the number of high achieving eighth-graders choosing to enroll at the high school.

1-to-1 can improve student performance in all curricular areas.

Longitudinal data on the effects of 1-to-1 access on standardized test scores and other measures of student performance are still fragmentary and limited at this point. However, research is beginning to reveal that ubiquitous access to technology can have a profound effect on student achievement.

A study of 259 laptop-using students at Harvest Park Middle School in Pleasanton, California, shows that students in 1-to-1 classrooms had higher scores than their non-laptop-using peers on standardized tests for English language arts, mathematics, and writing. They also had higher overall GPAs (Gulek & Demirtas, 2005).

The study also echoes previous research that shows students in 1-to-1 classrooms "spend more time involved in collaborative work, participate in more project-based instruction, produce writing of higher quality and greater length, gain increased access to information, improve research analysis skills, and spend more time doing homework on computers" (Gulek & Demirtas, 2005, abstract). The Harvest Park middle-schoolers, like students in other 1-to-1 programs, "report a greater reliance on active learning strategies, readily engage in problem solving and critical thinking, and consistently show deeper and more flexible uses of technology than students without individual laptops" (2005).

While these are promising results, the study is careful to point out that these improvements did not appear immediately. Any new technology or curricular reform has a learning curve, and schools should expect an adjustment period when implementing a 1-to-1 program. In the case of Harvest Park, that adjustment period was about one semester. By the end of the first year, "laptop students showed significantly higher achievement in nearly all measures after one year in the program" (Gulek & Demirtas, 2005).

As reforms go, this is remarkably fast and significant improvement, especially given that other education technology initiatives have had little direct impact on student test scores. Interestingly, the sixth-graders at Harvest Park seem to have demonstrated greater improvement than older students. Could this be because they're at the ideal developmental stage to take on these new technologies and approaches? More research is needed to isolate differential factors, but this result reflects what I have seen at The Peck School: younger students seem to embrace new resources and technologies more readily and enthusiastically than older students.

Gulek and Demirtas (2005, p. 29) cite other research in trying to explain why writing scores in particular seem to have improved so much among laptop-using students:

> The findings related to writing are consistent with results of a recent meta-analysis of studies that investigated the effect of computers on student writing (Goldberg, Russell & Cook, 2003). This meta-analysis found that students who use computers when learning to write are not only more engaged and motivated in their writing, but also produce work that is of greater length and higher quality, especially at the secondary level.

Given laptop-using students' enhanced ability to compose, revise, edit, and publish their writing, it makes sense that they spend more time with writing assignments and produce better work.

Other pertinent findings (Gulek & Demirtas, 2005, p. 7, 13):

Q: Does the laptop program have an impact on students' grade point average?

A: Results indicate that Harvest Park Middle School students in the Laptop Immersion Program attained higher GPAs than non-participating students in their respective grades. The greatest difference was observed in sixth-grade GPAs.

Q: Does the laptop program have an impact on students' end-of-course grades?

A: Results indicate that there is a substantial difference between laptop and non-laptop students in terms of their end-of-course grades. A notably higher percentage of laptop students attained A grades and a significantly lower percentage attained F grades in their English and mathematics courses. The largest difference between percent of laptop and non-laptop students obtaining A grades was in seventh-grade English and the smallest difference was in eighth-grade mathematics.

Q: Does the laptop program have an impact on students' standardized test scores?

A: Results indicate that a considerably higher proportion of laptop students scored at or above the national average in both the language and mathematics portions of the California Achievement Test Sixth Edition Survey Form (CAT/6 Survey) across all grade levels. The largest difference in NRT outcomes occurred between current sixth-grade laptop and non-laptop students in math, and current eighth-grade students in total language, when they were tested at the end of their first year enrollment in the laptop program.

Additional statistical evidence for the benefits of 1-to-1 can be found in the Education Development Center's three-year study of Project Hiller (Light, McDermott, & Honey, 2002, pp. 1–2):

> Standardized test scores rose significantly for Project Hiller students across all tracks. Analysis of ninth-grade scores for Cohort 1 indicated no difference between participants and their peers prior to Project Hiller; however, by years two and three of the project, participating students scored significantly higher than their non-Project Hiller peers. For example, within the honors track in specific regard to math scores, Project Hiller students scored 414.05 on the New Jersey State High School Proficiency Test (HSPT) versus 396.14 scored by their non-Hiller peers.

Supporters of Michigan's Freedom to Learn (FTL) initiative credit the program with improving grades, motivation, and discipline. Early returns from Michigan's statewide 1-to-1 program also reveal a strong positive influence on student test scores. Results from the January/February 2005 administration of the Michigan Educational Assessment Program (MEAP) test show that students in 1-to-1 laptop programs outperform their peers by a wide margin (Solomon, 2005, p. 4):

▶ In Bendle Middle School, the percentage of seventh-graders who scored "proficient" in reading increased from 29% to 41%, while the percentage of eighth-graders who scored "proficient" in math rose from 31% to 63%.

▶ In Leland Middle School, the percentage of students who scored "proficient" on the MEAP writing test rose from 53% to 84%—compared to a statewide average of 53%.

▶ Across the Eastern Upper Peninsula ISD, in just one year, the percentage of students who scored "proficient" in science increased from 68% to 80%, while the percentage of students who scored "proficient" in math increased from 57% to 67%.

Bruce Montgomery, executive director of the FTL program, points out the significance of these early returns (2006):

> Usually, such overwhelmingly positive results like this aren't seen for three or four years out. Clearly, FTL is doing what it is designed to do for our school children—enhance student learning and achievement in core academic subjects.

Mike Hester, principal of Hays (Kansas) High School, reports improved test scores since implementing a 1-to-1 laptop program (Apple, 2008):

> This year our math and reading test scores were up 12% to 17% over AYP (Adequate Yearly Progress), and we met the standard of excellence in social studies and science, scoring over the 80th percentile in both.

1-to-1 improves the home-to-school connection.

People who know I've been researching this subject often ask me what the real benefits of laptops are, emphasizing "real" as if they expect to hear nothing but vague promises and platitudes. Education technology skeptics point to the expense involved in acquiring enough laptops for a 1-to-1 program, not to mention the training, support, infrastructure changes, and curricular restructuring required. They cite previous failed school reform projects, relate anecdotes of students using laptops merely as powerful music-downloading devices, talk about studies on the difficulty of integrating technology into teaching, and on and on.

To these folks, my typical one word answer is always "Homework." When students have their own laptop, their homework is always with them. The dog can't eat it, it can't be accidentally tossed in the trash, and it's not likely to be forgotten on the bus or dropped in a puddle on the way home from school. All of the resources that students need to complete their homework go with them: online resources and references, databases and spreadsheets, e-books and other primary source material, and so on. It's all in one place and easily transportable from school to home and back again.

Improvements in student homework and the home-to-school connection are a consistent refrain among 1-to-1 leaders nationwide. Here are just two representative anecdotes:

> He can do homework in waiting rooms, on long car rides, on his mother's boring shopping trips—anywhere! He feels good about his accomplishments in a way I haven't seen for the past seven years. He's learning more material, and he's learning it faster. (Silvernail & Harris, 2003, p. 30)

> According to one principal, students who were reluctant to do homework became more willing to do it once it was on the computer. Students who did not have excellent handwriting skills could produce neat work, and in general, students had the ability to produce more professional-looking products. (Zucker & McGhee, 2005, p. 16)

Conclusion

According to the studies and school reports examined for this chapter, students who use laptops are more motivated and empowered, are more organized and engaged learners, attend school more regularly, advance their knowledge and understanding of technology, and become constructors and designers of information and ideas. Speaking from the vantage point of someone who's been an education technologist for more than a decade, I daresay this seems exactly like what we've been trying to accomplish all along. Don't be afraid to give power to the students.

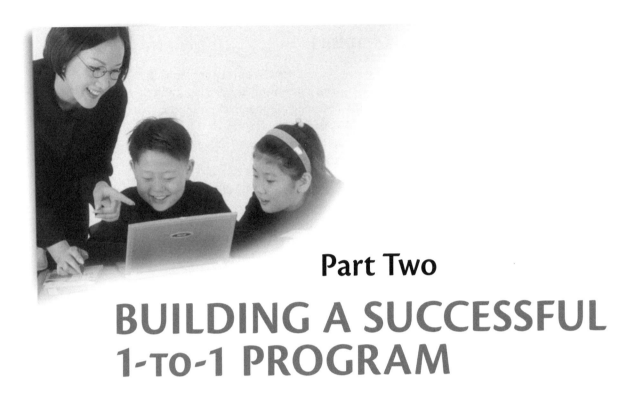

Part Two

BUILDING A SUCCESSFUL 1-TO-1 PROGRAM

MANY THINGS NEED TO BE CONSIDERED once the decision is made to introduce a laptop program. The first and usually most important step is thoughtful, in-depth planning that aligns with the school's mission and district and state standards. Planning is critical to a program's success and sustainability, yet it's often where shortcuts are made. Even when it's done well, the planning process is sometimes ended too quickly, and the program isn't steered in a structured way. Chapters 5 and 6 will help you ensure that all aspects of your new program have been considered and planned for.

Implementation is also a challenging process. Schools accustomed to running a wired network with desktop computers that never move from classrooms or labs can sometimes be unpleasantly surprised when hundreds of new users on wireless, mobile laptops are suddenly part of the mix. To avoid network meltdown, it's important to pay close attention to implementation issues and take advantage of the lessons learned by other 1-to-1 schools. Chapter 8 is full of helpful tips to reduce implementation headaches.

Previewing the Chapters

Chapter 5, "The Planning Process," examines all aspects of planning a 1-to-1 laptop program: forming and staffing a planning committee, getting multiple stakeholders involved, documenting the work, choosing among platform options, determining infrastructure needs and network capacities, and so forth. The chapter also looks at the importance of ongoing evaluation as the program moves forward, to ensure that it develops in the ways envisioned by the planning committee.

Chapter 6, "Professional Development for Teachers," discusses perhaps the single most crucial factor in the success of a 1-to-1 program. If teachers aren't committed to the program and comfortable with the technology, 1-to-1 laptops won't result in any significant improvement in student learning. Professional development is often overlooked or underfunded during the planning phase, so this chapter is a must-read for all program planners and administrators.

Leadership must be behind 1-to-1 for it to succeed. An active group of articulate visionaries have made 1-to-1 happen all over the world. I asked several of the wisest among them to contribute to Chapter 7, "1-to-1 Leadership." The chapter was largely written by esteemed 1-to-1 leaders Bruce Dixon, Leslie Wilson, Gary Stager, Milt Dougherty, and Ian Stuart.

Chapter 8, "Implementation and Logistics," covers many of the nitty-gritty logistical issues of implementing a laptop program: firewalls, virus protection and security, e-mail scanning, proxy servers, Internet filtering, passwords and privacy, network storage, backup, file sharing, updates, tech support, laptop cases, laptop storage, warranties and insurance, theft, and summer preparation for fall rollout. Interspersed throughout this chapter are sidebars from 1-to-1 pioneers describing how they've overcome these and similar logistical challenges.

Chapter 5
THE PLANNING PROCESS

Introduction

AS DISCUSSED PREVIOUSLY, one of the most essential components of all the successful laptop programs reviewed in this book is the planning (**P**) that took place before any laptops were purchased. Schools and districts differ in mission, instructional philosophy, teaching styles, demographics, and a myriad other factors. So, too, is the approach to planning 1-to-1 programs unique to the individual institution.

While I can't offer a surefire blueprint that will work for every school or district, I can identify a number of essential steps that will ensure your planning process is as effective and complete as it can be. These steps include taking adequate time to plan, bringing in multiple stakeholders, documenting all efforts, learning from other school or district laptop programs, making sure to consider all of the logistical challenges unique to a laptop program, and assessing progress along the way. This chapter will look at all these essential steps in the planning process.

> Many schools are spending large amounts of money on technology. Some are doing so without defining why they need technology in the first place. (Britto, Fish, & Throckmorton, 2002, p. 4)

Figure 5.1
Suffield Academy has one of the longest-running laptop programs in the country.

Planning: A Necessary but Complex Effort

1-to-1 laptops can become nothing more than a way for students to download and listen to music or take class notes when schools or districts neglect to plan thoughtfully and systematically. New programs can fail very quickly if leaders ignore the importance of:

▸ formulating a vision, with buy-in from multiple constituencies;

▸ hiring and empowering visionary educational leaders;

▸ providing adequate tech support, infrastructure, and computer repair;

▸ informing teachers that meaningful use of laptops in the classroom is a school-wide expectation;

▸ providing continuous professional development for teachers; and

▸ evaluating the progress of the program on a regular basis.

Individuals involved in 1-to-1 programs are unanimous on the importance of planning:

> A plan would have been nice! We had [administrators] who made the decision to supply laptops to our [students]. It was so impromptu that the technology department didn't have any input as to how these should be implemented.... We had no time set aside for staff development or maintenance issues and curriculum integration ideas.... Some of the teachers do okay integrating the technology. Others are using [laptops] as expensive notepads. (Personal communication from an anonymous technology employee at a public school district, January 15, 2005)

Given the multiple stakeholders involved—parents, teachers, students, administrators, school board members, taxpayers, political officeholders, and hardware and software vendors—and the differing needs and agendas they bring to the table, adequate planning is especially crucial for a large-scale technology implementation such as 1-to-1 laptops. Planners must carefully consider the funding needed, not only for initial purchases and immediate expenses, but also for the program's long-term sustainability. They need to take into account the high expectations of parents, taxpayers, the school board, and local elected officials, expectations that can easily rise to a level that no program, no matter how successful, could possibly fulfill.

Media attention can "spin" a new laptop program in a way that will leave school and district officials scrambling to correct misinformation and community reactions that result from it. Stakeholders interested primarily in school performance and adequate yearly progress may demand immediate return on dollars and other resources spent on laptops by way of higher student test scores, which may take a couple of years to show up.

Adequate, thoughtful planning can keep a school or district from being broadsided by these and other challenges of 1-to-1 implementation.

A Technology Plan That Is Not Driven by Technology

Some schools formulate technology plans that seem strong on paper but on closer look are driven by nuts and bolts and not by a vision of what the plan hopes to accomplish. These plans read like a list of jargon—bandwidth, protocols, platform, architecture, servers, cabling, topology, hardware, and IP scheme. With this kind of technology plan, the *educational use* of all this technology takes a back seat to *network operations*. Schools whose technology plans are written solely by technology experts without educational expertise will have networks that run reliably, as well as e-mail and Internet access for everyone, but meaningful use of technology in the classroom will be missing from those plans.

This doesn't mean that network, software, and hardware descriptions don't belong in the plan; they do. But they shouldn't be the primary focus of the document. Hardware, software, and network capabilities are all *support structures* that exist to facilitate classroom projects, communication, and learning. Successful technology plans must be driven by educational needs and learning goals, not technical specifications.

Just as we've seen that laptop programs can be different things to different schools, a plan for 1-to-1 computing should be carefully aligned with the particular goals and mission of each individual school or district. Separating technology from teaching and learning and not making it an integral part of your institution's mission and educational goals will not get you where you need to be. Ubiquitous technology needs to be supported not only physically but philosophically as well.

The Planning Committee—Who, What, How, and What Happens Next?

First of all, be sure you have a strong leader for your laptop initiative. This may seem obvious, but sometimes schools or districts don't spend the time to hire, promote, and empower the right person to be in charge. This person is most likely your technology director and ideally has one foot in education and one foot in education technology. To know what a teacher goes through in implementing a new program or technology, it really helps to have been a teacher yourself, since this gives credence to your ideas and improves the planning and implementation process.

If your laptop leader has more of a technical background than an educational one, be sure the leader schedules regular classroom observations as well as talks with teachers about teaching. Investing in a course or two and reading about pedagogy is also important. Your leader must have the trust of the teachers on the front lines to move your program ahead successfully.

Next, decide who will be on the planning committee and who will chair it. Choose members carefully and wisely, but be sure to include representatives from across your constituency. Your planning committee will also be your "vision" committee, because this group will formulate, decide, detail, market, implement, oversee, and assess how the program is put into practice in your school or district. Where your program goes will depend on how this group steers it, as well as how they turn over to other people the various pieces of the puzzle. Given the self-effacing culture of many schools and districts, however, it may be a good idea to play down this "visioning" aspect of the committee—at least publicly. Many educators espouse a "praise the class, not the individual" approach in their classrooms, and that may be the right tone to set here, too.

When creating and tasking the planning committee, keep in mind the particular culture of your school or district:

- ▶ What are its underlying operative beliefs?

- ▶ What are unique factors that frame, enhance, and mold where the school has been and where it's going?

- ▶ What are the educational, age, and socioeconomic profiles of the students being taught?

- ▶ What factors are unchangeable in your community and constituency?

- ▶ What's the predominant instructional philosophy of your school or district?

- ▶ How have other change initiatives been addressed? Why were they successful or not successful?

- ▶ How has technology worked or not worked in the past in your school or district?

Some of this will be found in your mission statement, but most of it will not.

Understanding your culture and what works will help you prioritize your efforts. For instance, if wounds from past innovations still haven't healed, analyze them carefully and seek ways to ease this new transition. Always keep in mind that your planning committee is leading that change. Perhaps change isn't even a word your organization often uses. If not, it's doubly important that you look for guidance from the leadership experts and researchers who have studied change. As leadership expert Michael Fullan notes, "For better or for worse, change arouses emotions, and when emotions intensify, leadership is key" (Fullan, 2001, p. 1).

Expert Advice

Make sure you're in agreement with your community about what's best for your program. Don't get caught up in unimportant details. You don't need to "teach the laptop"—not even keyboarding. Students will get it. This isn't about making miracles but about *providing access to student resources and tools*. So make sure the community is absolutely clear that when you're adding technology, it's a long-term investment in student learning. You *must* think about total cost of ownership. Make sure everyone understands this. Very rarely do schools talk about what the total return on investment is.

— Barbara Catenaci, Beaufort County School District, South Carolina.

Perhaps you already have a technology committee. Many schools and districts do—or did. This may be the place to start. However, in the past, this type of committee is likely to have worked on implementing a computer lab or computer network, both of which are separate from the day-to-day work of most teachers. A 1-to-1 program is a very different thing and requires an entirely new focus. 1-to-1 takes computers out of these dedicated spaces and distributes them throughout the school. As a consequence, your technology committee may need new ideas and new people to make it work for 1-to-1.

It's always a good idea to keep group and individual dynamics in mind. Kousez and Posner (1995, pp. 13–14) talk about "leading from the heart," an approach to leadership that is particularly appropriate in education. Most educators would consider their job a *calling* rather than simply a *profession*. Nearly all teachers have some story to tell about why they gravitated to teaching and what makes them stay despite the long hours and low pay. "Leading from the heart" reminds us to remain in touch with the emotional, and even spiritual, motivation behind the work we do. It helps us connect with those things that really matter to us. When leaders keep this in mind and approach the formation of a planning committee from this perspective, they can lead more effectively and empathetically.

For instance, how many doers and dreamers do you have on your committee? A planning committee tasked with formulating a vision for technology use in your school needs both. Everyone has some measure of these different human qualities, but some are naturally more comfortable being dreamers or visionaries, while others are more comfortable being doers. Dreamers are people who think big creative thoughts and ideas; doers want to get right to work on the tasks. You may find it helpful to assign certain roles and responsibilities to the visionary types and other tasks to the doers.

Many schools and districts have found that including key members of their parent body, board of trustees, and board of education can help the planning and marketing of a 1-to-1 program. A number of schools have pointed specifically to this strategy as a successful way to get parents on board and improve communications with all stakeholders. Whether and how this will work for you will depend on the culture of your school or district.

It's important to keep in mind, however, that while you need enough planning committee members to represent all stakeholder groups, the committee must remain small enough to manage effectively. You'll most likely have to assign pieces of the planning work to smaller task forces. While these task forces will be made up mostly of committee members, you may also include others from your school or district. This can be a good way to keep your committee manageable while generating input from others on specific, finite issues.

Surveying What Other Schools and Districts Are Doing

The good news for anyone considering the implementation of a new laptop program is that many good models and programs are already in existence (several of which we surveyed in Part 1). When the original Anytime, Anywhere group of schools started in 1996, there were no 1-to-1 models to follow. Fortunately, this group saw the wisdom of banding together and learning from one another, and the research and documentation they've generated in the past ten years provides us with many useful lessons and other keys to success. Today, we don't have to reinvent the wheel on 1-to-1; however, we do have to customize it to fit our schools' particular needs and purposes.

The references and resources section in the back of this book (Appendix B) is a good starting point for learning what other schools are doing with laptops and which models might work for you. The Lausanne Collegiate Laptop Institute, held each year in July in Memphis, is another good place to meet and learn from educators who are moving forward with 1-to-1 programs. This conference has grown quickly from 50 attendees in its first year, 2003, to more than 250 in 2005. It features several keynote speakers, dozens of concurrent sessions, and a host of laptop and tablet vendors ready to discuss your plans and needs and develop a customized solution for you. To learn more about this institute, go to www.laptopinstitute.com.

Schools with 1-to-1 programs seem particularly eager to share their experiences and know-how, so keep an eye out for articles about ubiquitous computing in *Learning & Leading with Technology, Education Week, Technology and Learning,* and other professional development publications. ISTE has several active special interest groups, such as SIG-TC, that deal with 1-to-1 issues, and most states have their own consortium of educational technology professionals, such as NJECC (New Jersey Educational Computing Cooperative) in New Jersey. Your state may also have an agency dedicated specifically to professional development and technology. For example, New York has BOCES (Board of Cooperative Education Services) and Pennsylvania has IU (Intermediate Units).

Independent school associations such as CAIS (Connecticut Association of Independent Schools), VAIS (Virginia Association of Independent Schools), and NYSAIS (New York State Association of Independent Schools) hold regular educational technology conferences that can inform your planning. ISTE's annual National Educational Computing Conference (NECC), the largest ed tech conference in the country, has a laptop strand that can be very helpful. Similarly, the yearly conference held by edACCESS, while geared more toward the nuts and bolts of technology rather than classroom implementation, can provide you with valuable grassroots support and information.

Expert Advice

It's my opinion that schools spend way too much time on direct training of computer skills. Our model is messier in that some students may seem to struggle at first because they don't have a firm tech base, but after a few months their confidence surges. Students build a lot more self-confidence when they have to figure things out themselves. So don't spend a lot of time on the laptop itself, because the focus should be on the learning. Be patient and allow the program to evolve naturally and slowly, so long as your school culture can survive that; some schools may demand immediate evidence of success. If you let your laptop program evolve over time, it will be much stronger as a result.

— Howard Levin,
The Urban School, San Francisco

Starting on the Same Page

Whenever a school or district sets out to enact a program with as many potential implications as 1-to-1 laptops, it's crucial that everyone start on the same page. Consequently, you'll find it very helpful to gather core reports and publications from your school and assemble them in a binder for everyone on your committee. This may include your existing technology plan, the school's mission statement, the results of recent state assessments and No Child Left Behind reports, demographic reports on your students and teachers, and similar publications. Before moving ahead, it's important to know where you are and where you've been.

Next, you'll want to begin documenting your school's plans to implement a 1-to-1 program. Keep accurate records of all your committee meetings, communiqués, minutes, drafts, statements, and so on. Make sure these reports are action-oriented. Too many organizations have foundered in the planning stages of a new program because action items aren't regularly identified and no one is held accountable for seeing them through. You've probably attended plenty of meetings like this, where everyone leaves feeling energized and enthusiastic but nothing ever seems to get done. Every plan, idea, and fact-finding mission should have a deadline or target date for completion, and an individual or group should always be assigned responsibility.

Good documentation accomplishes a number of things:

1. You want to make sure everyone present at your meetings, as well as those unable to attend, will be able to read and comment on the plans you're making and the solutions you're coming up with.

2. You want to keep a record of your committee's progress so that others can understand its function and direction.

3. You may want to go back to these early documents at a later date to evaluate the progress you've made and the changes that have taken place to your original plan.

One of your committee's first tasks should be the creation of a mission statement for your laptop program, and this document should be added to your binder. It should be as specific as possible about the aims of the program and should tie each element and target to concrete educational objectives. What exactly do you expect to improve on or enhance with the addition of laptops in terms of measurable results for teaching and learning? What have you seen or read about at other schools that you think can work in your school and district and can be accomplished through 1-to-1 computing?

A word about privacy: some schools keep these planning committee documents private, and some do not. This again needs to be a decision based on your organization's culture and ground rules. However, carefully consider whether or not THWADI (That's How We've Always Done It) is the operative reason for many of your plans and decisions. If it is, actively search for new voices and new ways of approaching this planning process. You want to bring people on board as early as possible, and giving them a chance to review and comment on the planning, as it happens, is often the best way to do that.

Key Elements to Consider When Planning a 1-to-1 Program

Here's a list of key things to consider when planning a laptop program. More information on many of these topics will follow in later chapters.

PLATFORM

Inevitably, one of your first and most important decisions will be choosing a platform for your 1-to-1 program. Your options include Windows-based laptops and tablet PCs (manufactured by Dell, IBM, HP, Toshiba, and others); Apple

Expert Advice

Pay strict attention to change management. There are two fundamental aspects to this: the people involved and the logistics of changing your technology.

I understand why some schools try to go whole hog on 1-to-1 during the very first year, but there is no real advantage to doing so in the long run. Schools that proceed too quickly may lose faculty members and experience unanticipated network problems, because everything, and everyone, is affected. The reality is that it's next to impossible to help the entire faculty integrate laptops all at the same time. If, instead, you ease into the implementation, you can use the previous year's groups to help prepare the next year's. Ultimately, both curriculum integration and classroom management go much smoother if you phase laptops in over time. Schools that don't do this often have to fire people two to three years down the road, because they end up with personnel they don't need once everything's in place. In fact, you may want to consider hiring people on a contract basis for a few years to help with your implementation.

Finally, make sure your manufacturer or vendor is a good partner and that you're not in it all by yourself. Confirm that the vendor is going to be there for you for the long haul—this relationship has to last.

— Alex Inman, Whitfield School, St. Louis, Missouri

laptops (iBooks and PowerBooks); Linux-powered laptops; thin clients; and Palm OS or Pocket PC handheld computers. There are pros and cons to all of these platforms and plenty of opinions about which are the best, safest, and most suitable for education.

Manufacturers will go to great lengths to convince you that they offer the best solution for the best price, so it's a good idea to prepare for this marketing onslaught. As you visit other schools with 1-to-1 programs, ask them why they chose the platform they did and whether they'd choose the same platform again. Consider your current hardware, network, and support infrastructure and look for solutions that will be easy to integrate into your existing systems. Also consider the "value-added" piece of the various platform options: will you receive a lot of support from your hardware vendor in terms of classroom setup, warranties, technical support, repairs, attractive pricing or leasing deals, and so forth?

If you're expecting parents to purchase the laptops, you'll want to make the proposal as attractive and complete as possible. This may take the form of a package deal, with the computer, case, insurance, technical support, and warranty all built in. Some schools have taken a tiered approach to this, offering different levels of support and coverage for different prices. More and more vendors are now offering package deals in which all the components of a "standard" 1-to-1 laptop program are included.

Laptop consulting companies that offer a soup-to-nuts menu have sprung up recently, and one of these may be just to your taste. However, it's good to keep a popular Internet acronym in mind here: YMMV (Your Mileage May Vary). Arm yourself with as much knowledge as possible before you start negotiating package deals and prices. Attend laptop conferences, visit other 1-to-1 schools, reach out to all the known hardware vendors (Apple, Dell, IBM, Hewlett-Packard, and so on), talk to your local technology consortiums, and keep up-to-date on the latest deals and offers.

As mentioned above, platform decisions should be considered in light of your existing network and support infrastructures. They should also be considered in light of existing human resources. If you have no one who understands Linux, for example, it's probably not a good idea to buy 200 Linux machines, even if they come at a really good price. If most of your computer technicians are Mac-illiterate, Windows-based laptops are probably your best option. But if you're a school with a long history of using Macintosh computers and have all those support pieces and relationships in place, iBooks make more sense.

Software resources should also be considered when deciding on a platform. Some vendors require platform-specific licenses. This means that even though you may already have 1,000 licenses for a particular product, those licenses may not be transferable to a different platform. Then, there's the issue of compatibility. Even though software has become much more compatible cross-platform than ten, or even five, years ago, there can be user interface and translation problems when moving to a different operating system. Microsoft, for instance, is infamous for not always keeping products such as Office current with its most up-to-date Windows operating system. Apple has historically done a better job of this, but Internet bulletin boards are full of anguished posts from frustrated Mac users complaining about the messy transition from OS 9.x to OS X. Again, review what software resources you have and want to keep and build that into your decision making.

You also have existing computer users to consider. Will teachers, students, administrators, and staff need to start from scratch and learn a completely different operating system from the one they've grown used to? Changing horses midstream is always difficult, but it's particularly challenging when 24/7 technology integration is your goal. If you decide to switch platforms, be sure you have identified a really compelling set of reasons for the switch and be prepared to explain and defend those reasons with skeptical teachers and staff.

Most servers will support a variety of clients, but the complexity of network administration seems to increase exponentially when you have multiple client platforms. In my experience, most schools with both Macintosh and Windows computers usually have one dominant platform in terms of numbers of machines. Regardless of which platform is in the minority, that platform seems to eat up the lion's share of the network administrator's time simply because it's separate and different. Even though major hardware and software products have come a long way in terms of compatibility, there are still plenty of programs that inevitably seem to cause problems when you're trying to update your anti-virus software, install new administrative software, upgrade your network switches, or perform other network maintenance. Avoid that complexity if you can by sticking with your current dominant platform.

INFRASTRUCTURE

Do you have adequate cabling and electricity in place to support your laptop program? Once you've chosen your platform, and even if you choose to go wireless, you'll still need adequate Ethernet cabling in your walls or ceilings, because the wireless access points and networked printers have to connect to something.

You'll probably want network "drops" (connections) in many rooms as well, to connect back to your main file server. Network drops for shared printers will be necessary, as will surge-protected electrical outlets for a classroom full of laptops. Despite recent advances in battery technology, some laptops will struggle to make it through a full day of school, particularly if students are using CD or DVD drives or powering peripherals through their laptop. Think ahead about how student laptops can be recharged efficiently during the day. At Peck, they've found that as long as students make sure their iBooks get a full charge overnight (as they are required to do) and turn their machines off during the day when they're not using them, the laptops will make it through most, if not all, of the day. Students should continually monitor their battery indicator. Spare batteries, power adapters, and outlets should be made available as needed.

If you plan to go wireless, locating the wireless access points so as to ensure uninterrupted coverage is also a critical planning need. At Peck, they originally set up their wireless network about five years ago and thought they'd done a pretty good job, but they've had to make a lot of refinements in the years since. They'd already pulled Ethernet cable through the walls, so adding wireless capability entailed installing Apple AirPort devices on ceilings and walls near existing network drops and having an in-house electrician bring electricity to the devices.

Two new buildings at The Peck School are outfitted with gigabit Ethernet cabling and newer network switches. Everything is designed to work with the network hardware that is in place. For this work, they contracted with a local systems integrator that specializes in the design and installation of new networks that integrate with an existing network infrastructure.

This company has helped determine the best location for switches and other network devices (with Ethernet this is mostly about distance—you can go about 300 feet from switch to switch without another device). The contractor also advised on the type and capacity of switches needed (leaving room for future growth), helped with cable installation, and provided Peck with a Windows server engineer who's made sure that everything will work on existing servers. The company has also redesigned the server room, which was moved to one of the new buildings. Peck has taken advantage of this new construction to relocate the wireless access points for the entire campus, fixing interference problems and eliminating "dead spots."

Adding cabling or wiring to an existing building requires going back to the original network plan and hiring a firm to run new cable where needed. The thickness and material composition of the walls, the distance between switches, the location of electrical wires, and other factors must be considered. Data cables have certain requirements different from those of phone cables. For example, data cables must not be crimped, bent, or stapled. Early in my career I worked for an organization that hired telephone contractors to pull data cable, and they'd stapled and bent the cable so much it no longer worked. This shouldn't happen today, because any professional cabling contractor should understand and have experience with both data and phone cable. Still, schools should be sure to hire contractors familiar with data cabling who offer warranties on their work.

NETWORK

What is the state of your network? Will it be able to handle the addition of, say, 40 mobile computers? How about another 300 mobile computers? Things to consider here include:

NETWORK OPERATING SYSTEM. Will your network and the operating system of the new laptops coexist effectively? The Peck School, for example, has both Macintosh and Windows computers, but the servers are Windows-based. They made this decision because they needed to run administrative programs that require Windows servers. With active directory and Macintosh network services, it all works for the most part. They did have to address printing issues and install a print server so that both Windows and Macintosh computers could find all the printers on the network. But network downtime is rare and usually has more to do with hardware failure (such as a network card) rather than an operating system problem. Still, this is an issue the school frequently revisits.

NETWORK BANDWIDTH. You may have enough Internet bandwidth through your existing service provider to serve your needs now, but what will happen when you add dozens of new computers to your local area network? This is particularly crucial if you hope to support the use of streaming media in the classroom. At Peck, they've previously used ISDN and DSL connections and now have a T1 line. As costs for high-speed Internet access continue to come down, the school takes advantage by purchasing a faster connection whenever possible.

INTERNET FILTERING. Since all schools that accept federal money are supposed to filter their Internet access, chances are you already have a filtering or proxy system in place. How will you add laptops to that system? Some all-in-one programs, such as Websense, may work for your program. At Peck, they use Symantec's SMTP gateway and its Enterprise Solution. For a yearly fee they purchase licenses for anti-virus protection and web and e-mail filtering for every computer in the school.

NETWORK SECURITY. You'll need to block ports, set up fire-walls, and consider what students may be able do and get to on your network. You'll have many different hardware, appliance, and software-based security solu-tions to choose from; you'll likely need to use multiple devices and approaches. You'll also need a good network manager to monitor and adjust your network settings continually.

Cautionary Tale

SPIM

Add SPIM to your list of jargon for the technology age. It refers to Instant Messaging SPAM that can infect your whole network when an IM user clicks on a message link.

WIRELESS CAPABILITY. Wireless networking is probably in your future if you don't already have it. Most new laptops sold today have wireless capabilities built in. Consider your networking options before making any big purchases: Is setting up a wireless network a possibility for your school or district? How many network access points will be necessary to ensure adequate coverage? Where would they be located? If you already have wireless access points in place, make sure they'll interface with the wireless devices on your laptops. Wireless networking comes with its own set of security considerations. At Peck, they set up passwords and hard code them on the laptops. They also discourage visitors from using the wireless network without permission.

ANTI-VIRUS, ANTI-SPAM, AND ANTI-SPYWARE SOFTWARE. Students will likely be taking their laptops outside the school network to their homes and other potentially unsecured locations. This increases the chances that viruses, Trojan horses, worms, spyware, and other nefarious programs may get onto their machines—and thence, onto *your* network. How will you scan these computers for viruses and protect your servers from infection from within? Be sure all your servers are continually updated and have the highest protection available. Also consider methods to scan every laptop on a daily basis.

Chapter 8 will offer further information on many of these items.

TECHNICAL SUPPORT

Schools often underestimate their needs for technical support. You'll almost certainly have to add personnel to support your laptop program, even if parents and students are purchasing their own laptops.

Technical support for laptops is different from desktop support for several reasons. Since laptops go back and forth from school to home, the risk of damage, loss, and malware infection is much higher. Some students and faculty will want to connect their laptops to their home networks as well as the school network, so the computers will have to be configured for both. For this reason, you should budget for at least one additional technical support person just for your laptop program.

As you add personnel, be sure they have the proper mix of people and technical skills. Supporting teachers and students should be their priority, not the hardware or network. In the words of education technology consultant Rick Bauer (personal communication,

October 15, 2004), "Technical Support = Empathy + Competence." A healthy dose of both from your technical support staff will go a long way toward ensuring not only that your computers are up and running, but that your students and teachers feel supported and respected as well.

FUNDING

We'll discuss funding options in more detail in Chapter 8. There are as many ways to fund a laptop program as there are school districts and schools.

Depending on which platform you choose, whether you lease or buy, and the types of support you'll pay for, costs for 1-to-1 programs vary widely. What should be clear from the outset, however, is that funding a laptop program is not just a one-time capital expense. It requires continuous, yearly funding that's likely to increase year-to-year due to inflation and other factors.

To ensure the continuity and stability of your program, it's a good idea during the planning stages to identify precisely how your laptop program will be funded for a set period of years. Three or more are recommended.

PROFESSIONAL DEVELOPMENT

Carefully consider how you'll bring teachers on board and how you'll expose them to effective models for integrating laptops into their teaching. Making sure teachers feel comfortable using laptops is crucial to the success of your program. If teachers aren't familiar with the online resources and integration strategies that work best in their subject areas, and if they aren't continually adapting their teaching practices to fit a learning environment where every student has a networked laptop computer, your program won't thrive and move ahead. Chapter 6 will delve into these issues in greater detail.

COMMUNICATION

Have a plan for communicating with all stakeholders, even while your committee is still formulating plans, goals, and approaches. Communication problems are common in many organizations, and they often stem from a failure to articulate institutional changes and visions.

Expert Advice

Give teachers laptops long before they're issued to students. Develop a strong, stable infrastructure and hire a top-notch tech support staff. Separate network and non-instructional decisions from instructional decisions. Invest in staff development. Visit other schools. Don't let students buy the laptops; the school should own them! Have a strong RUP (Reasonable Use Policy) and enforce it for both staff and students. Treat technology as just another classroom tool. Its use should be seamless and transparent, not a gimmick or gadget.

— John Durham, Cannon School, Concord, North Carolina

Sometimes schools hold onto information too closely while plans are still being made, feeling that it's not a good idea to broadcast half-formed ideas and invite criticism or ridicule. However, most experts say that frequent and timely communication is an important tool for change management and an indicator of the health of an organization. So don't be afraid to share what's going on even if your plan isn't completed. The professionals in your organization will appreciate it.

Encourage anyone with questions to come to members of the committee for answers, and budget time to answer these questions as they arise. Eliminating any perceived mystique or secretiveness in the planning process will help everyone buy into the program. Be respectful of those with differing opinions and let them have their say. They may be voicing worthwhile ideas and legitimate concerns others on your committee haven't articulated but that need to be considered as you move ahead.

SUGGESTIONS FOR MANAGING CUSTOMER EXPECTATIONS

Adapted from the action plan in Naomi Karten's book, *Managing Expectations: Working with People Who Want More, Better, Faster, Sooner, NOW!*

1. Guard Against Conflicting Messages. Identify changes you can make so that your standards and your actions are in sync.

2. Use Jargon with Care. Initiate a review of your most widely distributed written material, and make changes to eliminate possible gaps in clarity or precision.

3. Identify Communication Preferences. Analyze your customers' preferences, and identify changes that will enable you to work more effectively with them.

4. Listen Persuasively. Analyze each other's listening style, and identify changes that might improve the impact you make on customers.

5. Help Customers Describe Their Needs. Identify ways in which you can give customers something to serve as a focal point for explaining their needs.

6. Become an Information-Gathering Skeptic. Create a master list of questions that can guide you in challenging your customers' assumptions and your own.

7. Understand Your Customers' Context. Prepare a list of information-gathering questions to help you broaden your perspective of your customers' problems.

8. Try the Solution on for Size. Identify methods you can use to help customers "try on" the solution earlier in the project cycle.

9. Clarify Customer Perceptions. Identify changes you can make that will help customers better understand how you can help them.

10. Set Uncertainty-Managing Service Standards. Evaluate the advantages and pitfalls of your group's approach to setting service standards.

11. When Appropriate, Just Say Whoa. Identify situations in which you might just say whoa, so customers don't expect more than you can reasonably deliver.

12. Build Win-Win Relationships. Formulate methods for strengthening relationships with your customers, including at least one you view as difficult.

IMPLEMENTATION

Implementation issues are also described in detail in Chapter 8, but for now start thinking about your goals, requirements, and implementation date so that you can work backward from this target date when filling out your plan. Management experts talk about the "critical path" that all successful projects should take:

▶ identifying the individual tasks and requirements

- ▸ setting timelines and dates for each

- ▸ continually monitoring progress so that planners will know at once how each component may impact project completion

Using this technique will help your program stay on target. For instance, if a certain type of laptop case isn't available in the quantity you want for the first day of school, will this affect your critical path? What's Plan B? *Is* there a Plan B?

You should also keep your various constituencies in mind as you plan your program's implementation timeline: how will you bring your teachers, parents, taxpayers, board members, and the community at large fully on board? Planning informational evenings, press releases, and interviews with project leaders are measures other schools have taken to ensure that everyone affected by the program is properly informed.

ASSESSMENT

Schools often think they're done when laptops are finally handed out and the program officially begins. However, this isn't the time to disband your committee and congratulate members on a job well done. Instead, this is when managing change becomes most important. Your committee should continue to meet on an ongoing basis to address problems that occur and assess progress being made. You may at this point want to invite additional people, particularly from your teaching staff, to join the committee.

Once the hoopla is over, the press has moved on to other stories, and teachers start to integrate the laptops into their classrooms in small and large ways, the real learning begins. According to the anecdotal reports included in Part 1, most laptop-using teachers and students say they do *not* want to go back to their pre-laptop days. But without steady stewardship and continual assessment, 1-to-1 laptop programs can start to morph and move away from your original educational goals, becoming nothing more than a program of electronic pencils.

Be sure, then, that there's a process in place to monitor the ways laptops are being used in the classroom. Make it clear to teachers that they're expected to use the laptops for meaningful learning, not merely for automating classroom routines. As will be detailed in the next chapter, regular and ongoing professional development is the most important component of this process.

Conclusion

We all know examples of educational initiatives that didn't work. Inadequate planning is nearly always a factor in these failures. If you can make your program planning a continual, reiterative process, your 1-to-1 laptop program stands a very good chance of becoming integral to your institution's overall educational mission.

Chapter 6
PROFESSIONAL DEVELOPMENT FOR TEACHERS

Introduction

TEACHERS ARE KEY to the success of any 1-to-1 program. While students will readily gravitate to their new laptops and use them willingly to download music, write reports, and organize their work, teachers are often a bit harder to get on board. If they aren't convinced of the value of technology in general and of 1-to-1 laptops in particular they'll be slow to make the changes in pedagogy and classroom management that take the greatest advantage of a 1-to-1 environment. Thus, many of the potential benefits of your investment in laptops will be lost. While students will still be able to do meaningful work with their laptops, their experience in the classroom won't change very much if teachers don't embrace the new technology.

If first-time visitors to a big city don't have a map, a plan, or a tour guide, they'll probably happen upon a few interesting things at random but will likely miss the local Louvre, the city's best restaurant, a fascinating historical site, and so on. Similarly, without some type of guidance from their teachers, students with laptops will find some things to interest them and occupy their time, but they'll probably not use them in the most educationally effective and transformative ways possible. To ensure that teachers can play the role of trusted "guide on the side," they need professional development that's relevant to the content area and age group they teach and that helps them consider how laptops can enhance and transform what they're doing in the classroom.

Figure 6.1
Teachers at The Urban School all have laptops.

Professional Development—Vital to 1-to-1 Success

Nearly everyone agrees that professional development in technology integration is essential for teachers who want to learn how to adapt their instructional practices to the digital tools increasingly available to them. But finding the time and resources necessary to fund this vital training—which must be iterative, sustained, and understood by all parties to be an individual and institutional priority—has proved to be one of the key challenges of education technology integration. The need for timely and comprehensive professional development is only heightened in a 1-to-1 program. As Barrios writes, "Lack of targeted, sustained support for teachers in integrating technology with the curriculum has been identified as a major barrier to a successful one-to-one computing environment" (2004, p. 16).

Teachers new to 1-to-1 must be provided with meaningful examples of laptop integration that relate specifically to their content areas. These models will help them recraft their lessons and projects to take advantage of ubiquitous access. They also need help with classroom management and technology management issues. 1-to-1 programs can thrive or disintegrate on this one issue alone, so it's absolutely crucial that program planners carefully consider how they'll provide teachers with technical support and training in integration.

Critical questions to consider include:

▶ How can you encourage teachers and administrators to buy into the need for continuous and intensive professional development in technology?

▶ When, how, and how often will this professional development occur?

▶ Who will lead these professional development sessions: the early adopters among your staff and faculty, outside consultants and trainers, or a combination of the two?

▶ Who will follow through and evaluate the effectiveness of this professional development, and who will assess how well teachers are transferring it to the classroom? How will you respond to teacher feedback and customize the training to particular needs and project interests?

▶ How much will this professional development cost, and how will you pay for it? Will faculty be compensated for the training, will substitute teachers need to be hired, and will salary increases and incentives be tied to its successful implementation in the classroom?

▶ How and when will follow-up and reach-out to teachers occur after training sessions?

Some 1-to-1 schools have used survey tools and other pre- and post-laptop assessments to track changes in teacher attitudes and student perspectives regarding technology use in the classroom. This can be very helpful in planning and monitoring professional development efforts. If you do this, be sure to continue the assessment for several years to avoid being overly influenced by the honeymoon effect that can occur when new technology is first introduced. Conversely, you don't want to overreact to the frustrations that may be caused by initial technical problems and program growing pains.

Professional development comes in many different forms, and not all forms are equally appropriate and useful for learning how to integrate technology. Some of the best ed

tech workshops I've attended were the ones that gave participants plenty of time to work in groups, laugh about common problems, and share stories from the classroom regarding integration successes and failures. At one such workshop, the leader had us working in groups of three or four to tackle student technology lessons, giving us a student's-eye view of what teachers were asking their students to do with technology. This workshop opened many eyes.

Some of the worst workshops I've attended, on the other hand, were those where teachers were told to follow step-by-step, rote instructions. In fact, I myself have led workshops like this (before I knew better!), and while everyone left knowing something new, most later returned to me with many questions and a total lack of confidence in their own ability to explore and try new things with the technology. In other words, when I wasn't there to tell them which key to press, they felt lost and frustrated.

While linear, discrete instruction is often an important element of professional development workshops, teachers also need to be given time to reflect, work in groups, and share ideas and experiences. Remember to allow for some "Aha!" moments for your teachers, just as you would for your students.

Teacher Buy-In

Teaching is one of the most stressful of all professions. Turnover is high. Early burnout is common because teachers are, generally speaking, overworked, underpaid, and under-valued by our society. Teachers feel pressured from many sides: from students, parents, and administrators, as well as from state and national governments. Standards must be taught and adhered to, students are being tested like never before, and it all keeps coming back to the work of the classroom teacher.

Consequently, it's never a good idea simply to present teachers with a classroom full of laptops and a whole new set of expectations without first preparing them and soliciting their input. Teaching practices and classroom management strategies will (and must) change in a 1-to-1 environment, and teachers need to be supported throughout this transition.

It's crucial first of all to convince teachers of the value of teaching with laptops and demonstrate how this technology can help their students. Some ways to do this include:

▶ Give all your teachers laptops before you give them to students. Let them get familiar and comfortable with their digital assistant as a user before asking them to facilitate student use.

Lessons Learned

The Urban School's Approach to Professional Development

The Urban School leveraged the relationships between students and teachers with this innovative professional development program:

A key to building faculty skills and interest was offering summer technology workshops that were project-based. We offered a week of non-agenda-based tech support workshops. Teachers met with me before the workshops began and came into them with their own project plan. They chose something that would have immediate applicability in class. We hired student tutors and paired them with the teachers to help with the projects. We told the students not to touch the keyboard but to simply be a guide, and not do the work for the teachers. We did this for three years, and it was a great success.

— Howard Levin, The Urban School, San Francisco

▸ Train a cadre of tech-savvy students to support teachers. Be careful to set expectations appropriately: students should always be respectful of their teachers' needs and their level of technology expertise. Not all teachers will feel comfortable seeking technical support from students, particularly early on in the program. Allow teachers to opt out if this is a problem for them.

▸ Reach out to master teachers and early adopters of technology who have led previous innovations and seem open to exploring new approaches. At The Peck School, one of the math teachers immediately took to the use of the electronic whiteboard and communicated his enthusiasm to other teachers so energetically that it became contagious. This grassroots movement was all the more powerful because it was started by a fellow teacher who was not previously known as much of a techie. Encouraging this type of peer-to-peer sharing is an excellent way to inspire buy-in.

▸ Have your technology coordinator or facilitator schedule informal drop-in sessions and post a welcoming sign on his or her door so that teachers know they can come in with even the simplest and most embarrassing of technical questions, such as, "How do I turn this on?"

Expert Advice

Don't expect everything to work perfectly the first day. Every teacher is different, and it will take time to train them all. One year you're doing word processing, the next year electronic grade books. You're not going to come to the end of it. It's always going to be more expensive than you thought. Don't get frustrated. Find your ed tech colleagues and network and meet with them. Share. Commiserate. Pass around information.

Some schools see one another as competitors. Technical people don't seem to. Don't go it alone. Look around and communicate with others who are doing the same things you are.

— Elizabeth Cohen, St. Thomas, Coral Gables, Florida

▸ Hang out in the faculty room or near the copier or coffee-maker. Take your laptop there and be ready to talk to people who come in. Teachers often have limited time during the day to relax and unwind. Be approachable and available when teachers have a moment to think and reflect, but be sure not to make anyone feel cornered or on the spot.

▸ Publish and present your programs' successes frequently, and make this a teacher-led process, not technology-department-led.

Surveys are a good tool for gauging teacher attitudes and soliciting feedback in an unthreatening, anonymous way. Conduct a survey before, during, and after you start up your laptop program. If done thoughtfully, surveys can help you identify and address concerns quickly and track your success in real time. Surveys should be anonymous and include both discrete responses and open-ended questions. Keep the length short and be honest about how much time it will take and how the results will be used.

Share ideas and strategies during meetings and other venues, but avoid putting too much paper in mailboxes and sending out too many e-mails. In the past, I've been too prolific in this regard, and it hasn't proved useful. Too much communication dilutes your message and elicits groans. Targeted information is best. If you know fourth-grade classes are studying colonial America, for example, go ahead and send teachers resources and links that you know will be appropriate to what they're already doing in the classroom. Be sure to tell teachers why and how you think these resources can be valuable to them;

don't ask them to click blindly through 20 URLs trying to figure out what's being offered on these sites.

On the other hand, don't err in the opposite direction and wait for teachers to come to you. General e-mails to all staff saying, "Come see me when you have time," will rarely be answered, since no one *ever* has enough time. Know your teachers, what they're teaching, and how they like to teach. If you have a curriculum map for each grade level, refer to it frequently and pay close attention to overarching themes and time frames. Going out to teachers with something specific and targeted to their curriculum, and timed so that they can use it right away, will really encourage them to see you as their ally. Remember that it's always easier to edit than create. Consider starting a document for a teacher with some preliminary information filled in—say, a student rubric for evaluating websites about China—and then ask the teacher if this would be useful.

Respect the learning curve of adults. Not everyone learns, understands, and assimilates information in the same way and at the same speed. Make a point of saving all e-mail correspondence to and from your teachers. In my experience, teachers will often come back having remembered something you sent them months ago, ready to discuss it but unable to locate their copy.

Reach out to those you know aren't on board. Sometimes schools and districts hesitate to do this, but I've found a good deal of success with this approach. If particular individuals at a meeting are clearly uncomfortable with what's happening, seek them out later and see if you can get them to open up. You can't solve every problem, but you can negotiate and compromise, and you'll get credit for simply hearing them out. Listen carefully to your teachers when they have questions or concerns, and attend equally to their words and body language. Don't interrupt, and don't talk until they seem ready to hear you. Repeat their messages back to them so that they know you've heard and understood.

Make sure your technical support staff is friendly, empathetic, nonjudgmental, and respectful of teachers' time and their level of technological expertise. Condescension is always easy to spot and can quickly destroy all your efforts at soliciting teacher buy-in. Leave out the jargon unless it's educational jargon that all teachers know and will respond to. Find ways to explain technical details without sounding technical.

Lessons Learned

Technology Fellows at Bancroft School

Noticing the proliferation of laptop programs for students and faculty in the area, Bancroft School in Worcester, Massachusetts, decided to test the waters with a group of committed faculty to see what laptops might bring to their own school. Administrators provided each of these "technology fellows" with a laptop, carrying case, and digital camera for a two-year pilot program. The school also paid them a stipend of $250 to attend a weeklong professional development seminar. After two years, this cadre overwhelmingly recommended to the administration that the laptop program be expanded to all faculty members. Their reasons included:

- "Productivity and organization increases, and there's less paperwork."

- "Lessons can be prepared anywhere on a laptop."

- "I can pick up my desk anytime and go anywhere to work."

- "It's much easier to connect to LCD projectors, so I include them in my lessons more often."

- "Laptops are easy to access, reliable, flexible, and liberating!"

— William Brooks, Bancroft School, Worcester, Massachusetts

Finally, use mandates sparingly. While it's important that administrators make it clear that technology use is an expectation, avoid heavy-handed, top-down approaches. Teachers should be reminded of school or district mandates only as a last resort.

Working with Adult Learners

Teachers are adult learners, so it's important to know something about adult learning styles and what research tells us are effective strategies in teaching them. According to Malcolm Knowles (1984, p. 12), a leading theorist in the field of andragogy (adult learning), the essential characteristics of adult learners include the following:

- they are self-directed

- they want relevancy in what they are learning

- they want to know the goals of what they are learning

- they want to do, not just watch

- they want time to digest, think, and take a break

- they want to fit the learning into what they already know

- they have a wealth of knowledge

- they prefer to learn in ways that maximize their own learning style

- they want to learn cooperatively

- they want to have some involvement with the instruction and evaluation

While these aren't particularly new ideas, we still sometimes conduct technology workshops using the same industrial age instructional models we were subjected to as children: putting everyone into heterogeneous groups across disciplines and grade levels, requiring everyone to follow a teacher-directed activity step-by-step, and providing little opportunity for peer sharing and discussion.

Leading effective workshops and professional development sessions takes careful thought and a constructivist, learner-centered approach. The best technology workshops:

- target the specific needs of the teachers participating

- give learners time to practice what's been taught and explore the tool for themselves

- put people in peer groups and allow them to do activities as a group

- fulfill a need that teachers recognize

- provide something intrinsically valuable that learners can use immediately

- include a "what did you learn and what will you do with it?" debriefing time

- have both an assessment and a follow-up component

- are fun!

Expert Advice

Take a semester to set goals. The next semester have everyone integrate two activities or projects. The first shouldn't be that big, nor should the second. Expect some degree of failure; if these first projects are anything other than a massive disaster, you've done a great job. Then, evaluate the process, and have teachers think about what worked, what didn't, and how to do it better the next time.

— Alex Inman, Whitfield School, St. Louis, Missouri

Another familiar concept—the idea of "learning communities"—can be a useful principle in designing professional development programs that effectively serve the needs of adult learners. You can foster the development of learning communities in many ways, particularly given the communication and technology tools now available.

E-mail, the Internet, blogs, wikis, instant messaging, listservs, Moodle, Blackboard, and a host of other free and fee services represent ways teachers can be encouraged to reach out to other educators and learn from their peers. Some ideas for using these technologies to promote learning communities include:

E-MAIL. E-mail can be used to facilitate asynchronous communication and sharing. You can use it both within your institution and with colleagues around the world. Some e-mail systems, such as FirstClass, offer group mailboxes that work like virtual conferences. When individuals send an e-mail to a group mailbox, the message is available for everyone to read and respond to. For example, at The Peck School, students have a highly successful conference called Student Council. Everything from salad dressing to sports to the homecoming dance is open for discussion. This forum gives all of our students a voice, a sense of community, and some say in how things are done at the school.

Expert Advice

Skills are more readily internalized when professional development for educators takes place both *in context* and in *learning communities*. Technology skills taught in the context of a specific project and combined with teachers working communally— discussing, learning together, testing different possibilities—can be a catalyst for generating new ways to use computers in the classroom.

— Dr. Donna DeGennaro, Montclair University, Montclair, New Jersey

BLOGS. Blogs, a word derived from "web logs," are open, online journals or bulletin boards that allow anyone interested in a particular topic to post ideas and opinions and respond to other people's postings. Blogs have exploded in popularity in the past few years. There are now literally millions of them, covering every conceivable topic. Meta-blogs such as Technorati continuously monitor the "blogosphere"; to see an example of recent postings on the topic of 1-to-1, go to www.technorati.com/tags/1to1/.

WIKIS. Wikis are user-generated, collectively authored databases of information that take particular advantage of the hyperlinked nature of the world wide web. All wiki entries are open and editable by any user. The most famous wiki, Wikipedia (www.wikipedia.org), is an online encyclopedia that accepts contributions and clarifications from anyone. While there's some controversy over wikis' susceptibility to anonymous "vandalism" as well as questions about the accuracy of the information gathered in them, wikis' very openness is their best security measure, since chances are high that inaccurate, biased, or inflammatory postings will be quickly identified and edited.

INSTANT MESSAGING (IM). Instant Messaging is a synchronous communication technology that has quickly become wildly popular with students—but not so popular with teachers. While legitimate security and classroom management concerns related to IM have led many schools to outlaw its use in the classroom, I believe IM is the wave of the future and will be gradually embraced by teachers and administrators because of its value as an interactive authoring and collaboration tool.

MOODLE, NICENET (both free), AND BLACKBOARD (fee-based). These classroom management tools are being used by schools and districts to organize and publish curricular materials, schedules, assignments, assessments, and student performance data. They're also used to create a forum for online discussions. In the New York City area, the NYCIST forum for independent school technology administrators and staff uses Moodle to set up online courses taught by members for members.

Professional Development Approaches— Varied, Frequent, Not Boring!

To be successful, professional development needs to be varied, iterative, and fun. There should be opportunities to share, take part in hands-on individual and group activities, and receive training that provides information and skills immediately usable in the classroom. Some typical professional development structures include the following:

BOOT CAMP

Some schools and districts use the term "boot camp" to describe a summertime workshop that immerses teachers in technology for several days or a week at a time. Content and focus will vary, but teachers are actively encouraged to pull together and learn from one another as they tackle a number of different technology projects and models.

To keep teachers energized throughout the process, the best boot camp workshops will set aside ample time, equipment, support, downtime, and refreshments. This type of workshop often gets strong, positive reviews. If this approach seems right for your school or district, consider the following:

▶ provide incentives or stipends for all participants

▶ survey teachers beforehand so that you can target areas teachers need the most help with

▶ ask teachers to bring a lesson plan they are already using and help them integrate technology into that plan

▶ provide adequate staff for coaching, facilitating, mentoring, and technical support

▶ schedule downtime for relaxing and talking with peers

▶ make the training fun by using team T-shirts, hats, entertainment, decorations— whatever will work for your school or district

▶ create a theme for the week

▶ make each "day" shorter than a normal school day, and stick to your timing

INFORMAL DROP-IN SESSIONS

This can take the form of short, 20-minute "make and take" lessons for your teachers. These sessions can take place when schedules are more flexible, such as before or after school (as allowed by your school or district). They should offer training in discrete tools or techniques manifestly useful to teachers, such as creating rubrics, using e-mail to increase productivity, and downloading images from digital cameras.

Ideas to consider include:

▶ setting the stage for a "tech café" atmosphere—drop in, relax, learn something, no pressure!

▶ making sure enough people and materials are available to help everyone. If necessary, prepare an interactive version of lessons that can be handed out and completed on a computer by the teachers themselves.

SHOWCASE SESSIONS—"BAGELS AND BYTES"

Before or after school, arrange drop-in sessions in selected teachers' classrooms to show-case particularly successful examples of technology integration. Prepare a handout that summarizes the salient features of a particular lesson or project, identifying the curricular and technology goals realized and offering a rubric or assessment piece as well.

You may want to videotape and edit parts of these projects and run these videos in a continuous loop while teachers address their colleagues. Alternatively, you may simply want a teacher to talk, show what was done, explain why it was valid, and relate what was gained from it.

Think carefully about how these projects might work for different subjects, disciplines, and grade levels, and be sure to share your ideas with teachers. These sessions should be short and open to all, and the bagels should be fresh—*not* soggy!

TEACHER KIOSKS

Clearly, there is a theme running through these various approaches: *teachers mentoring and learning from one another*. In a kiosk situation, teacher-presenters set up mini-workshops and poster sessions, allowing colleagues to walk around and browse for ideas.

Encourage your teacher presenters to

▶ provide information for how a particular project might apply to different grade levels and disciplines;

▶ prepare handouts, videotapes, and attractive displays;

▶ make sure there is adequate tech support before, during, and after the presentations.

Conclusion

There's no greater indicator of the success of your laptop program than teacher buy-in. Invest the necessary time, money, resources, and energy into making your teachers comfortable with the technology, and all of your classrooms will reap the benefits. Start with what your teachers need help with the most—the administrative and instructional work they do every day.

Important points to remember:

▶ Make sure professional development for teachers is relevant to the content area and age group they teach.

▶ Structure professional development in ways that respect and reward your teachers' time.

▶ Build in enough time for everyone to unwind, interact, and reflect.

▶ Provide a venue for learning communities to flourish. Teaching can be isolating, and professional development should help teachers connect with one another.

▶ Give *everyone* something to take away and use immediately, either in the classroom or for personal productivity. Remember that your teachers are likely to be on many different levels in terms of fluency and comfort with technology, not to mention their differences in instructional philosophies, subject areas, grade levels taught, and so forth.

▶ Avoid giving teachers either too much or too little to do during workshops, and have a backup plan in case things don't work or people are bored or stymied.

▶ Vary instruction techniques and formats, and encourage *everyone* to have fun!

Chapter 7

1-TO-1 LEADERSHIP

Introduction

TYPE *LEADERSHIP* INTO A GOOGLE PROMPT, and you'll likely get 189,000,000 hits—and the option to click on a definition as well. Perusing the definitions, you may notice many of them use a form of the word to describe leadership, e.g., "the ability to lead." This is a fairly good indicator of a complicated idea—that defining the word requires use of the word itself. Typing *leadership* in Google Book Search produces 57,400 hits. It seems like we've struck a nerve.

Leadership is a multilayered concept that is tough to define and even tougher to execute effectively. Add to that the complexity of organizations with varying missions and purposes and their need for differing styles and approaches to leadership, along with the ability of leadership to instill success or engender failure, and the number of books and websites on the topic makes perfect sense.

Figure 7.1
Leaders provide the catalyst for successful 1-to-1 initiatives.

What Is It?

For our purposes, however, we're talking about 1-to-1 leadership: leading 1-to-1 initiatives at schools, districts, or states so that teaching and learning flourish, deepen, and progress. It's providing leadership that encourages, nurtures, supports, and furthers meaningful use of digital assistants. When leaders understand, accept, and embrace the educational possibilities of laptop learning, they provide the catalyst, glue, infrastructure, foundation, and grease for successful 1-to-1.

> **1-TO-1 LEADERSHIP DEFINED**
>
> 1-to-1 leadership is the process and the action of envisioning, supporting, growing, nurturing, and sustaining the use of digital assistants in an educational setting to achieve meaningful, high-order teaching and learning.

Leadership must be behind 1-to-1 for it to succeed. This is a given for any school improvement program in general and even more the case for something as far-reaching, integral, and resource-hungry as 1-to-1. Look at programs that didn't work—and there are several—and you will discover mixed, uncommitted, or even negative support from leadership for every one. However, successful support for 1-to-1 varies from leader to leader.

Let's take a stab at a definition of effective 1-to-1 leadership and test it throughout this chapter. 1-to-1 leadership is the process and the action of envisioning, supporting, growing, nurturing, and sustaining the use of digital assistants in an educational setting to achieve meaningful, high-order teaching and learning. We'll come back to this at the end to see if it makes sense.

About This Chapter

During the writing of this book and after, I was fortunate to meet many leaders and advocates of 1-to-1 at conferences and through organizations such as the Anytime Anywhere Learning Foundation (www.aalf.org), the One-to-One Institute (www.one-to-oneinstitute.org), and Lausanne's Laptop Institute, which is now sponsored by AALF (www.laptopinstitutte.com), as well as via listservs and searches. An active group of wise, articulate visionaries have made 1-to-1 happen all over the world. I asked several of the wisest among them to contribute to this chapter—and I'm happy to say they said yes! These leaders are Bruce Dixon, Leslie Wilson, Milt Dougherty, Gary Stager, and Ian Stuart. A full detailing of their credentials will follow in the introduction of their essays and sidebar.

The Historical View

We're starting with a leader of 1-to-1 who possesses a unique long view. Back in 1990, leaders and supporters at the Methodist Ladies College (MLC) in Melbourne, Australia, had an innovative and unusual idea: provide laptops to girls starting in third grade. True visionaries in the sense that they envisioned something that didn't yet exist, they formed a unique partnership to provide laptops to the students. The full story is available in the book *Never Mind the Laptops* by Bob Johnstone.

Bruce Dixon was a key early leader and visionary integral to getting MLC's program started and to its continuation. With more frequent flyer miles than anyone I personally know, Bruce Dixon traverses the globe on a nearly continual basis and is constantly in demand by schools, districts, conferences, and organizations that ask him to speak. He is also president of the Anytime Anywhere Learning Foundation. If you hear Bruce is speaking somewhere, do plan on hearing his compelling stories—you won't be sorry.

I asked Bruce if he could tell us what essential ingredients for leadership need to be in place for 1-to-1 to work and if these ingredients changed in his mind since his initial 1-to-1 involvement in 1990. His description of the type of leadership needed then and now is right on target and important if we are to have 1-to-1 be not just a "me too" effort, but a deep and meaningful approach to teaching and learning.

An Expert Speaks
BRUCE DIXON ON LEADERSHIP THAT MATTERS

Leadership can be a somewhat nebulous concept. In an educational context, it's an idea that provokes many conversations and plenty of policies, but not always enough action. To many, leadership can simply mean maintaining a status quo, particularly in schools that are perceived as "successful," which to many is in fact management, as opposed to leadership. In lower-achieving schools, the opportunity for reform presents more fertile ground for visionary leadership, though not every school or district is fortunate enough to be granted this opportunity. Add technology to the mix, and the impact of leadership is even more stark. Since the very first laptops were introduced to students in schools nearly two decades ago, leadership has underpinned 1-to-1's growth and in doing so has taught us much about how it may have an impact on effective school reform.

The first generation of 1-to-1 leaders were the pioneers, and they had great courage and imagination. These were leaders at the school and district levels who believed that ubiquitous access to a laptop was something so important that they would risk failure to make it possible for their students. These were leaders who had not seen what might be possible, but still imagined it. These pioneering leaders were risk-takers who believed that school could be a better place for their students if they had access to their own personal portable computers; and they were committed to showing their staff, parents, students, and their wider community that it was something they should do.

Often, they were what we might call Hero Leaders—extremely charismatic people who were able to build support for their 1-to-1 initiatives through the strength of their personalities. While they achieved a lot, when they left a position, so too often did much of the momentum that their vision had generated. Without them, however, we might still be walking our students down to labs once a week for their computing experience, and so we owe them much for their courage and vision.

The next generation of leaders was in many ways also a group of followers who often adopted the idea of giving their students laptops for a variety of reasons, most often because they genuinely thought they knew what might be possible in an immersive, technology-rich learning environment. By this time, the vision was more concrete than simple imagination. However, while some of this generation had a coherent leadership vision, a number also adopted 1-to-1 because it seemed like the "thing to do," or because the school down the road had done it. A number of schools that were led to 1-to-1 in this way had problems, which is to be expected, often because their vision was neither sustainable nor shared. These programs often became a technology access initiative rather than a more coherent and comprehensive foundation for pedagogical reform.

However, as time has progressed, we are now seeing a much more mature model of leadership driving 1-to-1 initiatives. Leadership is now investing in vision development that is genuinely shared across the whole school community, and, most importantly, that seeks to sustain rather than just initiate innovations such as 1-to-1. As the imperatives for this different pedagogical perspective are now becoming more urgent, leaders' familiarity with what anytime anywhere learning should look like is becoming more widespread and profoundly understood. The extent to which 1-to-1 can enable unprecedented personalization is now accepted, the benefits of students' building understanding in a constructivist learning environment is now clearly understood by many educational leaders, and the inevitability and benefits of learning in an immersive technology environment are no longer the subjects of long debate.

Additionally, today's leaders seek to broaden vision ownership beyond themselves or a chosen few. We now more fully understand the importance of building a vision that is truly shared across faculty, students, and the wider community. We understand the value of creating not just icons of innovation, but rather, an innovative culture that sees the search for better ways to leverage technology to improve the learning opportunities for students as the norm for all staff, not just for a few. We now know of the critical importance of the role of leadership in maintaining a long-term *focus* around staff beliefs and attitudes toward innovative practice, and this is leading to new dimensions of changes in teaching practice, which are becoming much bolder and more ambitious. With this emerging generation of leaders, we are finally starting to touch the edges of real reform, and ultimately the leadership that makes that a reality will be the champions of significantly more worthwhile and significant learning experiences for our students in the future.

That is, indeed, the leadership our young people deserve.

—Bruce Dixon

The Holistic View

Leslie Wilson is the forward-thinking visionary leading the One-to-One Institute. This institute is an outgrowth of Michigan's Freedom-to-Learn program and takes the lessons learned and the knowledge gained from that successful endeavor and casts the net further. The One-to-One Institute serves schools, districts, and states in the United States and around the world. Wilson's consultancy, Wilson Public Sector Consulting, LLC, serves the education industry. Wilson has written a succinct, insightful, thorough essay, laying out the ingredients and approaches for leading successful 1-to-1 initiatives.

An Expert Speaks

LESLIE WILSON ON LEADERSHIP FOR 1-TO-1 PROGRAMS

Leadership for 1-to-1 teaching and learning in 21st-century schools calls for a holistic, dynamic approach. For a successful implementation, the administrator must generate a shared leadership model within the school. The collective and individual strengths of each stakeholder will be called upon for designing and launching a 1-to-1 program. Adaptability and flexibility will be essential for day-to-day, short-, and long-term goals and activities.

Dancing with "change" will soon become the norm, not the exception. The driving force within collective leadership is the school's focus on student learning. At the heart of the school's leadership is a collective vision, which calls on the spirit; learning, which embodies collaboration; and action, which produces vitality. From these perspectives, leadership development shifts from individual-centered to collective-centered, from teacher-driven static curriculum and instruction to broad dimensions of learning based on student inquiry and production of dynamic content. The 1-to-1 classroom continuously evolves around students' personalized learning experiences. Teachers empower learners; leaders empower teachers.

A 1-to-1 program leader first must create a successful foundation by developing a shared vision for education technology within the school. The administrator must lead the effort through honest communication; sharing expected program outcomes; modeling technology integration; and building an effective, supportive infrastructure. An engaged leader strives to grasp the culture changes affecting stakeholders by understanding the new processes, environmental shifts, accelerated pace, and robust technology integration that characterize true 21st-century schools. Facilitating consistent professional development and understanding the impact of change for individuals is a significant piece of this leadership work.

Michigan's Freedom to Learn (FTL) administrators' professional development is a hybrid of education technology research, specifically that of 1-to-1 teaching and learning, and the Mid-continent Research for Education and Learning's (McREL) Balanced Leadership.

1-to-1 engagement causes a dramatic shift in educational practice presenting opportunity and challenge. The leaders' ability to navigate and guide a transformed ecosystem is critical for success.

Planning is crucial. For some, the changes from a traditional to a 1-to-1 approach will be embraced. For others, the divergence will seem to attack core values and beliefs. Those in the latter group need the collective leadership to address their fears while encouraging risk-taking in a safe environment. McREL calls this "leading second-order change" in schools and cites important leadership responsibilities necessary for facilitating second-order change (MacDonald, 2005; Waters, 2003). Those responsibilities coincide with what we have learned about leadership needs for implementing 1-to-1 programs.

Following are ten focus areas for successful leadership of 1-to-1 programs:

1. VISION

The development of a shared education technology vision among school leaders and stakeholders is essential. Reflecting the community at large, the vision must complement the district's values and overall mission. It must be accompanied by an action plan that is practical and aligned to goals, time lines, and funding specifics.

For this process to be successful, the leader needs a solid understanding of the research on technology integration related to student achievement, curriculum, and instruction. The leader can then articulate and clarify beliefs about education technology and the 1-to-1 approach. It is important to share study results that support this kind of implementation to enlighten stakeholders. It is recommended that 1-to-1 leaders provide information and data that demonstrate the need to shift from the traditional, industrial-age education approaches to those that help students engage the 21st-century global marketplace. The imperative for schools to meet 21st-century teaching and learning standards is grounded in research.

Sharing and working with that knowledge base must guide expectations. The latter must be realistic and grounded. It is also important that leaders make clear that technology in and of itself does *not* increase student achievement. It is the seamless integration of a guaranteed curriculum, instruction, and technology that drives student progress. Also important to the 1-to-1 vision is students' equal and consistent access to technology as part of their individualized instructional program.

2. DEVELOPMENT/DESIGN

Planning for a 1-to-1 program is essential. It is important to create procedures for pilots, evaluations, and adjustments prior to full-scale and final implementation. States and districts have had success when first implementing pilots with goals and evaluations to help nail down successful, expanded, future implementations. Essential to planning are decisions in the following areas: specificity of the project; request for proposals (choice of vendors); hardware; software; infrastructure; classroom management (physical and tactical); batteries; device storage; acceptable use and board policies; student use (home/school/travel to and from school); technology support; professional development for administrators, teachers, technology personnel, parents/caregivers, community members; database management of resources; back-up; disaster recovery plan; and Internet access/safety/filtering.

Data collection for evaluation of the pilot(s) is necessary. The information can be used to adjust the program where needed. Providing evidence of program success and limitation is helpful for stakeholders' understanding and buy-in.

Short- and long-term goals for program expansion and adjustments must be part of the development and design process. The strategy can be much like that demonstrated by a quality research and design team in a successful corporation. It will be a work in progress that is entrusted to a team that reviews ongoing program feedback and interim assessments. Time for sharing findings, troubleshooting, and making modifications will be needed.

The initial 1-to-1 implementation will include a specific set of students, teachers, schools, and classrooms. Understanding the project's impact for initial and future implementers and later expansions is very important. It is necessary to be aware of how 1-to-1 students and teachers will engage the learning setting to which they will migrate after being in a robust technology environment.

1-to-1 experienced students bring a unique set of skills that demand a collaborative, project- and inquiry-based, dynamic learning environment. Organized consideration and planning must be attended to as students move from their initial 1-to-1 classroom to the next grades. Leaders must have systems in place to ensure that students' levels of achievement continue even if they move from a 1-to-1 environment back to a traditional classroom.

The leader and team must have plans for the following:

- facilitating the early implementers' migration to the next grades; for them teaching and learning has been transformed

- scheduling how students and teachers keep/hand off the laptops for next three to four years

- planning professional development for current and future 1-to-1 teachers, technology staff, and administrators

- program expansion, including costs and resources

- refreshing model for devices

- students' migration to higher grade levels—from elementary school to middle school, from middle school to high school (students with 1-to-1 experience have different learning skills and expectations than those from traditional classrooms)

3. CURRICULUM/INSTRUCTION

Leaders must ensure that curricular design, pedagogy, and school environment utilize the right technologies to maximize teaching and learning. As stated earlier, having a *guaranteed* curriculum with common and measurable learning standards for all students is an essential foundation for student achievement in 1-to-1 environments. Teachers' primary pedagogical shift will come in knowing how to integrate technology with curriculum and instruction *meaningfully*. This occurs through consistent, ongoing professional growth opportunities, which include teachers' practicing, sharing, reflecting, and debriefing within a structured learning community.

Understanding the difference between low-level and meaningful integration will guide expectations for curriculum/instruction/technology assimilation. Keyboarding, word processing, and basic presentation development are examples of low-level integration. Project-based learning; independent research; problem-solving; student collaboration; and data analysis, synthesis, and reporting are examples of meaningful fusions of technology, curriculum, and instruction. Michigan's experience shows that it takes, on average, three years for a teacher to become a highly skilled expert in this practice. Ongoing, focused professional development, ideally using a coach/mentor framework, is necessary for institutionalized transformation to occur.

In a 1-to-1 environment the dynamics of management change dramatically from those in a traditional classroom. A unified set of expected student technology-related behaviors must be developed and should be consistently communicated and enforced between home and school. Leaders must understand and support these new expectations and standards.

Effective and just-in-time technical support is important to uninterrupted instruction. Leaders can help teachers become technology troubleshooters so that they are able to solve a number of technical glitches. This will facilitate consistent teaching and learning. Inevitably, technology does present challenges. It is also important for leaders to expect teachers to have backup plans in the event that the technology usage planned for a lesson becomes unavailable. This kind of flexibility and adaptability are key ingredients for 21st-century learners.

The leader can ensure a quality 1-to-1 instructional environment by doing the following:

▶ Ensure power supplies and sufficient surge protected power strips.

▶ Specify use of printers for students and teachers.

▶ Enforce an Acceptable Use Policy that includes acceptable software.

▶ Communicate disciplinary policies that apply to technology breaches.

▶ Employ filtering software.

▶ Make available a list of acceptable websites for student access.

▶ Define and implement a plan for device re-imaging.

▶ Provide swap-out devices for loan.

▶ Design and implement a technology troubleshooting plan.

4. PROFESSIONAL LEARNING

It is essential for leaders to ensure comprehensive, ongoing, focused professional development for those engaged with the 1-to-1 implementation. Veteran 1-to-1 groups know that teachers move from novice to expert over a period of three years. Leaders must assure that the training experiences are differentiated for the teachers' unique skill sets. Educators will move along the novice to expert continuum at different speeds.

1-to-1 computing generates constructivist, student-centered classrooms. Teachers need techniques to replace conventional teacher-centered strategies. In addition to the training around technology integration, leaders need to develop plans that include time for teachers to learn. Models include a combination of the following: after school and weekend development sessions, teacher release time, retreats, summer-months workshops, and online opportunities. Successful leaders also know of the importance and carve out time for teachers to discuss their craft around curriculum, technology resources, and best practices.

Leaders also benefit from professional development. They need an understanding of the technology and curricular matters involved in the 1-to-1 environment. The professional learning plan should span the period of time from pre-launch to when teachers have solidified real integration expertise. Professional growth options must continue beyond that point to complement the rapid pace and increased advances of technology and information. Coaching and mentoring frameworks have been very successful—particularly as teachers move from novice to expert in practice.

An effective process for moving to a 1-to-1 program is to provide teachers with devices and training for a span of time prior to the students' launch. This scenario gives teachers individual and collaborative opportunities to explore and experience teaching and learning possibilities using technology and related resources. Leaders can set expectations for this period of teachers' professional growth. The goal is to ready teachers to be able to engage the whole 1-to-1 classroom more effectively and efficiently.

School culture is dramatically affected in an enhanced technology environment. Training facilitates an understanding of this change. It is important for leaders to provide an environment of safety for teachers to try new ideas and practices without risk. All stakeholder groups need to benefit from professional development around 1-to-1 in order to facilitate program success. Groups should include, at a minimum, administrators, teachers, technology personnel, parents/caregivers, and community members.

5. PROFESSIONAL PRACTICE

Leaders must model the use of technology in their professional work. Continuous growth and development in this regard speak volumes to the leaders' constituency. Classroom visitations where teachers and students are engaging the 1-to-1 program are important. Regular communication and discussion among these pioneers will guide progress and program adjustments. The leader builds the environment for success. This usually means challenging the existing culture and norms. Basic to this are establishing lines of communications, systems for input and feedback, and efficient problem solving.

Change, such as that created through 1-to-1 programs, must be systemic. Each system, as part of the whole, must be working in the direction of fostering the transformation. Close attention and alignment are needed among policies, procedures, services, information, and technology engagement. There are not templates for these areas, as each will be unique to the school environment. What is needed is ongoing reflection, rethinking, and redesigning among the professional learning community.

Leaders must understand the social, legal, and ethical education technology issues. It is important for leaders to model responsible decision making related to these matters.

6. OPERATIONS

Leaders must ensure the integration of technology to support overall district systems for learning and administration. As 1-to-1 implementations grow and expand, the districts' abilities to respond to robust technology use will affect teachers' consistent work toward ubiquitous integration. The more that school leaders and officials understand, support, and engage the implementation, the greater the chance for project success and growth.

7. ASSESSMENT AND EVALUATION

It is important that a system of ongoing and annual evaluations be in place to assess program goal attainment and incremental measures of necessary project adjustments. The annual summative evaluations provide information regarding overall program success, needs for improvement, and focused areas of response about project efficacy. Research findings should be accessible to stakeholders. It is recommended that evidence of adjusting the program as needed be shared through ongoing communication systems.

8. COMMUNICATION

As with all things that involve change in schools, leaders' ongoing, consistent communication is critical. Sharing the research and knowledge base with district stakeholders is a must. The community will need to share, discuss, and understand the project. This includes the good news as well as the challenges. Multiple ways to share and discuss are recommended.

Ideas for communicating include structuring scheduled meetings to allow for different groups and stakeholders to have concerns heard and addressed, facilitating immediate support where needed, learning from others who have traveled this same path, being highly visible and available within the project, supporting the risk-taking pioneers, and providing printed or electronic newsletters/updates for constituents.

Repetition of key messages helps. Assert and clarify what is happening with the program through the avenues chosen for communicating. Remind the community of the reasons for the program launch, the focus on student preparation for the future, and the shared vision that provided the foundation for the effort.

9. THE IMPLICATIONS OF CHANGE

Leaders must understand and work with the impact of change for individuals involved with the 1-to-1 project. There are early adopters who will positively engage the project. There are those for whom this approach will challenge their beliefs and values about education. They will be recalcitrant. A responsive leader must work with the reluctant to help them overcome fears and promote their taking necessary risks. Toward this end, the leader can listen to and recognize differing perspectives, illustrate unfounded reasons for dissension, resolve issues (i.e., battery life, power strips, etc.), arrange for reluctant teachers to visit classrooms where the project is successful, provide skeptics the opportunity to witness the zeal of teachers and students who have embraced the changes, and orchestrate scenarios for teacher-to-teacher problem solving.

Adaptability, flexibility, and change-up will be essential for the shared leadership team. Unanticipated situations will occur with even the best-laid plans. As students become self-directed learners, teachers' practice will need to become more of a resource, coach, and guide. Recognizing when and how to shift will become part of the day-to-day game plan.

10. SUSTAINABILITY

Funding short- and long-term education technology goals is part of the vision. Districts cannot count on one-time funding windfalls to subsidize short- and long-term technology goals. In times of tightened school budgets, technology is often the first area hit by cuts. Real 21st-century school vision makes funding for education technology an imperative. With no available silver bullets, leaders must rely on focused and thoughtful funding planning with a collaborative team of district leaders. Using data to drive ed-tech goals, it is important for the district to look at its current technology resource allocations, return on investments, and total cost of ownership. Resource recapture, cost avoidance, and fund reallocation have become staple strategies for districts to find funds once they have made education technology a top priority. Leasing and parent/caregiver purchases through the school/vendor relationship are avenues that have gotten traction among 1-to-1 schools over the past two years.

PARTICULARS FOR THE PRINCIPAL

The principal is the key leader in a 1-to-1 environment. His or her leadership skills will directly impact the program's success. The following principal leadership activities are recommended.

▶ Lead the identification of the school's shared vision and purpose for the 1-to-1 program.

▶ Communicate consistently with all community members—the good news and the challenges.

▶ Facilitate cooperation, unity, troubleshooting, and collaboration among staff.

▶ Create professional learning communities for 1-to-1 teachers, parents/caregivers.

▶ Build a climate of culture shift and change.

▶ Ensure a safe environment for risk-taking, trial and error, and mistakes.

▶ Develop, design, and implement consistent content and schedule of professional development.

▶ Provide or facilitate just-in-time solutions issues.

▶ Respond to individuals' engagement of change.

▶ Visit 1-to-1 classrooms; interact with students and teachers.

▶ Model use of technology in building operations.

▶ Ensure technology support and process for problem-solving.

—Leslie Wilson

1-to-1 Advice from the Trenches

I first saw Dr. Milt Dougherty speak at the Lausanne Laptop Institute in Memphis several years back. His presentation was right on the mark for what 1-to-1 ought to accomplish and how, but what particularly impressed me was his position of leadership then—he was a superintendent! Having attended far too many conferences populated by the choir—the education technology coordinators, the teachers who integrated technology into their classrooms routinely, the directors of technology—but hardly any principals, school heads, or superintendents, I wanted more leaders in the room when we discussed the successes and challenges of 1-to-1. And here was a superintendent who got it! (Nowadays there are many more administrators who get it, granted. And there even are scheduled principal cohorts at Lausanne, NECC, and other conferences.)

Early leader-adopters like Dougherty can provide from-the-trenches valuable advice for the 1-to-1 journey. He speaks from the hands-on, real-world, day-to-day experience of being the leader where the buck stops. Dougherty is president of Milt Dougherty and Associates.

An Expert Speaks
MILT DOUGHERTY ON VISION AND LEADERSHIP

A quote from Proverbs goes as follows: "Where there is no vision, the people perish." While the origin of the saying indicates its ancient relevance, with the congruence of rapid change, technology, and new demands for educators, vision is also a key component of successful educational initiatives, and vision is more than ever the most important function of leadership.

For today's educational leaders to be creators of the future rather than protectors of the past, they must first understand that the world is a different place, and as the pace of change accelerates, their role as "scouts" out on the edge of the future takes on more importance. With the increasing amounts of information available, the leader's role is to review and assimilate that information deftly and bring it back to others within the organization to determine how best to use it to prepare for the future. As technology becomes more accessible for schools, its role and relevance also becomes a part of that discussion. Quite likely, part of the discussions involving leadership, technology, and relevance will include 1-to-1 laptop programs.

Though 1-to-1 laptop initiatives are more common today than just five years ago, the number-one variable aligned with their success is still the leadership associated with the initiative. Leaders help answer the question, "Why should we do this?" As Jim Collins writes in his best-selling book *Good to Great*, "When used right, technology becomes an *accelerator* of momentum, not a creator of it. The good-to-great companies never began their transitions with pioneering technology, for the simple reason that you cannot make good use of technology until you know which technologies are relevant and which are not." It is through due diligence, research, and discussion that leaders help their organizations determine which technologies are relevant, and in any discussion about individualizing education for students, surely the laptop becomes relevant.

Too often, though, once an educational organization has determined that student laptops are a way to restructure the teaching and learning processes of a school, people within the organization make the mistake of thinking the first step is acquiring the tools and training. My experience shows that step is at least number three in the process.

Before investing in hardware and staff development on how to use the technology, it is imperative that organizations front-load their initiative with discussions about today's educational challenges and what is needed to solve a problem they have. I call this [first] phase "articulating the problem." Once the problem is clear (for example, too many of our students are not prepared to function in today's work environment), then it's time to challenge peoples' mental models about how schools can and should operate. Once again, it is through leadership this epiphany evolves.

Step two, the challenging of mental models, requires special shepherding from the leader since nearly everyone has the same mental model about how schools do business. Only through the sharing of good information and discussions about how processes can and do change can any organization be ready to accept fundamental changes in how they function. If you have guessed that it is the role of the leader to provide the good information and facilitate the discussions mentioned here, you are absolutely correct.

Once steps one and two have been accomplished, the *relatively* easy part of providing tools and training can take place. While "relatively easy" may be a bit of a stretch, compared to making headway in the first two phases, this part of a 1-to-1 laptop program is pretty simple. Teachers and students must be provided the equipment and given adequate professional development on how to make good use of their new tools and training.

The last step in the progression of implementing a 1-to-1 laptop program once again relies heavily on the role of the leader. This step, which I label "doing business differently," requires both patience and modeling by the leader, as well as the continuation of providing good information and facilitating quality discussions about what the new information means.

Only through visionary leadership can any real restructuring occur. The leader must help provide the vision as well as be an activator to see that the vision remains the end game of an organization's efforts. As those things happen, the people not only avoid perishing, they may very well eventually reach education's promised land.

—Milt Dougherty

Now for Something Completely Different

I knew of Dr. Gary Stager for a number of years, having become familiar with his writing on 1-to-1. When taking the position at The Peck School in 2002, I especially was looking for ideas on 1-to-1, and Stager's writing impressed me anew.

His credentials are impressive. For 26 years, Stager, an internationally recognized educator, speaker, and consultant, has helped learners of all ages on six continents embrace the power of computers as intellectual laboratories and vehicles for self-expression. He led professional development in the world's first laptop schools (1990), has designed online graduate school programs since the mid-90s, is a collaborator in the MIT Media Lab's Future of Learning Group, and is a member of the One Laptop Per Child Foundation's Learning Team. Stager's doctoral research involved the creation of a high-tech alternative learning environment for incarcerated at-risk teens. His recent work includes teaching and mentoring some of Australia's "most troubled" public schools.

Stager is senior editor of *District Administration* magazine, editor of the blog "The Pulse: Education's Place for K–12 Debate," visiting professor at Pepperdine University, and an associate of the Thornburg Center for Professional Development. Stager is also the executive director of the Constructivist Consortium. In 1999, *Converge* magazine named Stager a "shaper of our future and inventor of our destiny." The National School Boards Association recognized Stager as one of "20 Leaders to Watch" in 2007.

Seeing Stager speak is an enlightening and energizing experience; his audiences are not bored. He takes the stage in a suit, tie, and sneakers, and is never afraid to upset apple carts, challenge traditional thinking, take on all opinions, and maybe contradict the last and even the next two speakers. He reminds us that few of the ideas we have discovered are new and brings us back to the importance of learners, while sometimes sacrificing the egos of teachers and tech coordinators.

An Expert Speaks
GARY STAGER ON "HARD AND EASY"

When I led professional development activities in the world's first two "laptop schools" back in 1990, the most unusual variable was not that fifth through seventh graders each had their own truly personal computer when neither I nor any of my colleagues did. The most unique characteristic of these two schools and dozens of others that followed was the way in which those laptops were used. Although it seems like prehistoric times, there were drill and practice programs, "educational" games, and productivity packages widely available even before the first Gulf War.

Despite this range of seemingly easier options, the original "laptop schools" embraced computer programming, particularly Seymour Papert's LogoWriter and its accompanying constructionist philosophy. The schools chose to do something hard with their laptops—something Papert might call "hard fun." This approach stands in stark contrast to those who embrace computers as productivity enhancers, test score improvers, or back-of-the-classroom amusements.

The laptop would be an incubator for powerful ideas—an intellectual laboratory and vehicle for self-expression. Since the personal laptop, as expressed by Alan Kay's 1968 plans for a Dynabook, was itself inspired by observing young children program in Logo, countless schools around the world embraced Logo and its potential. Large international conferences were held. Books were written, and millions of copies of Logo were installed. I embraced the Logo philosophy, led hundreds of teacher workshops, and even edited a journal dedicated to its implementation. However, at Australia's Methodist Ladies College (MLC) in Melbourne and the Coombabah State School in Queensland, something demonstrably different was underway.

I remember returning home from Australia in the early nineties and presenting projects programmed by children in LogoWriter to audiences at educational technology conferences in the United States. One of my heroes, a fantastic longtime Logo-using teacher, looked at the projects on display and remarked, "Oh! That's what it looks like when the students have time."

Many of us believed the intellectual and creative abilities of students would be amplified by Logo programming, but such goals often remained elusive where there just were not enough computers or time available to realize our aspirations. Students with their own personal laptop computer could now spend the time necessary for the task at hand. Each success would inspire project elaboration or the testing of a larger hypothesis. Errors in thinking or execution required complex debugging strategies.

While the laptop inspired previously reluctant students to become passionate learners, perhaps interested in schoolwork for the first time, children were able to integrate the skills and techniques taught them into personally meaningful projects. Such projects frequently outpaced the imagination of the curriculum. This was not only tolerated, but embraced as the catalyst for wholesale school reform and innovation.

Not only had the early "laptop schools" invested in computers, they did so in order to disrupt the status quo in a deliberate fashion. MLC Principal David Loader quoted Holt, Dewey, and Papert in memos to parents, essentially saying, "We love your children and the tuition that you send us, but frankly our school isn't good enough." This was quite a statement to send to the community, especially when one of the first two schools was a private school dependent on parental investment and the decision to "go laptop" passed a 27-member board by only one vote.

Loader and some of his pioneering colleagues were ready to learn from the laptop experience and make whatever changes in schooling that the experience required. The implementation of laptops was never referred to as a pilot, project, initiative, or experiment. There was an expectation that the provision of personal, portable, mobile multimedia computers for every student would pay educational dividends in excess of their cost and disrupt traditional pedagogical practices.

Attitudes towards class size changed overnight when 15–30 projects needed to be supported in every class. Within a year, English, history, geography, and religious education teachers demanded a three-hour humanities block during which all of the subjects could be integrated in a project approach. Forms of assessment and the curriculum changed. Students working on a humanities project had to engage in sophisticated mathematical thinking and computer science while their teachers observed the need to blur the artificial boundaries between subject areas *and* learned the value of collaboration.

Countless professional development opportunities were created. Even architectural plans needed to be revised since students were now mobile in ways never before anticipated. Teachers, who were required to pay roughly 25% of the cost of their own laptops, requested that vendors come to school to demonstrate the $5,000 laser printers some purchased with their own funds for use at home.

Teachers were reading books about educational theory and discussing the nature of teaching and learning informally over lunch. Older teachers nearing retirement, yet confident in their abilities, spearheaded the use of laptops and LogoWriter. These veterans were trusted and admired by younger colleagues with neither the technical nor pedagogical expertise to innovate on their own. Average teachers wrote papers to present at conferences and enrolled in graduate school. The status of teachers was elevated where it mattered most—in the heads of the teachers themselves.

Today, dozens of teachers from the original "laptop schools" are school principals, professors, and corporate presidents around the globe. Expecting professionals to use professional tools enhances their self-image and—surprise!—improves their professionalism.

The early "laptop schools" invested in a wide range of sophisticated professional development strategies that could provide and sustain momentum. Traditional workshops were available in addition to opportunities for school visits and post-graduate study. Veteran teachers were relieved of some teaching duties so they could mentor colleagues in their own classrooms.

Schools employed me, sometimes for months at a time, to do whatever I deemed appropriate for improving the quality of the school, and I had complete access to principals eager to consider my recommendations. Such willingness to learn, lead, and support serendipity has sadly diminished with each passing year, but in the early '90s, I was able to convince multiple schools that the only way their teachers could teach in new ways was for them to learn in new ways. So, on numerous occasions I took dozens of teachers away for what became known as "slumber parties" during which they would learn to learn with computers in exactly the ways we hoped their students would learn. If teachers wish to learn computer mechanics or how to use a particular productivity tool, they could enroll in the school's community education program free of charge. These learning opportunities were always on a teacher's own time and outside of school-based professional development focused on learning. Many teachers apprenticed with me in computer camps offered during school vacations. This benefited children and working parents in addition to creating an informal yet powerful professional development vehicle for a steady supply of teachers.

Successful school leaders sustained progress by continuing to innovate while ever mindful of the need to remind their employees and community to keep on pushing. The best school leaders create rituals to honor and preserve worthy efforts while challenging others to continue growing.

DOES EASY DO IT?

Today, I speak at a lot of 1-to-1 events and participate in panel discussions where a colleague will reflexively alert the audience, "This is hard." Such warnings seem a precondition before implementing laptops or even accepting the inevitability if 1-to-1 computing. It has never been a matter of if, but of when. Our deliberations too often descend into adolescent debates over whether laptops can go home or how many white boards to purchase (my answer: none) or how we will keep children off the Internet, all the while focusing on the constraints rather than on the affordances of this protean device. The laptop not only helps students learn what we have always wanted them to know, but allows them to know things that were impossible to know and to do things unimaginable just a few years ago. Sadly, as the technology has become cheaper and more ubiquitous, its use in schools has become more cautious and pedestrian. I rarely encounter the learning renaissance or explosion of classroom creativity I experienced pre-1996. This is not an indictment of the technology but of schools and leadership. It is not the technology that has failed but our imagination and willingness to engage in reflective practice.

Perhaps in the No Child Left Behind era, when public schools are being shamed and oppressed by standardized testing while independent schools embrace such draconian practices as a vulgar marketing tool, it is too hard to use laptops in transformative ways. It seems easier to pretend that the world has not changed or that understanding computer science is irrelevant to nearly every walk of life. Our schools can adopt technology policies that treat teachers and students like imbeciles and felons.

Maybe it's all *just too hard!*

In retrospect, asking parents to spend $3,000 in 1990 for each student laptop seems hard. Asking teachers to learn to program computers and teach students to do the same seems hard. Requiring teachers to spend their own money to help purchase a laptop while asking them to challenge all of their basic assumptions and beliefs about the nature of teaching and learning seems hard. Expecting principals to lead, inspire progress, and make change palatable to the community seems hard.

The crazy thing is that I don't remember any of the work I did in "laptop schools" as being hard. The work was so exhilarating, and the benefits of collaborating with joyful learners and curious eager energized teachers was so rewarding that it all seemed effortless. Easy as pie!

That's right: setting the stage for the tens of thousands of schools around the world who have since considered or embraced 1-to-1 computing was *easy!* Convincing parents to buy their child a laptop was easy. Teaching thousands of children and their teachers to program on floppy-based laptops with monochromatic displays and a megabyte of RAM was easy. Creating productive contexts in which innovation and progress would continue in my absence was easy because the adults saw with their own eyes how children are competent and deserve the richest range of intellectual and creative opportunities imaginable.

Now, if I can just convince a few more adults and policy makers how easy it really is to change the world!

—Gary Stager

ONE QUESTION FOR IAN STUART

Ian Stuart is on the front lines of a successful 1-to-1 school in Scotland. Check out Islay High School's website (www.islay.argyll-bute.sch.uk) and Stuart's blog (islayian.blogspot.com) for more detail about a tremendous model of taking leadership out of the offices and into the classroom—and of embracing students as true leaders.

Q: What is the most important thing a leader can do to start and sustain a 1-to-1 program?

A: I think the most important thing is to have understanding—an understanding of the fears and uncertainties, difficulties and problems.

I have used the Situational Leadership Model as used by Moss to keep me focused on the issues that individuals may be having and on what they need for any given task. It also gives them a reference point to say, "In this situation, I have a development need at this level." It's not a case of "I can't do" but a case of breaking the large task of ICT development down into very small steps, some of which people can do themselves, others with which people need support.

—Ian Stuart, ICT Coordinator, Islay High School

Conclusion

Now you've heard from several of the leading experts on 1-to-1 in schools. While there were differences in presentation and style, there were commonalities as well. These include:

▶ determining vision and ensuring the vision is shared by all

▶ ensuring that higher order learning is happening with digital assistants—raising the bar to achieve 21st-century skills and not just automating the classroom

▶ paying attention to planning and development

▶ understanding the long view and the importance of sustainability

If you look at the schools that have not continued their 1-to-1 programs, you will find that the vision was not shared by all, that classroom use of digital assistants did not consistently involve meaningful work that furthered thinking and problem-solving, that planning was truncated or not thorough, and that not enough effort was given to the requirements of the long haul.

It would seem that our initial definition probably holds up: 1-to-1 leadership is the process and the action of envisioning, supporting, growing, nurturing, and sustaining the use of digital assistants in an educational setting to achieve meaningful high order teaching and learning. Leaders who embrace this definition day-to-day won't have roads without bumps, but by learning from the wisdom of Bruce Dixon, Leslie Wilson, Milt Dougherty, Gary Stager, and Ian Stuart, they may benefit from the guidance of these successful leaders.

Chapter 8

IMPLEMENTATION AND LOGISTICS

Introduction

LAPTOP PROGRAMS ARE COMPLICATED VENTURES, with a whole host of logistical issues to plan for and resolve. Just the idea of having hundreds of portable computers roaming around campus, wirelessly accessing your network files and sharing resources, is enough to strike fear in the hearts of even the most resolute and confident of network administrators.

And if that isn't enough, these digital assistants will also roam *off* campus and be used in students' and teachers' homes, where network access protocols and security schemes may be entirely different. Then, they'll be brought back to campus, potentially carrying a whole menagerie of computer viruses, worms, Trojan horses, and adware eager to get onto your network servers. For network administrators, this sounds like the perfect formula for a full-fledged nightmare!

Damage, loss, and theft are also concerns. When school computers remained in a supervised lab and were used only for teacher-directed activities, screens didn't break when poked by a pencil, and computers weren't dropped, stepped on, run over, or used as a shield in a snowball fight. In those days, additional insurance wasn't needed for individual computers because they were included in the blanket policy that covered all school facilities.

This chapter will introduce you to some of the most important logistical challenges that typically come with a 1-to-1 laptop program. Once again, a number of great ideas are offered by educators working in the trenches who have faced and overcome these same logistical challenges.

Preparing Your School Network for 1-to-1

Since nearly 100% of schools and districts across the country have Internet access today (U.S. Department of Education, 2004), it follows that most of you reading this book will already have a computer network in your school or district. However, if you're in the early stages of planning a 1-to-1 laptop program, you may not yet have specific policies and procedures in place to cover computers that go back and forth between school and home networks.

As so graphically illustrated above, adding a laptop program will *greatly* increase the complexity of managing your network. It will probably require adding technical staff, and it will definitely add to the workload of your technology department. Planning for these logistical challenges is crucial to the long-term success of your program.

Expert Advice

Our small network simply wasn't ready for laptops. We did fine the first year, when we had merely a handful. But when we rolled out 300 laptops in the second year, the network fell apart—viruses, wireless problems, printer problems, you name it. Our unreliable network caused the faculty a great deal of frustration that year, but we've made tremendous progress since then.

— Karen Douse, Harpeth Hall School, Nashville, Tennessee

Just as you need a technology director to lead technology integration efforts throughout your school or district, you also need someone to manage, update, adapt, secure, and run your network. This network manager should be certified in a number of operating systems and networks and will need regular professional development opportunities, including workshops and certification training. You may already have a good network manager in place, but it may be necessary to hire additional network administrators to handle the new services and security challenges that come with a 1-to-1 program.

The following are some basic computer network issues to consider when planning for 1-to-1.

FIREWALL

By now, most schools are using some sort of firewall to block ports and secure their network from unauthorized access or use. However, 1-to-1 will put added strain on your entire network, so it's best to review your current firewall to be sure it's up to the task.

For instance, if you don't want students to be able to use instant messaging during the school day, have you blocked all of the ports associated with IM? IM can "jump ports," so you may need to consider multiple measures, such as a firewall appliance, software solutions, or locking down workstations. Some of the most popular firewall appliances used by schools include Packeteer, Barracuda, and SonicWall. All of these products have their pros and cons, and they may or may not be compatible with your network architecture, so do your homework and choose carefully. As always, your most valuable asset will be a well-informed network manager who keeps up with security trends and emerging threats.

Do you have, or plan to have, Voice over Internet Protocol (VoIP) running on your network? If so, be aware that a variety of new threats are specific to this technology, and your firewall needs to be robust enough to handle them. Be sure that the company you choose to install your VoIP products will provide you with specific security advice and protection so that outside IP-specific attacks cannot get through.

VIRUS PROTECTION

Do you run an anti-virus program automatically on all of your computers? How are program and virus definition updates managed? While it's fairly easy to administer a virus protection program for all school-based workstations, it's more difficult to make sure student laptops that log on and off the network at odd times during the day are similarly protected and updated. At Peck, they have anti-virus software set to update automatically during the day, and generally this doesn't intrude on schoolwork.

The timing and management of anti-virus updates are important issues to consider. You'll need to determine what level of inconvenience users are willing to tolerate. You may be forced to make some tough decisions here, balancing the need to limit disruptions and downtime with the need to protect your data and network resources.

OTHER NETWORK SECURITY ISSUES

How have you balanced the security needs of your network with the needs of your students and faculty to use their computers as fully as possible? If, for example, you want to control students' ability to install programs on their laptops and stop certain system functions, can students still go home and use their laptops with their home Internet connections? If you're giving students 24/7 access but drastically limiting their ability to research through the Internet and download files, are you crippling the laptops' usefulness?

Cautionary Tale

The Kutztown 13: Monitoring Gone Awry

In Kutztown, Pennsylvania, lax network security measures at the local high school resulted in students' exploiting the very technology that administrators had set up to monitor student computer use to monitor the *administration's* computer use instead. The technology staff had not only chosen an easy-to-guess password for the administrator's account, but they had also taped it to some administrators' computers. Several students—being the natural explorers that we know they are—found and shared it. You can read about what happened next by going to www.wired.com/news/technology/0,1282,68480,00.html.

The moral of the story: guard your administrative accounts, change the password frequently, and monitor your monitoring software as much as you can.

There are certainly different schools of thought on this. Several of the schools interviewed for this book "lock down" their student laptops, preventing students from changing any configurations or adding software. At The Peck School, they originally went this route, too, but found it too cumbersome and limiting, especially because they wanted to encourage students to use their laptops at home. While Peck does risk students making problematic changes to their computers, it's a fairly simple matter to reimage the computers as needed and start all over.

Are security configurations regularly checked to make sure they're set and working the way you want them to? Many security products default to a security level that's either too high or too low. Tweaking these levels to respond to user needs and complaints will often be necessary, and this should be done several times a year.

Do you run a remote desktop product to check on network activity and computer use? This is done at Peck, and it's been quite useful as a monitoring tool. For instance, when students are working in groups, teachers will use the remote desktop utility to check their students' screens to be sure they haven't wandered away from the subject at hand. Other schools use ARD (Apple Remote Desktop) and similar products to monitor appropriate use and check on student progress on assignments and projects. This unobtrusive approach to offering formative feedback and advice precisely when it's needed works especially well with adolescents, who often want to save face and not ask for help in front of their peers.

Expert Advice

Managing a laptop program is a huge logistical task. One major area of concern is the stress that laptops put on the networking infrastructure. We had to add a packet shaper and e-mail spam filter. While we might have purchased these even without a laptop program, they became essential when we got our laptops.

— Fred Bartels, Rye Country Day School, Rye, New York

E-MAIL

Do you have an SMTP gateway that scans your e-mail for viruses and spam? Have you set it up to filter both incoming and outgoing mail? We typically think of security threats coming from the outside, but if any of your laptop users has "caught" a worm or Trojan horse, he or she may unknowingly be sending out viruses or worms to others.

Does your Internet service provider (ISP) offer any anti-spam or anti-virus protection? This seems to be a growing trend and can provide another layer of security. At The Peck School, they have two levels of security: a Symantec SMTP gateway and Trend Micro's security products running on the ISP's T1 connection.

Is your e-mail set up to allow downloading and uploading of attachments? Provided your other security components are in place, this is usually safe and is an excellent way to get around defective floppy disks and CDs that aren't readable. Students can simply attach files to e-mails and send them to themselves or their teachers, going back and forth from home as needed. You may have to establish size limits on attached files and also block the uploading of certain types of files, particularly executables. There will be a fine balance required here, however: too many limits will make it difficult for users to get their work done efficiently.

INTERNET PROXY SERVERS AND FILTERS

Do you use a proxy server? Your laptops will most likely connect to the school network through a proxy server. You'll probably need settings for both home and school. At Peck, they've set up home and school Internet connections on the iBooks. Macintosh's Safari is smart enough to know the difference and provide the proxy settings at school and not use those settings at home when Home is checked. Our network manager and technical support specialist make sure the settings are created and then adjusted over the summer so that the laptops will work seamlessly once the students get them in the fall.

Do you filter your Internet access? This is a federal requirement, so most districts do. How often is your filter updated? Do you also log everyone's Internet use? At Peck, they use Symantec's Enterprise solution, which includes an SMTP gateway for all e-mail traffic and web content filtering. Since Peck is a K–8 school, administrators believe their students need this kind of protection. They've also used Websense to filter Internet content. Both products are easy to configure and update and allow users to prevent or allow specific web addresses as needed. This means that if a teacher wants to use a particular website that for some reason is filtered out by one of our categories, we can add that site to our "safe" list. Many similar filtering products are available on the market.

PASSWORDS AND PRIVACY ISSUES

How are you keeping your data secure internally? This means making sure no one can see anyone else's files. Password protection and user grouping are two ways to protect data. At Peck, they assign teachers and administrators to groups and then allow those groups to get "rights" to certain files on the network. Users can see their own personal files, but they can only see other people's files when they've been given permission to do so.

How often are passwords changed? Do you allow short or long passwords? Can people reuse old passwords? Are letter and number combination passwords required? At Peck, passwords for e-mail, the network, and Internet access are all in effect. Since they're multiplatform (the laptops are Macintosh, while most of the servers are Windows), they haven't implemented and prefer not to use a one-password approach. This means users have to remember to input multiple passwords.

Some schools and districts have used LDAP (Lightweight Directory Access Protocol) to simplify access to all servers, but Peck hasn't done this and has no LDAP-accessible applications. With an LDAP solution, users logging onto your network need just one password, instead of several, to gain access to all services. When applications are LDAP-compatible, they share the password. It's like having a master key for all the doors in the building. Without this solution, students and teachers must input separate passwords for different resources: a password for the network, a password for the Internet, a password for e-mail, and so on.

Have you addressed FERPA (Family Educational Rights and Privacy Act) with regard to your network and electronic data? Check out the following site to learn the FERPA guidelines you need to consider: www.ed.gov/policy/gen/guid/fpco/ferpa/index.html. In general, FERPA guidelines require schools to make sure that only teachers and administrators who need to access student data can do so. Student records are password-protected and locked away from inadvertent viewing. You may have to check the access rights of your network groups to make sure they are in compliance with FERPA.

NETWORK STORAGE

How much storage space per user is allowed on the network? If you allow too much, you may find the temptation to save inappropriate files too great for some.

The approach at The Peck School is to start everyone off with 100 megabytes and add more storage based on requests. When teachers and students are working on videos, the school has in the past given them more. Lately, however, they've decided it makes more sense to have users save video files to their own hard drives and then burn them to DVD or compress them with QuickTime and save on a CD. It's an issue the school continues to grapple with, and most likely they'll have to go to larger storage options in the future. iMovies have really taken off as an educational vehicle, and that means you'll need more storage for these big files.

FILE BACKUP

Is everything on your network backed up regularly? While you don't need a daily backup of every single file, you do need your entire network backed up on a regular schedule. If applications and databases aren't regularly backed up, a reinstall in the event of a server crash will mean a reconfiguration of all of them. This will require you to restore all program updates and possibly many months of records and changes (if these records and changes are even recoverable).

Have you tested your restore lately? Even if you back up regularly, you need to test the restore of these files to make sure your backup is running reliably and the restore feature works. You'll have to consider your network and bandwidth here. Peck's solution is to make sure everyone backs up files to the network. The school doesn't back up on the fly or during the day when wireless files are going back and forth. They back up about 2 a.m. when no one is on the network and there's no wireless activity.

BLOCKING FILE TYPES AND FILE SHARING

Do you block certain file types—such as MP3s and other media and game files—from being freely passed around your network? This is a big issue and deserves careful consideration. At Peck, students are allowed to download legally purchased music to their computers. However, if any of their music or any other files they may have downloaded causes the computer to crash, only the normal applications will be reinstalled when the computer is reformatted. It's a fine line. The school wants its students to "own" their computers, but students need to understand that the primary use of their laptops should be school-related.

Expert Advice

Equipment issues are the flip side of having a good 1-to-1 laptop program. The equipment itself doesn't hinder the program, but viruses, spyware, and other nuisances do. Rather than spending 60% of my time on curriculum and 40% performing triage on equipment, I've found that this ratio has flipped since we brought the laptops online.

— Sandy Kennedy, Berkeley Preparatory School, Tampa, Florida

Do you block the sharing of hard drives on your network? If you allow this sharing or simply don't monitor it, you may find students setting up their own peer-to-peer file sharing system to pass music files back and forth. You should block or turn off this feature unless there's a compelling educational reason to have it available.

PROGRAM UPDATES

Are all your mission-critical software products regularly updated? Is a log kept of this information? Are there special authentication issues related to laptops used in more than one network environment? There should be a regular update log and approach that can be accessed and viewed by your technology department, and more than one person should be trained on how to do these updates.

TECH SUPPORT AND MAINTENANCE

What's your priority—your network or your laptop users—as far as support and maintenance is concerned? The answer may seem obvious, but there will be times when you have to make this difficult call.

For example, what if a critical network update becomes available during the middle of the school day: do you shut down the network right away to install it, or do you wait until most users have logged off and left the school building? At the schools where I've worked, we've almost always chosen the needs of computer users over the network. It's important that your teachers know they're your priority even when you have to make a call now and then in favor of the network. You want technology to support the learning, not keep the learning from happening just to save time.

Other Considerations

Preparing your network for the addition of dozens or even hundreds of new and mobile users is job number one for a new laptop program. Many other considerations, however, will be just as important to your program's start-up. Here are several of the most important:

PROTECTIVE CASES

You'll have to determine how best to protect your laptops when they're carried around at school and transported to and from home. Protective cases are crucial for safeguarding your big investment in laptops.

Many schools have opted for an "always-on" solution, which is a protective case that's attached to the laptop body and surrounds it at all times. This type of case is custom-fit to a particular laptop model and is generally not transferable to other models. Many schools have had success with these cases, even though some have reported that students occasionally do take the cases off. An always-on case will work best if it allows students access to all the ports and connections they typically need. Transportation to and from school with this type of case requires a backpack, ideally one with extra padding.

Another solution is a hard-sided case. This is what The Peck School has used. The school originally negotiated a volume price for an expensive hard-sided case and asked parents to purchase it, through the school, on the day laptops were distributed. Peck later found a similar hard-sided case for much less money and worked with a local luggage store to customize it with foam cut to the size of our iBooks. This worked well as long as students put only the laptop, nothing else, in the case and left it in the case as much as possible. However, the school may consider going to the always-on case in the future.

Expert Advice

We use always-on cases. Our insurance claims dropped 60% when we switched to them. The biggest challenge is trying to get users to keep them in their cases. When they're pulled out, it puts a lot of stress and torque on the system board and other parts of the computer, and the system board welding comes loose.

— Alex Inman, Whitfield School, St. Louis, Missouri

STORAGE

There will be times during the day when laptops aren't in use—lunchtime, sports, after-school programs, and so forth. Consequently, you need to consider where the laptops can be safely and securely stored when they're not needed.

At The Peck School, they were able to retrofit cubbies to the building that houses the seventh- and eighth-grade classrooms. Cables and locks were affixed to these cubbies, allowing students to thread the cables through the case handles and lock the laptops to the cubbies for secure storage.

A certain amount of policing is still necessary, however, to make sure laptops are securely locked in place and not left around the school. At Peck, teachers who see an unsecured or unattended laptop will "kidnap" it and bring it to the division or technology head. The student will then have to retrieve it and face the consequences.

WARRANTIES AND INSURANCE

When purchasing laptops, ask for an extended warranty. This will cover normal wear and tear on your computers. Of course, not all laptop mishaps will be covered by a warranty: soda spills, animal interference, failed stress-testing experiments, and accidental drops, to name just a few. This is where insurance—either purchased by the school or paid for by individual parents—can make a big difference.

Some schools self-insure their laptop program, combining school funds and parent contributions and setting this money aside to pay for repair and replacement not covered by the manufacturer's warranty.

THEFT DETERRENCE

Schools can purchase identifying tags and permanently glue them to laptops to help recover lost or stolen computers. Each tag includes an identifying number as well as the toll-free telephone number of the company providing the tag. Anyone finding a lost or stolen computer can call the company, which then notifies the school or district.

Registering the IP or MAC addresses of computers while they're logged onto the network has been helpful for some large school districts and schools that have experienced internal theft. This allows the network manager to scan for the IP or MAC address of the lost or stolen computer and track its use. To work, however, this deterrence solution requires a managed network as well as managed switches so that the precise location of all laptops logged onto the network can be determined.

INSTANT MESSAGING

Imho im=nbt (In my humble opinion, instant messaging is the next big thing.)

Instant messaging, along with text messaging, has become *the* communication medium of choice for the millennial generation. Up to now, most schools and districts have limited IM or outlawed it altogether, as it *can* be highly intrusive in a traditional classroom. However, it may prove to be the best way we can reach millennials and encourage their thoughtful collaboration if we, as educators, can figure out how to use this tool judiciously. A few schools have already begun experimenting with it as a way to offer students on-the-spot technical support and engage them in group conversations on school-appropriate topics.

Instant messaging offers its users a significant degree of anonymity. This disconnect from normal social interaction can be both a boon and a danger. Young people report that it's easier to say difficult or personal things via IM than to say them in person. That's one of the reasons students will often say things online they don't mean or wouldn't say in person. Sometimes these messages are vulgar, threatening, or sexually explicit. Thirteen-year-old boys have said that it's easier to IM a girl they like than talk to her in person. Sixteen-year-old girls have said they prefer to break up with a boyfriend using IM.

Is this avoidance of difficult situations and real-world communication healthy? What are the long-term effects on students' communication skills and emotional development? We don't know the answers to these questions yet.

The Peck School blocks IM and will continue to do so until the school can identify a valid educational project that requires it. Even then, they'll probably turn it on only for that project. IM is a double-edged sword: the reactive and disruptive nature of this style of communication, along with its potential to be used for cheating, must be carefully considered and planned for if it's to find a place in most school settings.

Summer Preparation for Laptop Rollout

The following is a description of what The Peck School does at the end of every school year and in the summer to prepare for laptop rollout in the fall:

APRIL–MAY

- Order computers as needed in time for summer delivery (Peck is on a 4-year replacement cycle for laptop computers).
- Negotiate deals and add-on features.
- Purchase extended warranties for all laptops.
- Interview and hire part-time summer tech staff.

JUNE

- Retrieve laptops from seventh- and eighth-grade students.
- Check inventory of hard-sided cases and order new cases as needed.
- Order theft deterrent plates.
- Assess the condition of eighth-graders' laptops to determine if repair or replacement bills need to be sent to parents.
- Order spare batteries and power cords as needed (they keep spares as loaners for students).

▸ Schedule faculty laptops for reimaging and updating (they're more flexible with faculty laptops, because teachers continue to use their computers over the summer to plan and develop curriculum; also, many teachers take summer workshops and seminars and need their laptops).

JULY–AUGUST

▸ Reimage all laptops, updating and reinstalling software as needed, checking for damage, and cleaning and repairing (some are repaired in-house, others are sent out).

▸ Image new computers, affix theft deterrent plates, and input serial numbers and information into hardware inventory database.

▸ Assign laptops to new and returning students. This process includes

- database assignment by serial number and internal number;

- updating and printing database forms, including the laptop assessment sheet to be signed by student and parent (see Appendix A);

- printing out labels with student name, laptop number, and name and address of the school, and inserting them into self-adhesive "luggage tags" affixed to the computer case;

- determining cubby assignments (cubby number and lock combination are stored in the inventory database as well as typed into our student information database).

▸ Prepare laptop pickup packages for students, including laptop, power cable, Ethernet cable, locker, locker cable, and luggage tag.

▸ Set up network, Internet, and e-mail accounts and IDs for all students and faculty.

▸ E-mail and call all seventh-and eighth-grade parents to explain laptop rollout. Parents and students are responsible for

- purchasing a laptop case;

- reading and agreeing to the school's laptop policies and procedures, which includes sharing the costs for repairs not covered by warranty;

- participating in an orientation session;

- signing an inventory and assessment sheet that describes the condition of the computer (see Appendix A).

Monitoring and Maintaining Laptops throughout the Year

Once laptops are in the hands of students and teachers, program administrators need to monitor usage actively and act quickly to fix problems as they arise, so that curricular plans and schedules aren't disrupted by technical difficulties. Here are some of the most important things Peck does to ensure that laptops are being appropriately and effectively used:

Lessons Learned

Keep Track of Your Spare Parts

Keep a variety of spare parts on hand to minimize disruptions. Identify them by engraving an assigned number on every item, and log them in and out. Peck used to hand out chargers without assigned numbers but discovered that students were freely borrowing chargers from one another and returning someone else's instead of their own. It turned into a huge problem. Students now have to return the specific charger they were assigned.

▶ The school regularly reminds students about the appropriate care of laptops and the ethical use of all school computer equipment and resources. Peck uses the student-friendly acronym LARK to help students remember that all use of school hardware, software, e-mail accounts, and Internet access needs to be

L (Legal)—Only software and music that's been purchased can be downloaded; sources can only be used if they're cited and used appropriately.

A (Appropriate)—Everything viewed, sent, downloaded, and used on school laptops must be school-appropriate, not just to seventh- and eighth-grade students but to kindergarten students and grandparents as well.

R (Responsible)—Equipment and resources must be used carefully and responsibly to avoid the damage that results from neglect and poor handling.

K (Kind)—All e-mails and other electronic communications must be respectful and considerate of all parties; sending chain mail or any type of offensive or insulting material to anyone is never kind.

▶ We review and redistribute our Acceptable Use Policy (see Appendix A) several times per year and make sure students understand and adhere to it.

▶ Peck has found that a proactive approach to damage control and hard disk maintenance can be very helpful. While the Acceptable Use Policy and Laptop Guidelines (see Appendix A) state that students should bring any damage or problems immediately to administrators' attention, this doesn't always happen. Collecting computers several times per year allows Peck to assess computers for wear and tear, repair and correct problems, and update the assessment sheet.

Implementation Challenges—The Experts Speak

Here are some first-person accounts of implementation challenges faced by other 1-to-1 programs.

SUFFIELD ACADEMY (SUFFIELD, CONNECTICUT)

Dean Ellerton, director of technology at Suffield Academy, lists these as the key challenges that his school has faced with its laptop program:

REPAIR "UPTIME." The more you rely on laptops, the more "downtime" is not tolerated. We've had to beef up staff (both adult and student technicians) to look at broken laptops in a timely fashion, and we've had to maintain a good number of hot-swap loaners, so that students are never without a functioning laptop.

NETWORK PERFORMANCE. The more we use laptops in our classrooms and at night in our dorms, the more we realize that our program is really about 1-to-1 access to our network. So we've had to make sure our network is robust and reliable. In 2003, we updated all of our network electronics to be fully switched, 100 Mbps (with gigabit uplinks). We also replaced all of our wireless access points with 802.11 g (54 Mbps) to gain network access speed.

INTERNET BANDWIDTH. We've struggled to keep up with the expectations of our users with regard to the size of our Internet pipe. They were so used to a dedicated cable modem or DSL connection at home, our pipe, which was originally just a T1, seemed small to them. Our first solution, and we still use this, was to install a packet-shaping appliance to "massage" the traffic and allow or squeeze it depending on its academic or recreational value. We've subsequently added more actual bandwidth. Most of our traffic is http traffic. We now have a dedicated business-level cable modem (6 megabits per second) that we use exclusively to pull http traffic. This is hooked to a Linux-based proxy server to also help maximize our productive use.

SECURITY, VIRUSES, AND NETWORK CONTROL. Wireless access adds another layer to our network complexity and opens us up to new security threats. In 2003, we redid our network's logical structure to install many more VLANs (e.g., one per building, wireless, etc.) for increased control. In addition, we use an authentication and control appliance to control access to our network via centralized log in and MAC-based access controls. We also use this to moderate client and port on/off times for bedtime. When viruses became the massive issue they are now, we started an anti-virus server for the students and supplied the licenses (Sophos). In addition, we also use the control appliance to scan clients automatically as they log onto our network and place them into Quarantine VLAN if they've failed to keep up-to-date with virus definition and other security updates.

SPAM. We installed a campus-wide spam filter appliance to help unclog our e-mail server (95% of what we get is spam). This comes with a user-based quarantine (they get e-mailed once a day with a list of their spam) and user-defined whitelist.

INTERNET FILTER. Our school doesn't filter Internet content, but we do monitor activity. We use a product that looks at all Internet traffic, classifies it, and provides reports to an administrator as to the acceptability of the activity (as defined by our AUP).

STORAGE. Our students store massive amounts of files. We just installed a SAN to hold all of it; we now have terabytes' worth of disk space. This doesn't cover DV movie files, however, which we store locally and back up to FireWire drives.

BACKUP. The more we store, the more we back up. We now back up to large hard disks and then to tape from there. It takes a dedicated server and all day to do it!

RECREATIONAL USE. Like everyone else, we're struggling to come up with strategies to monitor and control recreational use, primarily chatting. We've made some areas of school, such as the library, chat free, using our firewall and packet-shaping appliance. However, the community hasn't yet electronically prohibited chatting or games at other times. While we tell students that they shouldn't be doing it in class or in evening study hall, we don't yet electronically whack them for it.

FORNEY (TEXAS) INDEPENDENT SCHOOL DISTRICT

Roger Geiger, director of technology at Forney ISD, offers these suggestions for 1-to-1 program start-ups:

1. Don't try to roll out the laptops during the first week of school. There's already too much going on.

2. In Forney, we pay for the insurance, and parents pay a $250 deductible if the laptop is seriously damaged or lost. Parents are also responsible for all non-warranty damage up to $250. So far, after a year and a half, we've had no damage charges below $250.

3. It's important to decide where you'll secure laptops when not in use during PE, lunch, band, and so forth. If students don't need their laptops at home, where can they leave them at school? Our laptops are too big for most of our lockers. On our elementary campus, we've stationed mobile laptop carts in each classroom so that laptops can be locked up and charged. When we expand the laptop program to the secondary level, we'll need to come up with a similar solution.

Expert Advice

St. Thomas students get a laptop, a case, usually a USB drive, and a three-year warranty covering accidental damage. It's non-negotiable. We give interested parents information about insurance specifically for laptop use and tell them to look into their own household insurance policies to see if they cover damage not considered accidental. They have to buy the always-on protective case we prescribe. This works out well: our vendor takes the orders, and parents pay the vendor directly. The vendor ships the laptops here, and we image them. This is a lot easier because they have built-in wireless cards.

— Elizabeth Cohen, St. Thomas School, Coral Gables, Florida

4. Working with laptops can eat up class time if teachers aren't prepared—boot up, shut down, program glitches, and so forth. You need to decide how you'll provide classroom tech support.

5. What do you do when the laptop battery runs out? Even with extended life batteries, ours sometimes run out of juice by the end of the day, and there's no good place to charge all of them in a regular classroom. The mobile laptop carts are our current solution, but we may revisit this when we expand the program.

6. If you don't want students to load non-approved software to their laptops, you'll have to lock them down to make it impossible. But if they take their laptops home, they'll need to be able to load printer drivers and connect to their home ISP, so you

have to remove the load restriction. How do you prevent them from loading the stuff you don't want them to load? At Forney, we've locked our laptops down completely this year, making the support situation much simpler. The students can't use their laptops to get on the Internet at home and can't load home printer drivers, but neither of these are necessary for using the electronic textbooks that we've loaded onto their computers.

Conclusion

After reading about the myriad logistical issues that must be addressed when you add laptops to the mix of technologies at your school, you may be thinking that a laptop program is too daunting a proposition. But take heart. Adding laptops to your network will indeed increase its complexity and require strategic planning, extra time, and flexible, committed personnel. What we've learned from the leaders of 1-to-1 programs around the country can help all of us succeed in rising to these challenges.

Part Three

TEACHING AND LEARNING IN A 1-TO-1 ENVIRONMENT

GIVING STUDENTS UBIQUITOUS ACCESS to computers changes the classroom learning environment in a variety of fundamental ways. For a laptop program to be successful, teachers need support and encouragement so that they can embrace those changes and modify their instructional practices and classroom management strategies.

Reflective teachers will find this to be a natural process—deconstructing familiar approaches in the light of new tools, resources, and theories of learning and then merging those that work more effectively with daily practice.

Ubiquitous access to computers changes what teachers can do and expect, and it changes the way students can respond and engage. The chapters in Part 3 will help you start making those changes so that you can take advantage of what 1-to-1 has to offer.

Previewing the Chapters

In Chapter 9, "Current Learning Theories and the 1-to-1 Classroom," Donna DeGennaro surveys current research on how students learn and applies it to the 1-to-1 classroom. She offers teachers practical suggestions for making the most of this new learning environment. Dr. DeGennaro has bridged theory and practice throughout her career, having provided technology leadership and instruction at several Philadelphia schools. She has held research and teaching positions with several Philadelphia area colleges and is assistant professor of curriculum and teaching at Montclair State University in Montclair, New Jersey.

Chapter 10, "1-to-1 Tablet PC Programs That Work" was written by Dave Berque of DePauw University, the most qualified person I know to discuss this topic. The chapter outlines the unique benefits and some of the pitfalls of tablet PCs and includes case studies of three leading tablet PC programs. Also included are insights, tips, and cautionary tales from tablet PC leaders at these schools, as well as advice and reflections from teachers and students.

Chapter 11, "The Shift (Web 2.0 and Beyond)," discusses the move toward learner-centered environments. Nothing jumpstarts The Shift quite like 1-to-1. Because when every student in the room has a digital assistant, he or she does not have to look "up" to the teacher for resources or ideas—the student has resources at his or her fingertips. This chapter examines some of the approaches and pedagogies that can work when 1-to-1 is an integral part of teaching and learning. It's for educators who are bold and reflective, concerned about growing and not about staying put.

Chapter 12 covers "Classroom Management Strategies for 1-to-1": classroom setup, just-in-time technical support, loaner laptops, software for monitoring and managing the classroom, content filtering, policies and consequences, and a number of other management tips and ideas from laptop experts. The 1-to-1 classroom presents teachers with issues and challenges that non-laptop classrooms don't have; however, thoughtful planning and flexible teaching can help you turn them into valuable benefits.

A sample lesson plan for a 1-to-1 classroom is offered in Chapter 13, "Teaching with Laptops—A Model Lesson." Elizabeth Cohen, director of technology at St. Thomas Episcopal Parish School in Coral Gables, Florida, shares a project-based lesson plan that is facilitated, enhanced, and extended through the use of laptop computers.

Chapter 9

CURRENT LEARNING THEORIES AND THE 1-TO-1 CLASSROOM

Donna DeGennaro

Introduction

ACCORDING TO the July 2005 PEW report, *Teens and Technology: Youth Are Leading the Transition to a Fully Wired and Mobile Nation* (Lenhart, Madden, & Hitlin, 2005), young people increasingly use the Internet, interactive simulations, IM, and text messaging as a natural part of their everyday activities. While this study primarily reflects out-of-school technology uses, imagine what can happen when students are given 1-to-1, 24/7 access to laptop computers. The question becomes: how can educators effectively bridge out-of-school technology practices with in-school 1-to-1 laptop learning?

When it comes to technology, most of us have heard the familiar refrain, "Technology can facilitate good teaching and learning when used appropriately." But what does this really mean? We've read examples of effective technology integration, yet sometimes we still have trouble visualizing and explaining it, particularly in an environment where every student has a machine. We're left to ask ourselves: What's the relationship between good teaching and learning, and how can technology be used appropriately to support these practices? What exactly *is* "appropriate use of technology"?

To begin to answer these questions and understand the value of 1-to-1 laptop learning, we must first take a look at current theories of how people learn and what this implies about the proper design of learning environments. Armed with this knowledge, we can then begin to consider how 1-to-1 laptops support these principles and implications and define appropriate uses for this technology resource.

Figure 9.1
Classrooms with laptops everywhere are de rigueur at The Urban School.

How People Learn

A seminal work titled *How People Learn* deftly summarizes current theories about learning and the design of learning environments (Bransford, Brown, & Cocking, 2000). This book reports on the ongoing efforts of cognitive scientists and educational researchers to explore the nature of learning. The work has resulted in the publication of a set of guiding principles about learning as well as the implications of those principles on the design of community-centered learning environments (see Table 1).

A new NSF-funded learning center known as LIFE (Learning in Informal and Formal Environments) is bringing together cross-disciplinary researchers to build on this work. The center's aim is to study the social, cultural, cognitive, and affective dimensions of learning and how transformative education technologies can support the principles reflected in Table 1 (Bransford, Brown, & Cocking, 2000).

TABLE 1. Guiding principles for learning and implications for learning environments.

PRINCIPLE	IMPLICATION
1. Students come to the classroom with preconceptions about how the world works. If their initial understanding is not engaged, they may fail to grasp the new concepts and information that are taught, or they may learn them for purposes of a test but revert to their preconceptions outside the classroom.	Schools and classrooms must be learner-centered.
2. To develop competence in an area of inquiry, students must: (a) have a deep foundation of factual knowledge, (b) understand facts and ideas in the context of a conceptual framework, and (c) organize knowledge in ways that facilitate retrieval and application.	Schools and classrooms must be knowledge-centered.
3. A "metacognitive" approach to instruction can help students learn to take control of their own learning by defining learning goals and monitoring their progress in achieving them.	Schools and classrooms must be assessment-centered.
4. Learners' brains develop not in isolation, but rather as a function of social interactions with others in the environment.	Schools and classrooms must be community-centered.

© 2000 National Academy of Sciences. Reprinted with permission.

The terms *learner-centered, knowledge-centered, assessment-centered* and *community-centered* can take on various meanings. Their distinct definitions in this context are important to explicate.

LEARNER-CENTERED ENVIRONMENTS

It's important to note first that "learner-centered" is distinct from "student-centered." Learner-centered environments focus on students' prior knowledge and experiences as well as their cultural backgrounds, because students come to the classroom with a particular understanding of how the world works. Educators can maximize student success by finding ways to uncover what students know and how they've come to know it.

In terms of technology, the significant questions are: What technology literacies do learners come with? How have previous and ongoing experiences with technology shaped their learning and communication styles? How can we begin to tap this experience and knowledge in effective ways and make the best use of ubiquitous access?

KNOWLEDGE-CENTERED ENVIRONMENTS

Knowledge-centered environments focus on sense-making and deep understanding of concepts. A knowledge-centered activity provides students the opportunity to uncover the "big ideas" as they work on real-world problems and scenarios. Basic skills and factual knowledge develop within larger conceptual frameworks rather than through lecture and memorization.

In a knowledge-centered environment, students use meta-cognitive skills to "explore, explain, extend and evaluate their progress" (Bransford, Brown, & Cocking, 2000). Meta-cognitive skills are essential to fostering the kind of active exploration and application of knowledge that is needed to extend and transform students' initial preconceptions.

In terms of technology, the significant questions are: How does technology support and facilitate student knowledge development? How do continuously accessible technology applications foster student negotiation of meaning and deep understanding of information and concepts?

ASSESSMENT-CENTERED ENVIRONMENTS

Assessments can be formative or summative. Formative assessment engages students and teachers in a continual feedback loop, requiring both to reflect on the learning process that's taking place in the classroom. Teachers reflect on the observations they make of classroom activities and student performance on formative assessment tasks, while students reflect on their own learning process and performance or the learning process of a peer.

This type of meta-cognitive activity is most valuable when teachers and students use these reflections to revise their work and improve their performance. For teachers, this can come in the form of altered curricular designs or the use of new learning resources. Students can use this reflection to critique and revise their research questions and apply in new ways the information they've accumulated.

Summative assessments, on the other hand, provide a quantitative and qualitative picture of where students are at a particular point in their learning process. Summative assessments include tests, quizzes, portfolios, or other means of gathering information about student progress.

In terms of technology, the significant questions are: How can technology assist teachers in administering, scoring, and reflecting on formative and summative assessments? How does technology mediate students' ability to participate in their own (and their peers') ongoing formative assessments?

COMMUNITY-CENTERED ENVIRONMENTS

When we think of creating a classroom community, we often have images of establishing rules in order to have "good classroom management." While community-centered does refer to the norms and expectation of participation, it is more complex than this. For one, identified norms of participation should reflect the culture from which the students come. Different ways that students act at home and in their communities can directly impact how they will successfully participate in school. Another important aspect of community-centered environments is that they embody characteristics of Vygotsky's (1978) notion of social learning. This view requires creating classrooms that foster norms of interactions that allow learners to move from actual to potential developmental levels of understanding ("zones of proximal development") by working with others. In this view, initial and evolving mental development become more visible when students have opportunities to share understandings and negotiate meaning amiably, as well as cordially reason and argue with each other (Darling-Hammond & Bransford, 2005).

In terms of technology, the significant questions are the following: How can technology be helpful in building effective community? How does technology support norms of sociable knowledge sharing, negotiation, reasoning, and argumentation?

It's important to note that all four of these guiding principles focus primarily on *what is being learned* rather than *what is being taught*. These principles establish a conceptual framework that centers on what *students* are doing in the classroom rather than what teachers are doing. However, this should not be understood to imply that students must always work in groups, nor does it mean that students should never receive structured guidance from the teacher. From understanding and accommodating learners' backgrounds, to helping learners construct knowledge out of new information, to finding opportunities for continuous reflection and revision, this framework lays the groundwork for conceptualizing appropriate uses of technology that will support what we have learned about how people learn.

Using Technology to Support Learning

To begin our consideration of appropriate uses of technology, let's imagine a scenario that typifies how youth today interact with and co-opt the technology tools of our increasingly wired and mobile nation.

> A student, Kellie, is at home at her desk. Kellie's laptop is in front of her, her cell phone is to the side, and her iPod is nearby playing her favorite tunes. As she listens to the music, she types away on the laptop. She's not doing just one thing on the computer but several. Her IM window buzzes with messages and replies from six buddies chatting all at the same time, and several other windows sit open in the background. IM is currently the focus: she and her friends are discussing their fantasy football results for the week. They argue over who the best players are and who they'll choose next time. While still IMing, Kellie toggles back and forth between browser windows to investigate player stats, results from last week, and predictions for next week's games.
>
> As the conversation continues in IM, Kellie hears her phone buzz. Another friend is text messaging her to ask what she's up to. Kellie texts back and invites her friend to join the IM chat. Now she has seven buddies. Without missing a beat, Kellie and her friends continue to discuss the best configuration of players for the fantasy team. There are points of agreement and points of contestation. They can immediately back up their opinions with facts gleaned from the web (as well as their combined fantasy football experience). Playing Madden—a simulated football franchise, league, and game—they come to understand all elements of the game in a very realistic way, which in turn informs their decisions on players.

This scenario illustrates some of the many ways that members of the millennial generation integrate technology seamlessly into their everyday lives to communicate, build and share knowledge, make decisions, and participate in social networks. Today's children are natural multitaskers, and technology gives them the tools to do what comes naturally and pursue these many important activities simultaneously. To older generations, this kind of multitasking behavior may seem bewildering and pernicious, an endless series of distractions and diversions that feed on and reinforce children's chronically short attention spans. But what is really happening here is that children are assimilating the givens of our media- and technology-driven society and using them in their own ways to learn what they need to learn to navigate and take their places in that society.

Yes, they are learning—this isn't just play or socialization. In the informal, technology-mediated learning environment described in this scenario, the activities are learner-centered, knowledge-centered, assessment-centered and community-centered. The scenario is learner-centered, in that it's focused on the interests of the participants and depends upon and activates the knowledge and skills that the participants bring with them. It is knowledge-centered, in that these young people are actively searching for and applying information in a goal-driven process. It is assessment-centered, in that the participants are constantly challenging each other and evaluating alternative approaches and perspectives, which naturally cause them to reflect on and rethink their own preconceptions. Finally, it is community-centered, in that there are particular norms of social participation with technology that afford the children an opportunity to negotiate their decisions about their players, while raising the level of learning through the social process.

For many of us, it may seem quite a stretch to compare what happens in this informal learning environment to what happens (or should happen) in the more formal school learning environment. While it's true that this scenario says something important about the way children use technology today to help them understand the way the world works, these children aren't really building on or extending the kinds of conceptual frameworks that are implied by and necessary to academic learning, are they? These students are using new information and their own prior knowledge, but they aren't really gaining a deep comprehension of the topic or synthesizing it to make a compelling argument. Transcripts of this IM chat might reveal substantial reflection on and revision of previous ideas, yet these buddies may not be consciously reflecting on their personal learning or that of their peers.

Nevertheless, these are differences in degree, not in kind. At the most fundamental level, this scenario embodies most of the principles posited by current learning theories and can tell us much about effective and appropriate uses of technology in a laptop-equipped classroom.

Bridging the Gap between Informal and Formal Learning Environments

This scenario can help us bridge the gap between the learning activities that young people naturally pursue at home and with their friends and the learning environment that teachers create in the classroom. Let's take a parallel scenario and apply it to a 1-to-1 classroom setting.

In the description that follows, the teacher is engaging students in a project-based learning (PBL) activity. Project-based models are designed to immerse teams of students in the exploration of a real-world problem or issue. Students are required to build on their previous experiences and knowledge to come up with a solution or create a product that they then present to others. These projects are self-directed and research-based and require students to collaborate and employ problem-solving skills. The end products or presentations should illustrate that students have extended their understanding by actively engaging with the subject matter and using the information they've gathered to create or communicate something new.

Kellie is now in a 1-to-1 laptop classroom. As at home, she has many technologies and applications at her fingertips (whether that includes the cell phone or the iPod is something to consider for another time!). Instead of working with her peers from a distance, she now sits shoulder to shoulder with her classmates, who have their own laptops at hand. In addition to IM and Internet, Kellie and her classmates will use a variety of software programs in the process of completing this activity.

The students are divided into groups to address a community problem: water pollution. They read stories about the rise in pollution levels and develop an inquiry question that will lead them in a search for the reasons behind this phenomenon.

Kellie's group begins by assessing the situation. They study the details of the pollution reports and record questions they have. They use a graphic organizer program (such as Inspiration) to create a concept map of this information and to identify the "bid ideas" that frame these individual details. Each student in Kellie's group does this individually, and then they all use IM to negotiate the central problem and agree upon an inquiry question for their group.

The teacher is "lurking" online, adding comments and questions and pushing groups to clarify their thinking. The teacher does this from a distance for several reasons: this allows her to listen in on each group more or less at the same time and discover what previous knowledge each student brings to the learning activity. It also permits her to save this initial "record" of student understanding for both formative and summative assessment. Based on their teacher's feedback, the student groups complete their concept maps and formulate their inquiry question.

The next day, the students come in ready to begin the research process. They open the graphic organizer program on their laptops and review their concept maps. The teacher then introduces them to Artemis, an educational search engine designed to help students keep their inquiry question in mind as they pursue web research. The students use their laptops to access Artemis and begin their search for information. A list of suggested websites organized by their teacher is available in the background.

Students sit close to each other and share and interpret what they find (distributed cognition). This type of activity encourages the negotiation of current and constructed knowledge. The teacher interjects comments on occasion to ensure that students are clarifying what they've written and reflecting on how they've arrived at their proposed solution.

To see the results of their suggested solution, the students use a simulation program (such as Model-It) that will allow them to see multiple representations of the data. Students enter the pollution data to bring the simulation to life. The simulation simultaneously illustrates data in pictures, graphs, and numbers and shows potential outcomes in multiple forms.

Students draw conclusions about what they see and analyze the effectiveness of their proposed solution by making connections among these multiple representations. Students determine if any missing pieces or additional information will be needed to complete their simulations.

The circle continues until the students come to the end of their allotted time. They close by using their laptops to create a final multimedia presentation that shares their findings with the class.

This scenario draws upon several learning theories and models of teaching. In this activity, learning is *distributed* (learning happens across people, tools, and artifacts), *situated* (learning is a social process that occurs in the context of a shared activity), and *constructed* (new learning is built from previous knowledge).

This is a project-based activity, but other teaching models will also work successfully in a 1-to-1 environment. Some of these teaching models include cognitive apprenticeship (Brown, Collins, & Duguid, 1989), case-based teaching (Schank, 1991), and anchored instruction (Bransford et al., 2000). For more information see: www.edtech. vt.edu/edtech/id/models/.

The most important lesson to learn from this scenario is that rather than trying to apply traditional models of teaching to a 1-to-1 environment, we should look for ways to exploit ubiquitous access to make the learning environment more learner-, knowledge-, and assessment-centered. The flexibility laptops afford students gives them the ability to move in and out of applications as they organize the larger picture, agree upon the details, collaborate with their peers and teachers, and test solutions in ways not possible without interactive technologies.

The flexibility fostered by good instructional design in a laptop environment requires enormous levels of responsibility on the part of both students and the teacher. Hand out the laptops without careful curricular planning, and students will find distractions for sure. However, if students are guided to use the tools in ways that emulate case-based scenarios, project-based learning, constructionist learning, anchored instruction, cognitive apprenticeship, and inquiry-based learning (Oliver, 2002), 1-to-1 laptops can have a strongly positive effect on learning.

A Final Thought

Technology can be both a benefit and a detriment to learning. It has been shown to be most beneficial when it's embedded in, and closely aligned with, curricular objectives and goals (Kulik, 2003). Moreover, technology use is most effective when it's used as a support for inquiry-based, problem-solving, and knowledge-construction activities (Oliver, 2002).

Some specific examples of such uses are the following:

▶ computer-based animations and simulations that create multimodal opportunities for students and teachers to see, understand, and explain complex concepts;

▶ software tools that assist students in filtering and organizing data collected from the Internet; and

▶ web-based applications that provide organizational support for online research within the context of previously designed inquiry activities that help learners solve real world problems.

Without this conceptual framework, technology has the potential of being used simply to perpetuate traditional forms of teaching and learning. In particular, students can be plugged into computers to do "drill and kill" tasks that aren't so different from those in traditional workbooks, and teachers can use multimedia technology to make their "sage on the stage" lectures more colorful and stimulating. Though there may be valid reasons to use such strategies in particular instances, these take little advantage of the great resources afforded by ubiquitous access (Bransford, Brown, & Cocking 2000).

In fact, when computers are used to reinforce low-level thinking skills, they can do more harm than good (Wenglinsky, 1998). The most appropriate uses of technology are those that align with current learning and models of teaching that incorporate what we have come to know about how people learn (see Table 2).

TABLE 2. Learning Theories and Models of Teaching

LEARNING THEORIES (Kearsley, 2005; Papert & Harel, 1991)	
THEORY	**DESCRIPTION**
Affordance	Learning is guided by a "stimulus array": that is, the environmental setting provides clues necessary for the perception of what to do and how to do it. Learning environments should be realistic, unconstrained and provide perceptual cues.
Behaviorism (S-R)	Learning happens in discrete steps through carefully planned stimulus (questions) and response (reinforcement).
Constructionism	Learning occurs through the building of knowledge structures. The learner must be intentionally and actively engaged in constructing a product, which can be physical or abstract.
Constructivism	Learners engage in a continuous process of knowledge-building by using cognitive structures (mental models or schemas) as well as current or previous understandings to construct new ideas. The process includes hypothesizing, decision making, and knowledge transformation, and requires learners to engage with cases and context-bound problems.
Cognitive Flexibility	Learners are flexible, adaptable and have the means instinctively to reorganize knowledge under continuously changing circumstances.
Distributed Cognition	Learning happens across individuals, tools, and artifacts in a given space. Tools and the organization of the tools are instrumental in how knowledge is shared and distributed.
Situated Cognition	Learning begins with activities and perceptions rather than abstract concepts. Further activity mediates the learner's conceptualization or cognition.
Situated Learning	Learning is an inherently social process that takes place within the context of social and cultural activity. This theory is grounded in affordance and social development theories.
Social Constructivism	Students' previous knowledge and experience influences their social activity. Through this social activity, students draw upon their understanding of the world to create an understanding of what is considered "reality" or perceived as reality.
Social Development	Social interactions play an essential role in learning and the development of cognition. Learning happens first on the social level and then on the individual level. Moving from level to level depends upon the zone of proximal development (ZPD). This theory builds on social learning theory.
Social Learning	Social learning refers to the interrelated and dialectical relationship among cognitive, behavioral, and environmental components of a given situation. A key component to social learning is the observation and modeling of behaviors, attitudes, and emotions of participants within the learning environment. Attention, memory, and motivation are also essential components of social learning.
Radical Constructivism	Learning is constructed based on our mental schema and experiences of how the world works. Knowledge can only be constructed from that basis.

(continued)

TABLE 2. Learning Theories and Models of Teaching *(continued)*

MODELS OF TEACHING	
MODEL	**DESCRIPTION**
Anchored Instruction	Anchored instruction draws upon situated cognition. Specifically, anchored instruction "anchors" students in realistic cases or problems. Students identify the problem and are given a specific role toward completing an assigned task. Students use information revealed through a story to find solutions. An example of this approach was developed by John Bransford and the Cognitive Technology Group at Vanderbilt University (Bransford, Sherwood, Hasselbring, Kinzer, & Williams, 1990). Using a series of video case studies, students work in groups to solve a problem. All of the information needed to solve the problem is provided in the structured video story.
Case-based Teaching	Case-based teaching finds its roots in both direct instruction and social constructivism. Teachers carefully structure the direction of activities and students work in groups to answer questions and negotiate decisions about the case. Both Roger Schank (www.engines4ed.org/hyperbook/misc/rcs.html) and Daniel Edelson (www.engines4ed.org/hyperbook/nodes/NODE-197-pg.html and http://josquin.cti.depaul.edu/~rburke/pubs/burke-kass-aaai94.pdf) have created model examples of such activities.

In their examples, students are placed in a real-world case related to a specific topic or discipline. CBTs combine learner and knowledge-centered characteristics. Students draw on their past experience to answer questions and make decisions, but these past experiences are challenged when the system offers alternative solutions and when their classmates offer various interpretations of the case. Students are then required to research the case and use the information they gather to reconsider or support their position.

Final decisions about the case are socially constructed and agreed upon. This implies that students must have a deep understanding of the content and be able to argue for the decisions they make and convince others that their particular solution is the best one. |
| **Cognitive Apprenticeship** | Cognitive apprenticeship is grounded in social constructivist learning theories. This model is also based on the concept of traditional apprenticeship: there is an expert and an apprentice. The teacher and learner role-shift throughout the learning process. The expert role can be played by the teacher, an outside expert, or a cognitive tutor (www.carnegielearning.com/products.cfm).

The expert's job is to model real-world activities in a way that aligns with the apprentice/learner's ability level. Specifically, the expert uses modeling, coaching, and fading strategies, while helping the learner move from novice to expert. The apprentice observes the master and copies her actions on a similar task. The expert coaches the apprentice through the entire process. Coaching takes the form of provided hints and corrective feedback as well as explicit explanations of how and why tasks are done in a particular way. As the apprentice becomes more skilled in the task, the master gives more and more authority to the apprentice by "fading" into the background.

Learners need to articulate mastered knowledge by talking through their thinking process and drawing upon shared knowledge in appropriate ways throughout the activity. In this way, the teacher assesses where students are and how well they are internalizing new concepts and information to connect with meaningful learning. |

(continued)

TABLE 2. Learning Theories and Models of Teaching *(continued)*

MODELS OF TEACHING	
MODEL	**DESCRIPTION**
Constructionism	Constructionism falls between social and radical constructivist learning theories. Constructionism contends that students learn best by creating a physical or conceptual model. Rather than limiting this model-building to contexts or cases, as in constructivist activities, students in a constructionist environment are responsible for creating their own problems. Students can work in teams or individually. Either way, in order for the students to succeed, they will need to search continuously for information and knowledge that can be applied to their problems. Students are ultimately responsible for justifying why and how they "build" things.
Goal-based Scenarios (GBS)	Goal-based Scenarios is an instructional approach developed by Roger Schank. Grounded in situated learning and more instructor-directed than PBL, these structured computer simulations place the learner in an embedded instructional activity where learners take on a specific role to complete well-defined tasks and goals. These activities are learner-centered, in that they are intended to be designed around student interests and knowledge. The expectation is that establishing this connection with the learners' interests will motivate them. GBS are knowledge-centered because they require that students acquire and apply knowledge throughout supportive, scaffolded activities. Students move through simulations, while simultaneously accessing the Internet to gather data, and keep electronic journals to record observations and reflections and apply the knowledge they have gained from each simulation.
Inquiry-based Models	Inquiry-based models require the learner to develop a question of personal interest. The learner then seeks data and knowledge that inform the question. The inquiry process continuously evolves through a cycle of raising questions, testing solutions, discovering what works, and asking more questions to gain a deeper understanding of the problem at hand.
Project-based Models	In project-based models, teams of students explore real-world problems. Based in radical constructivism, students draw upon their own experiences and knowledge to create a product or presentation that they share with others. These projects are self-directed and research-based and require students to use problem-solving skills. The presentations should illustrate that students have called upon the knowledge of the world's best thinkers and gathered and organized data into graphs, organizers, and other effectively communicated representations.

Chapter 10

1-TO-1 TABLET PC PROGRAMS THAT WORK

Dave Berque
*Introduction and Conclusion
by Pamela Livingston*

Introduction

WHEN IT CAME TIME TO WRITE the second edition of this book, a chapter on tablet PCs seemed essential. I called upon Dr. Dave Berque. Professor and chair of computer science at DePauw University, Berque has focused professionally on human-computer interaction, pen-based computing, and instructional technology. His pen-based groupware system for sharing and annotating content during class was revamped as the commercial version DyKnow Vision. Berque has received grants from the National Science Foundation and Hewlett-Packard, is a contributor to *Tablet PCs in K–12 Education,* was the 1997 Carnegie Foundation for the Advancement of Teaching U.S. professor of the year, and received the 2007 Mira Techpoint Award for Education Contribution in Technology. A consultant for DyKnow, Berque is also highly recommended as a speaker because of his knowledge of higher education and K–12 teaching and learning.

In explaining the benefits of tablet PCs to a group of educators several years ago, I described how Kanji learners must draw strokes for Kanji characters in a certain order, writing on a long strip of paper to demonstrate to the instructor knowledge of the order of the strokes. During a session at Lausanne's Laptop Institute, I'd seen Berque describe how a feature in DyKnow allows the instructor to replay the Kanji character strokes, eliminating the inconvenient hard-copy paper showing each stroke separately. The educators present laughed good-naturedly; they were not yet teaching Kanji. They couldn't imagine embracing the extra cost and complexity of tablet PCs for one application. Of course, there are many applications available for tablet PCs, even more so now than at the time of the session, but educators, being practical professionals, need to see and understand what's possible before embracing any new technology.

Figure 10.1
A student at the American School in Bombay uses a tablet PC as a routine, yet vital, ingredient in his education.

WHAT IS A TABLET PC?

In general terms, a tablet PC is a notebook computer with a display screen on which users can "write." The computer's operating system allows digital "ink" to be written or drawn on the computer screen by using a special pen. This process is called "digital inking," and hand-drawn items can be saved like any other computer document. Handwritten text can also be saved "as written," or it can be translated into typed text.

— from *Tablet PCs in K–12 Education*, p. 9

Rethinking an existing laptop classroom has helped me more fully consider the possibilities of tablet PCs. Several years ago, while working on my master's thesis, I observed three seventh-grade students using traditional laptops in a history class. The teacher gave a trigger that notes should be taken; all students had laptops on their desks. One student rapidly typed an outline as the teacher spoke, turning ideas into bullets and numbers, and grouping all the concepts hierarchically with amazing speed. Another student asked others around her a few things as the teacher spoke and typed a few notes on her laptop. A third student shut the laptop screen, took out a notepad, and used the laptop as a hard surface, hand-writing notes, which included some symbols and arrows.

The three students obviously had different learning styles and when given the opportunity chose different tools and approaches to learning. I wonder now how these three students might have worked if they had had tablet PCs with convertible screens. The speedy outliner would still have had a full-sized keyboard—but this student would also have been able to go back later and star key points and ideas by hand. The second student, who talked to others and typed some notes, would similarly have had a keyboard but would also have had the ability to mark notes on the screen on the spot or when reviewing the notes later. The last student, who hand-wrote his notes, would still have been able to write, but unlike with the paper notebook he had used, he would have hand-written his notes on the tablet PC and had a fully searchable and indexed document. An added bonus for this imaginary tablet-PC-empowered classroom would be that the students could upload their notes and ideas to the classroom projector for sharing with the entire class.

This chapter outlines the unique benefits and some of the pitfalls of tablet PCs and includes case studies of three leading tablet PC programs. Also included are insights, tips, and cautionary tales from tablet PC leaders at these schools, as well as advice and reflections from teachers and students. If you are an educator, as you read this chapter you may want to think about your own classroom (either with laptops or without), your curriculum, and your students. If you teach with laptops now, you may wish to think about a different dynamic, where typing *and* writing, words *and* symbols, and text *and* drawings are all part of the landscape for you and your students. What options might be available with tablets, and how might tablets help your students become independent learners and critical thinkers? Keeping your mind open to the possibilities for tablet PCs can bring about a deeper, more empowering educational experience for your students.

Pens and Pedagogy: A Natural Fit

Traditional laptop computers are well suited for working with text. However, educational content often includes material, such as maps, graphs, charts, drawings, and diagrams, that can be difficult to input using a keyboard. Examples of these non-text-based materials include editing marks (writing), supply-demand curves (economics), inclined planes (physics), map annotations (history), molecular structures (chemistry), and Kanji characters (foreign language). Creating and manipulating this type of content using a mouse and keyboard is a tedious process that requires students and teachers to focus on the *process of inputting* the content. Unfortunately, this focus on process often comes at the expense of thinking *about the content* and its *significance* to the topic being taught. In an educational environment, this is the antithesis of what technology should do, because it shifts the focus away from the material being learned and toward the technological mechanisms for inputting and manipulating this material. Tablet PCs address this problem by providing a natural, intuitive input mechanism for freehand content in various subject areas, as shown in Figure 10.2.

The remainder of this chapter illustrates ways tablet PCs can play an important role in a 1-to-1 program. We begin by providing some basic information about tablet PC hardware configurations. This discussion is followed by an overview of software that best leverages tablet PCs. The software overview is followed by the heart of the chapter: a set of case studies that show how tablet PCs are being used at St. Ursula Academy (a private Catholic school in Cincinnati, Ohio), the American School of Bombay (a private World

Figure 10.2
Freehand educational content from Microsoft Word and DyKnow Vision.

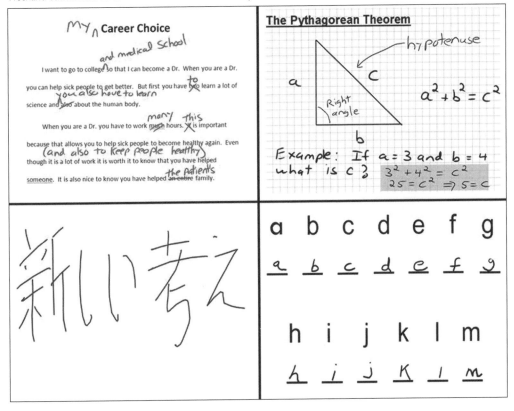

International Baccalaureate School in Mumbai, India), and Hunterdon Central Regional High School (a public school in Flemington, New Jersey). The chapter concludes with a brief discussion of future tablet PC trends and points to resources that provide more information about current and future educational uses of these devices.

Tablet PC Hardware

Tablet PCs are essentially laptops with pens. Therefore, much of what you already know about deploying laptops in 1-to-1 environments holds true for 1-to-1 tablet PC deployments. For example, planning for limited battery life and providing a reliable network infrastructure are crucial regardless of whether your students are using traditional laptops or tablet PCs. This section focuses on additional hardware issues to consider when deploying tablet PCs instead of traditional laptops.

Figure 10.3
Convertible tablet PC in laptop mode.

Figure 10.4
Convertible tablet PC in tablet mode.

Most tablet PCs fall into one of two primary models: convertible and slate. The convertible model looks like a standard laptop and comes complete with an attached keyboard. However, in addition to using the keyboard, the user can draw digital ink directly on the screen of the tablet PC with a special pen. Because a convertible tablet PC screen is attached to its keyboard via a swivel pivot (instead of via a hinge as is typical for laptops), the tablet PC screen can be twisted and positioned to lie flat on top of the keyboard. Thus, a convertible tablet PC can be converted into a device that allows the user to write on the tablet PC screen as easily as she or he would write on a paper notebook. Figure 10.3 shows a convertible tablet PC being used in laptop mode and Figure 10.4 shows the same device after its screen has been rotated and folded flat to cover the keyboard.

The slate model is an alternative type of tablet PC. Whereas convertible tablet PCs have an integrated keyboard, slate tablet PCs require an external keyboard (attached via a USB cable or docking station). Because there is no permanently attached keyboard, slate models tend to be lighter than convertibles. On the other hand, convertibles tend to be more popular in situations where users make regular use of both the keyboard and pen. Because students tend to make regular use of both input modalities during class, the convertible model tends to be preferred for student use in 1-to-1 tablet PC deployments. The schools that are profiled in the case studies later in this chapter use varied makes and models of tablet PCs; however, they have each independently settled on a convertible model. Lessons from each of these deployments clearly show that the pen is not a replacement for the keyboard. Instead, it is better to think of the pen as a very helpful supplemental input device that will be used heavily for certain types of content.

Screens on typical convertible tablet PCs vary in size from about 10 inches to 14 inches measured diagonally. Smaller and lighter units may be advantageous if younger students need to carry the devices regularly between home and school. Weight has been further cut in many models by eliminating an internal CD/DVD drive in favor of an optional external unit that can be used when needed. Smaller devices have an advantage when used in a 1-to-1 deployment. Anyone who has taught in a standard computer laboratory full of large displays knows that the teacher can feel disconnected from the students due to the visual barrier the screens present. Especially in classes with students who are young (and short), it can be hard for the teacher to make eye contact with the students, who are often hidden behind large monitors. Regardless of their screen size, all tablet PCs provide a line-of-sight advantage (compared to a traditional laptop or desktop computer) when the tablet is lying flat in pen-input mode. Smaller tablet PCs provide this advantage even when the screen is positioned vertically to facilitate typing.

Many students and teachers have noticed another unanticipated benefit while using a convertible style tablet PC in a 1-to-1 environment: the swivel screen makes it easy for a student to share work with others. It is common to see a student twist his or her display toward a peer during a collaborative activity, and students can swivel their screens toward a teacher who is standing nearby.

Tablet PC Software

As noted earlier, tablet PCs are essentially laptops with pens. Because of this, all standard Windows software runs on a tablet PC. However, the full educational potential of a 1-to-1 tablet PC deployment is realized through the use of software applications that exploit the power of the pen. Some of these applications (including standard Microsoft Office productivity tools) can be used in a variety of disciplines, while others are subject matter specific. The remainder of this section samples both types of software.

CROSS-DISCIPLINARY TABLET PC SOFTWARE

Microsoft Office tools such as Word, PowerPoint, and Excel each provide support for digital-ink annotations when they are run on a tablet PC. Ink annotations are freehand drawings made with the tablet PC's pen directly on the

Figure 10.5
St. Ursula students collaborate with tablet PCs using swivel screen.

Cautionary Tale

The Case of the Missing Pen

Tablet PCs typically have a special slot that stores the digital pen when it is not in use. However, it is unbelievably easy to put the pen into a pocket or purse accidentally instead of storing it in the slot. Once this happens, the likelihood of the pen becoming separated from the tablet PC is high—and a tablet PC without a pen is about as useful as a … laptop. Many models of tablet PCs include tethers that can optionally be used to attach the pen to the tablet chassis. While the tethers are typically not installed by default, it is highly recommended that you require students to tether their pens in order to cut down on pen loss. Purchasing a few spare temporary loaner pens for each classroom can also help to cut down on lost class time when a pen does get lost or damaged.

tablet PC screen (see Figure 10.2 for some examples of ink annotations). For example, a teacher may draw diagrams directly on top of PowerPoint slides while explaining concepts during class and may annotate students' typed documents to give feedback on writing after class. Similarly, students may be paired off during class, with each student providing inked feedback on his or her partner's written document.

Students who are already accustomed to typing class notes in Word may now incorporate diagrams and sketches into their Word documents. Alternatively, the students may take notes using Microsoft OneNote (or its free and simpler counterpart Microsoft Journal). While these tools both support typed input, they are more pen-centric than Microsoft Word. OneNote also has features that allow handwritten and typed notes to be easily categorized, organized, and searched. The organizational benefits for students can be great.

DyKnow Vision and its companion program DyKnow Monitor have been designed specifically for use in 1-to-1 classroom environments (see box). While the tools can be used with traditional laptops, they are particularly well suited for 1-to-1 tablet PC deployments. The tools provide many of the note-taking and organizational benefits described earlier, but also include features that are specifically designed to enhance the classroom experience, including the delivery of teacher's notes to students; student annotation of teacher content; classroom interaction through multiple choice polls,

DYKNOW TOOLS

Several of the case studies presented later in this chapter use DyKnow software to support their 1-to-1 tablet PC deployments. This software has been used to support such subject areas as mathematics, writing, economics, physics, history, and foreign language. When using DyKnow Vision, the teacher may extemporaneously draw sketches on a tablet PC. The teacher may also use a convertible tablet PC (or a standard laptop) to type material and may import prepared content, including PowerPoint slides and live webpages. All information sketched, typed, or imported by the teacher appears immediately on each student's display.

Each student may use a keyboard or pen to make private annotations to the teacher's material to augment concepts or to solve problems posed by the teacher. Portions of one or more student workspaces may be viewed by the teacher or shared with the entire class to promote discussion. Alternatively, the students may be engaged by multiple choice polls, focused chat sessions, or through a feature that allows the teacher to permit a student to "draw on the board" from his or her seat. The teacher may also have small groups of students share virtual sheets of paper that they may use for collaboration. Webpages containing interactive activities may also be embedded in the DyKnow notebook and shared with the class. Using companion DyKnow Monitor software, teachers may focus attention by blanking student screens, watching their progress, or limiting the programs students can run or the websites they can access.

Each student's DyKnow Vision notebook may be printed or saved for later study. The notes may be replayed stroke-by-stroke, allowing students to review class work in a dynamic manner and allowing teachers to understand a student's problem-solving process. Teachers may also use the system to review, grade, and electronically return student work. At the teacher's discretion, audio may be captured for review and replay.

group work, chat, and other activities; after-class note review and replay; and computer monitoring to focus students' attention.

CONTENT-SPECIFIC TABLET PC SOFTWARE

A number of tablet PC software programs have been developed to support teaching and learning related to a specific content area. Several of these tools are included in two collections of programs: the Microsoft Power Toys for Windows XP Tablet PC Edition and the Microsoft Education Pack for Tablet PC. Among the most popular of the tools in these collections are the Writing Practice Tool for Tablet PC (useful for grade-school writing practice), the Tablet PC Music Composition Tool, Microsoft Physics Illustrator for Tablet PC, and Equation Writer (useful for mathematics classes).

The Tablet PC Music Composition Tool is illustrative of the new opportunities tablet PCs provide. Using this tool, teachers or students can input music using a special notation and the tablet PC pen. As notes are hand drawn, they are recognized by the software and converted to standard printed musical notation, as shown in Figure 10.6. The music may then be played through the tablet's sound card, thereby allowing the class to hear the results of the composition immediately.

Figure 10.6
Tablet PC composition tool.

Expert Advice

Articulate Your Vision

Administrators at the American School of Bombay recognize the importance of explaining their 1-to-1 tablet program to all their constituencies. The school website states, "Handheld computing defines the trend in the evolution of technology. It symbolizes the idea of anytime/anywhere learning and has changed the face of the world of business, medicine, and other professions. In our endeavor to prepare our students for the increasingly technological world, we have made a commitment to personal computing and the integration of handheld computing in our classrooms. Tablet PCs extend the possibilities of notebook computers and provide the power of a notebook in handheld form. No functionality of a notebook-computing device is lost. On the other hand, the tablet PC adds an important set of functions without detracting from the common laptop paradigm." Articulating this clearly on their website helps parents, teachers, and students understand that the school has chosen to leverage this new technology for solid pedagogical reasons.

Case Study

TABLET TAKE ONE:
THE AMERICAN SCHOOL OF BOMBAY

The American School of Bombay is a private, coeducational PK–12 school with approximately 700 students. The school is a fully recognized World International Baccalaureate (IB) School located in Mumbai (formerly Bombay), India. The American School of Bombay has a multinational student body consisting of 47 nationalities, including 29% Americans, 15% Indians, and 56% third-country nationals. While there are more limited 1-to-1 programs in other international American Schools, as of this writing the American School of Bombay is the only overseas American School with an ongoing commitment to a 1-to-1 learning program that is integrated across the K–12 curriculum.

THE TABLET TRANSITION

The American School of Bombay began its 1-to-1 program by issuing laptops to all Grade 3 teachers and students in 2001. The following year the program was expanded to Grades 7, 11, and 12. In 2002, all secondary school teachers were also provided with laptops. In 2003–2004, the 1-to-1 program was expanded to include the entire secondary school (Grades 6–12). This was also the first year of the tablet PC program with all students in Grades 6–11 required to have tablet PCs. Currently, students in Grades 6–12 (and all teaching staff, regardless of grade) use tablet PCs as part of this program. In total, more than 450 tablet PCs are deployed to students and teachers. The machines include models made by Dell, Toshiba, and Fujitsu. Information about the American School of Bombay's tablet PC program was provided by Shabbi Luthra, director of Technology at the school.

KEY TABLET USES

According to Luthra, teachers and students at the American School of Bombay use several key software packages to leverage the power of their tablet PCs. The most important of these are DyKnow Vision and Monitor, Microsoft Journal and OneNote, Adobe Acrobat, several programs from the Microsoft Education Pack for Tablet PCs (Equation Editor and Ink Flash Cards), and several programs from the Microsoft Experience Pack for Tablet PCs (Ink Art, Ink Desktop, and Snipping Tool). In addition, ink annotations are frequently used from within Microsoft Office products. For example, teachers use the tablet PC pen to make editing marks and grade assignments that have been submitted in a variety of formats, including Word, PDF, and Excel.

Students in language classes and science classes use Microsoft Journal and Adobe Acrobat to complete assignments. Students in mathematics classes use DyKnow Vision and Excel to solve problems during class. The middle school is focusing on writing across the curriculum, and a lot of pen-based editing is occurring there as well as in the high school. Luthra also reports that DyKnow Vision is being used to support note taking; collaboration; and after-class note review across subject areas, especially in mathematics, science, and foreign language classes. In addition, the middle school is using DyKnow Monitor as a classroom management tool when required.

▶ A TEACHER'S PERSPECTIVE

Jacques A. Weber
American School of Bombay, French and Spanish

1. **What do you see as the greatest benefit of using tablets in your classroom?**

I have thought about this question quite a bit, and as hard as I try to narrow ideas down to one single benefit, I think it really comes down to two very important ones: (1) classroom efficiency and (2) working in the students' arena.

Our school has pretty standardized policies for file naming, locations of files and software, tablet usage, etc. I like to further reinforce that with my own classroom tablet policies, such as specific details to be included within file names, when to log on to what software, appropriate use of machine translation, and so on. In the traditional classroom, students would be working with papers, which can be misfiled, and binders and books, which can be lost. The sheer reduction of paperwork helps to avoid some of these common pitfalls, not only for the students, but also for the teachers who, of course, might also misplace a document. Students can turn in their assignments electronically as soon as they have finished them instead of bringing the paperwork to class. In essence, we have moved from touch-and-go paper mismanagement to complete file management. This, of course, all changes if you misplace your laptop; but that's what backups are for!

The other important benefit is working within the students' arena. I feel that I am at a bit of an advantage, being a younger educator who has grown up with computers and who actually used a laptop in high school. In today's world, knowing how to use a computer to its full capabilities is almost a prerequisite to a job in the corporate world, so we are making sure students start learning from an early age. Naturally, elementary and secondary students feel much more comfortable with computers than their peers from three decades ago and seemingly regard the digital world as a place where they are at a distinct advantage over their teachers. The fact that I feel just as comfortable as (if not more comfortable than) they do, allows me to work with them in "their space." I find this to be a distinct advantage as an educator in a tablet school.

2. **Thinking of your practice as a teacher, what changes, adaptations, or philosophical adjustments have you had to make now that tablet PCs are part of teaching and learning in your classroom?**

As far as curriculum and philosophy are concerned, I have had to make few adjustments. I have always included technology as much as possible in my curriculum and policies. In my previous school, we did not have PCs in class, but every student had at least one computer at home. Consequently, I insisted that students use the class website, submit electronic homework, type up all work, do regular research online, etc. Having the tablet PCs in the classroom now has just added a layer of convenience (i.e., I get more immediate results from work that is to be completed electronically).

A natural adjustment, of course, is classroom management and ensuring appropriate use of the Internet in the classroom. There is a fine line between draconian oversight of student behavior in the classroom and respectful but efficient guidance. This is, arguably, the most difficult part of using a tablet in class, and the dynamic changes by class. As a matter of fact, the dynamic within the same class can change throughout the school year as students occasionally try to tune out. The key is learning to keep an eye on students while always ensuring that lessons are thought-provoking and engaging.

3. What advice might you have for teachers just starting out using tablets?

My response would be targeted to two audiences: those comfortable with computers and those more comfortable with pen and paper.

First, to those comfortable with computers: Make sure you keep an ear to the ground so that you can keep up with the latest trends and fads, both negative and positive. For instance, I regularly hear about new websites and resources from students and often wind up sharing with them websites that I know about. When working in groups, I also often hear students discussing a shortcut or a different way of doing a certain task. In short, don't be afraid to learn from your students, too! As for the negatives, keep an ear out for new software and ways that keep students from staying focused in class. GoogleTalk is a good example of software that can distract students, but you can also turn it to your favor and use it for a discussion activity.

Now, for those new to computers: Most importantly, don't be nervous! While what I mentioned above may seem a bit daunting, it becomes easier after a while. Just like learning any new skill (e.g., a musical instrument or a foreign language), there is an initial struggle that you will battle through—but eventually you will overcome this; once you have, things will come to you more quickly and naturally. Also, once you feel more comfortable with the ins and outs of your machines, you should work on becoming more comfortable with multitasking. In the *Times of India,* I recently read that people are now fitting 31-hours worth of work into a 24-hour day. As uncomfortable as that may sound, that seems to be the trend in today's business world, and the youth of today are learning even earlier how to pack even more into that 24-hour period.

▶ A TEACHER'S PERSPECTIVE

Jason Roy
American School of Bombay, mathematics

1. What do you see as the greatest benefit of using tablets in your classroom?

The tablet makes class time much more productive. In the old days, if I wanted students to access certain information, I would first have to copy it down onto the blackboard, and the students would then have to copy it into their notebooks (this is all before anything productive could happen with that information).

Now, with tablets and DyKnow, I can instantly send them the background information; students spend zero time copying needless information from the board. (Obviously, there are times when I want students to copy something down to help them memorize it, and I can still do this, too.)

2. Thinking of your practice as a teacher, what changes, adaptations, or philosophical adjustments have you had to make now that tablet PCs are part of teaching and learning in your classroom?

CLASSROOM MANAGEMENT: I think the computers are awesome, but I also realize that they create a great temptation for distraction. I guess I feel like this hasn't changed my practice too much. Students have always been distracted in schools. Five years ago, students who were not engaged in my class might try to work sneakily on another class's homework, read a book, gaze out the window, or just doodle, while today they can just go to their Facebook page.

I try to make my lessons as engaging as possible and plan them out from start to finish. In this planning, I make sure the students will be involved in whatever is going on all the time. It is never just me talking for more than a minute or two at a time. If I notice a couple days of unusually distracted classes, I might initiate a conversation about presence (being in the moment) and how studies have shown that we (as humans) are not very good at attending to more than one thing at a time and that even I can get easily distracted by the Internet. These usually go very well.

LESSON DESIGN: I try to use DyKnow to have the students doing mathematics as fast as possible. I also try to harness the potential of being able to have all the students access the Internet. So, in the middle of a class, we can all spend ten minutes looking at a web applet. It is also easy to incorporate social bookmarking tools and other sites that students can use later. One day, for example, when we were looking at matrix multiplication, I found three different sites that explained how to do the algorithm geared to three different learning styles. It allowed me to have the students access the links I had found in order to deepen their learning.

I also make sure to integrate the various DyKnow feedback mechanisms into my classes every day. I particularly like polling questions (Using Eric Mazur's Peer Instruction Model) and panel submission. It is also really great to have students display their work on the board (using the wireless projector) and then talk about how they solved the problem.

3. **What advice might you have for teachers just starting out using tablets?**

First, embrace the tablet and spend time learning how to use it. The technology is not going to go away! Your students will likely know more about the tablet than you do, so take advantage of this fantastic resource. They will love to show you what they know. If I ever wonder how to do anything, my first line of attack is to ask the nearest tech-savvy student, and then I go to Google or Wikipedia.

Start small. You are not going to be the most amazing tablet teacher the first day you are handed a tablet. Before using the tablet every lesson every day, consider using the tablet for a couple of lessons a week or for a few minutes every lesson. Remember

Expert Advice

Support the Parents

The American School of Bombay has instituted a series of hands-on Parent Tech Connection workshops. These monthly meetings are used to address a variety of technology issues that are of interest to parents. Topics vary from month to month and have included Internet Safety, Using Online Databases, Introduction to DyKnow, and A Tablet PC Primer. The latter workshop is conducted in a hands-on fashion and is intended to familiarize parents with the ways in which their children use this tool. While most parents are familiar with standard laptops, fewer have had prior exposure to tablet PCs. The parents appreciate learning about this tool so that they can help their children to use it effectively at home. This is especially important at the American School of Bombay because students first receive a tablet PC for 24/7 use in the sixth grade. Thus, parental support is more important than it would be if the students were first introduced to tablet PCs at a higher grade level.

that the students love their tablets and are hence going to want to use them for everything.

Spend serious time rethinking how you are delivering information. Are you the only one talking, or are students actively participating and constructing their own knowledge throughout the class period? The closer your classroom is to active student participation, the easier it will be to move to tablet use.

Resist the urge to be a tablet policeman. Instead, focus on creating engaging lessons, and the tablet problems will solve themselves.

RECOMMENDATIONS

Based on her experiences with the American School of Bombay's 1-to-1 tablet PC program, Luthra has developed a set of recommendations for other schools.

▶ Provide teachers with tablet PCs prior to giving them to students. This will help the teachers to adjust before they have to support their students.

▶ Support teachers with intensive training on the use of tablet PCs and supporting software tools.

▶ Focus professional development on changes required in pedagogy to support teaching and learning. At the American School of Bombay, professional development and training in technology are provided through departments and required tablet PC training sessions. All high school teachers are required to demonstrate a lesson that integrates the use of DyKnow and tablet PCs as part of this professional growth and evaluation program.

▶ Provide access to wireless projectors in all instructional spaces. These projectors have been widely adopted at the American School of Bombay as a way of helping teachers to be more mobile in their classrooms.

PITFALLS AND PROGRESS

As a tablet PC pioneer, the American School of Bombay encountered some problems with its initial tablet PC deployment in 2003. Faculty and students experienced performance shortfalls with the first-generation tablet PCs that were available at the time, tablet PC hardware was deployed before appropriate supporting software packages were identified, teachers needed more professional development, and there was no clear program in place to assess the effects of the deployment.

Each of these problems was subsequently addressed. The current generation tablet PCs rival traditional laptops in terms of performance. On the software front, significantly more educational software is now available that exploits the power of tablet PC pen-input. By leveraging newer hardware and software, training teachers, and assessing their deployment, the American School of Bombay has become a model 1-to-1 tablet PC program.

▶ A STUDENT'S PERSPECTIVE

Sunanda Vaidheesh
American School of Bombay, class of 2008

1. Thinking about your work in the classroom and at home, what do you think is different when using a tablet PC as opposed to before you used a tablet PC?

First, in comparison to before I used tablets at school at all, I am much more efficient in my work habits. Since all my work and resources to help me get my work done are centralized in one location (no more binders and sheaves of paper fluttering around in my locker), I can quickly access what I want and find the tools I need to complete my task with a few clicks. While a project for my sixth-grade history class might have required that I create an elaborate hand-drawn poster to illustrate my knowledge, I can now create a PowerPoint presentation with all the images and text necessary to create an engaging presentation in a shorter period of time.

Additionally, there are a lot more options for how I want to engage with my education: a PowerPoint presentation is simply one—and the most basic—example of how it could be done. In the past six years, I've created and edited numerous videos, flash animations, and other multimedia presentations, to visually present my knowledge. They have allowed me to tap into my various strengths and develop some of my weak points.

However, the biggest difference has been the level of engagement that I've had with my classes. While some teachers are quick to assume that when I am on my tablet in class, it must be because I am checking my e-mail or Facebook, using my tablet in classes in fact enabled greater classroom engagement in many ways. In economics, when a certain graph from the textbook doesn't really seem to make sense, with a couple clicks we can Google (yes, it's a verb!) alternate explanations. Moreover, we can really see the practical application and relevance of our classes to our lives with our tablets. The accessibility of information (literally, at our fingertips) just makes us more able to see the connections between what we're learning and why we're learning it.

Last, the tablet also gives students a large deal of responsibility for their own learning. With regards to organization, it really *does* prepare us for the real world—where information, tasks, and responsibilities will be thrown at us from all directions, and we're expected to balance it all. Sure, we have the right tools to help us; but more than that, the tablet and our tablet program has made us much more able to handle the complexities of managing multiple responsibilities at once. The tablet particularly helps this as it enables greater mobility, for one thing, and it gives us greater freedom to figure out how we learn best. No longer is it handwriting *or* typing—it allows us to play to our strengths and work with the learning style we're most comfortable with.

My last—and perhaps most crucial—point about responsibility is that with the tablet program, it is also up to us to find the relevance in what we're doing. The teachers certainly help us, but in the end, it's that eager psychology student who, in his spare time, reads the psych blogs he subscribes to and shares it with the class, who really encapsulates this idea of taking responsibility for your own learning.

2. **What advice would you have for other students using a tablet PC for the first time?**

Honestly, don't stress out too much about how you're going to manage keeping track of everything, because, in time, you'll find that exploring new technologies and finding new ways to approach the same task are innate for any iGeneration student. It's also important to find your own niche with your tablet. Just because your friend has jazzed up his desktop so that his summer countdown is flashing 24/7 doesn't mean that that's the only way of keeping track of important dates. At the same time, talk to your friends about how they stay organized and share with them new tools you discover. Along with the tablet PC and the tablet program come the need to share and collaborate—so, take bits and pieces of what you hear and see to find a system that works for *you*.

Another important thing to remember is that time management is *everything*. Of course, checking your friend's Facebook status is more interesting than AP calculus, but you do have to figure out when the best time for multitasking is and when's best for focused concentration. Personally, I know that I can review for a psychology exam while keeping my Outlook inbox running in the background because the material clicks quickly but that I can't do math homework in the same way—I need all the concentration I can get. However, one of my close friends is a math whiz and does it the other way around. It really depends on how you work best.

On that note, figure out what way of note taking or test studying is best for *you*. If you think linearly, type up your notes in bullet or outline form; if you're a visual learner, use your stylus to draw out a mindmap or check if your online textbook comes with animations or videos that will help. The key is to figure out what works best for you.

As far as the tablet itself, while using the stylus for note taking is effective for some, don't feel compelled to do so just because it's there. Sometimes typing just ends up being more effective! Though, with regards to organization, there are a couple great tablet-only tools that really do make things easier—for example, Ink Desktop, which lets you scribble reminders and to-do lists with your stylus directly onto your desktop. Give them all a try and just have fun exploring!

Also, I really wouldn't recommend eating a plate of spaghetti (or worse, soup) with your tablet cradled on your lap. It just never really works out to anyone's advantage.

3. **What advice would you have for teachers just starting to teach in a tablet PC classroom?**

First, it is very important for teachers to recognize that in a tablet PC classroom, there is no *one* wielder of information and that mythical "right answer." The instant accessibility of information is great because to a certain degree, teachers and students are on the same level in terms of access to knowledge.

Multitasking is *not* all evil. I'm aware that no teacher likes to admit that there are times in his or her classes when 100% focus isn't required, but blocking all computer use for fear of multitasking is not the solution. Some of the best classes I've had with regards to addressing this issue are those in which there is a mutual agreement between teacher and students that there are times when we can pay attention while also keeping our Outlook open, in case any emergency student council e-mails come in, and other times when our full attention is needed. By giving us the responsibility to stay on task, we also respect the teacher a lot more.

When in doubt with technology, always ask your students. Someone *will* know why it's not working.

Don't require students to type—or to use their styluses—in class. We end up being more productive when we figure out which aspects of the tablet are more useful to us than others.

Have *fun* with it! When we see that our teachers are excited about using the technology or just about class in general, our enthusiasm automatically rises.

Case Study

TABLET TAKE TWO:
ST. URSULA ACADEMY

St. Ursula Academy is a private, Catholic, college-preparatory secondary school for young women. The Academy is located in Cincinnati, Ohio, and has just over 700 students in Grades 9–12. St. Ursula also offers a special program for young women with dyslexia and other learning disabilities. Students in this program are college-bound and participate in the school's standard, rigorous college-preparatory curriculum with extra support provided as needed. Kim Henninger, Director of Technology at St. Ursula, provided information about the Academy's tablet PC program.

THE TABLET TRANSITION

St. Ursula began providing standard laptops to all teachers in 1997 with replacement laptops provided in 2000 and again in 2003. In 2005, each teacher was provided with a tablet PC instead of a laptop. During this time frame, computers were made available to students during class through computer laboratories. As usage increased, the number of these laboratories grew from a single fixed-seat laboratory to four fixed-seat laboratories and six laptop carts. Significantly, the proliferation of these facilities was driven by teacher demand.

Figure 10.7
A St. Ursula teacher and two students using tablet PCs.

After gaining experience using computer laboratories and laptop carts, the faculty requested that the school move to a 1-to-1 program. The board of trustees approved this request in December of 2005, with implementation planned for the following academic year. Unlike the American School of Bombay, St. Ursula moved directly to a student 1-to-1 tablet PC program without first implementing a 1-to-1 laptop program. However, like the American School of Bombay, teachers had the opportunity to become comfortable with tablet PCs before they were provided to students.

The first group of incoming ninth-grade students received tablet PCs in fall 2006, and the second cohort received their units in fall 2007. As a result, approximately 500 HP tablet PCs are now deployed to all teachers as well as to all ninth- and tenth-grade students. By the fall of 2009, every student in the school will have a tablet PC, at which point more than 800 tablet PCs will be in service. In the meantime, spare tablet PCs are made available for use by the occasional eleventh- or twelfth-grade student who is enrolled in a class where the majority of students are participants in the 1-to-1 tablet PC program.

Expert Advice

Provide Special Support When Needed

St. Ursula Academy holds a half-day tablet PC workshop for incoming students just prior to the start of classes. The school also holds a three-week summer workshop in June for students who are in the learning disabilities program as well as for other students who would benefit from additional support. Participants in the three-week workshop receive their tablet PCs as part of the session and spend time during the workshop using the devices just as they will when school starts. By providing these workshops, St. Ursula helps to level the playing field, especially with respect to new technology that is more likely to be unfamiliar to incoming students. The dual pen- and keyboard-input mechanisms supported by the tablet PC can level the playing field even further by providing alternative methods for representing and processing information. For example, a dyslexic student who struggles with typed text may find that making simple sketches can be an empowering supplement to traditional note taking.

KEY TABLET USES

Henninger reports that the tablet PCs have been fully integrated into academic work at St. Ursula. Students use the tablet PCs in all subjects to write papers, take notes, conduct research, take tests online, access readings, create projects, and submit homework. She says that the most important software applications across the curriculum are PDFAnnotator, DyKnow, Microsoft Journal, Blackboard, and Microsoft Outlook. Discipline-specific tools such as SmartMusic are used in specific classes as well.

As noted above, several of the tablet PC uses reported by Henninger do not leverage the pen-enabled nature of the tablet PC. This underscores the point that a tablet PC provides all of the functionality of a traditional laptop. However, Henninger has also noted several instructional uses of tablet PCs that would not be possible with a standard laptop. For example, students at St. Ursula annotate digital texts using PDFAnnotator outside of class and take hand-written notes and complete fill-in exercises and other pen-based interactive exercises using DyKnow during class. Henninger believes that these in-class activities result in a changed paradigm that is characterized by increased student reflection and comprehension. She explains that this is due to the fact that teacher content is immediately available to students for capture, annotation, and review on their tablet PCs. Mindless copying verbatim from the board is eliminated.

Paradigm changes can also be seen in science laboratories at St. Ursula, where students use the tablet PCs to sketch what they see under a microscope, using tools such as Windows Journal, and in science and mathematics classes, where students use their pens and DyKnow to solve problems that are shared with the entire class to promote discussion or that are shared with only the teacher for grading. Tablet PC pen-input is also being leveraged in foreign language classes in a variety of ways. For example, pictorial slide presentations are used to give students opportunities to practice the language by naming the objects in the diagrams.

▶ A TEACHER'S PERSPECTIVE

Emily Rosen
St. Ursula Academy, geophysics and physics

1. What do you see as the greatest benefit of using tablets in your classroom?

I think that the greatest benefit of tablet use is the opportunity they provide for increased collaboration in the classroom. The tablet helps to make the classroom more of a student-centered learning environment in that it makes it much easier to receive student input, share student work, work in groups, research topics of interest, provide feedback, and so on.

2. Thinking of your practice as a teacher, what changes, adaptations, or philosophical adjustments have you had to make now that tablet PCs are part of teaching and learning in your classroom?

Since implementing tablet PC use into my teaching, I have had to make several changes. I find that I use group work and research in the classroom more now than I ever did before. This makes the classroom more interactive. For example, before using the PC, when I introduced Newton, I would simply list some historical information about his life so that my students could get a feel for his life and contributions before beginning to learn his laws. Now, I have my students work in groups to do some quick research on his life. They write down the three most interesting things they learned about him and submit their work, and we project and share these facts with the class.

Simple activities like this keep my students much more engaged than they were before we had the tablet available for classroom use. After carefully researching which technical applications have been found to best improve science education, I find that I use online simulations and real-time graphing (Excel) much more often so that the students can visualize things that are not tangible or easily available for an experiment (e.g. atomic structure). I do not think that using the tablet has forced me to make any kind of philosophical adjustments. I have always felt that the classroom should be an interactive, student-centered environment; and the tablet PC has only made it easier for me to work on establishing this environment in my classes.

Figure 10.8
Microscopes and tablet PCs—integral to science for St. Ursula students.

3. What advice might you have for teachers just starting out using tablets?

It is very important to be patient. Think of the tablet simply as a tool that can assist you in your teaching. Tablet use can be implemented slowly. It is not necessary that you are familiar and comfortable with all applications of the tablet before using it in the classroom. Learn one program or application at a time, and slowly integrate these things into your teaching as you see fit. There are times when the tablet may not fit well into your lesson, and that is okay.

▶ A TEACHER'S PERSPECTIVE

Adam Niemes
St. Ursula Academy, information technology

1. What do you see as the greatest benefit of using tablets in your classroom?

I think the greatest benefit of using the tablets in the classroom has been the ability for the students to use the pen to write out their notes instead of typing them. I think with students using computers in the classroom to take notes, it has detracted from their ability to learn the material as typing notes is not as effective as writing them by hand for some students. With the tablet, however, they can still have that tactile learning by writing the notes out using the tablet technology. I also think using innovative technology, such as tablet PCs, has been a benefit to students to keep them up with the latest technological advances. It is very important for students to learn early how to save their files correctly and where to save them. It is critical for all students to know how to maintain the integrity of their data as this will be crucial later on in life in nearly every potential career.

2. Thinking of your practice as a teacher, what changes, adaptations, or philosophical adjustments have you had to make now that tablet PCs are part of teaching and learning in your classroom?

I don't think there have been many adjustments with the integration of the tablet PCs. The only adjustment that I have noticed with using the tablet is the organization process. Be sure to keep your files very organized and keep track of where things are at all times.

3. What advice might you have for teachers just starting out using tablets?

Try to integrate the tablet PC in class every day. Definitely use your tablet every day for a few weeks before starting out. It will take some getting used to, and playing around with it will really help you become more comfortable using it and fixing problems if they occur.

RECOMMENDATIONS

Henninger's experiences as St. Ursula lead her to offer the following advice to educators at other schools that are considering tablet PCs as part of their 1-to-1 solution.

▶ Do not underestimate the added value that a tablet PC brings as compared to a standard laptop. The pen-based input supported by a tablet PC is what allows the students to use the tablet PC as a notebook, binder, and textbook all in one.

▶ Consider using tablet PCs to implement a range of classroom activities that address the needs of students with varied learning styles, including visual, auditory, and kinesthetic. For example, the pen-input afforded by a tablet PC makes it easier to use teacher-drawn and student-drawn sketches to reinforce the written word.

▶ Take care of the teachers first. It is crucial for the teachers to be comfortable with their tablet PCs and supporting software before the devices are provided to students.

▶ Take time to look at what other schools are doing with tablet PCs and then adapt what you learn to your local environment.

▶ If you already have a traditional laptop 1-to-1 program, anticipate that students will use tablet PCs more than they use the laptops; plan in advance for problems that may result from the increased usage. For example, with increased usage comes decreased battery performance over time (consider providing replacement batteries after two years), and increased wear and tear (consider keeping spare units on hand).

PITFALLS AND PROGRESS

The 1-to-1 tablet PC deployment at St. Ursula Academy has progressed relatively smoothly. The only significant problem being encountered that is specific to the tablet PCs is pen breakage. Other problems, such as the need to develop a mechanism for backing up student work and issues related to short battery life, are also experienced in traditional 1-to-1 laptop programs.

A number of surveys have been administered during the St. Ursula's 1-to-1 tablet PC rollout. The results of teacher surveys clearly demonstrate that the tablet PCs are being heavily used in all content areas. Student and parent survey results show that both groups are very pleased with the 1-to-1 tablet PC program. Many student testimonials praise the tablet PC program; the students often specifically note that they are more organized because of their tablet PCs.

Observations of students by faculty and technology staff corroborate these student reports. Two years into this program, it is clear that each constituency recognizes the added value that tablet PCs bring over traditional laptops. It is equally clear that everyone is looking forward to the day when the program covers all four class years at St. Ursula.

▶ A STUDENT'S PERSPECTIVE

Nora Elson
St. Ursula Academy, class of 2011

1. **Thinking about your work in the classroom and at home, what do you think is different when using a tablet PC as opposed to before you used a tablet PC?**

   Now I have a lot more resources! Before if I was, for example, reading for homework and I didn't know what a word meant, I used to skip over it; but now I pull up the Internet and find it. Sometimes for biology I search for labeled pictures of the certain animal we're talking about; it helps to see the same diagram but from a different source.

2. **What advice would you have for other students using a tablet PC for the first time?**

   I would say, don't be so afraid. I was terrified I would break it, but you should really have fun with it! Explore all the programs that are on your tablet!

3. **What advice would you have for teachers just starting to teach in a tablet PC classroom?**

Definitely try to involve the tablet as much as possible because it has so many possibilities and the students are interested in them. I would try to figure out as much as possible from not only the tech people but also from the students.

▶ A STUDENT'S PERSPECTIVE

Tori Cardone
St. Ursula Academy, class of 2011

1. **Thinking about your work in the classroom and at home, what do you think is different when using a tablet PC as opposed to before you used a tablet PC?**

I think that the tablet PC helps me stay more organized over the school week. I can keep all my assignments in one spot, and I can organize them in a way that makes sense to me. The tablet PC also makes it easier to have all of my resources available at one time; I cannot forget anything at home. The pen tool on Microsoft Word and Journal makes my notes more organized because I can color-coordinate, highlight, and draw pictures right into my notes. It also makes my backpack lighter on the trips to and from school since I don't have any books to carry.

2. **What advice would you have for other students using a tablet PC for the first time?**

I think the biggest advice I could give to other students would be to be very patient with your tablet PC. If you are having problems with something, ask one of your classmates about it, and chances are they've had the same problem at one point or another. I would also recommend that you back up your files very frequently. Most people disregard this rule because they do not realize how incredibly important it is, but if your tablet crashes, you will be ecstatic when you still have all your files.

3. **What advice would you have for teachers just starting to teach in a tablet PC classroom?**

My advice for the teachers starting the program would be similar to the advice for the students. My number-one piece of advice would be to be patient with your students and let them go to the technology department if and when it is necessary. I would also advise them to have extra copies of the day's work on hand in case their students need to use a pen and paper.

▶ A STUDENT'S PERSPECTIVE

Rachel Tonnis
St. Ursula Academy, class of 2010

1. **Thinking about your work in the classroom and at home, what do you think is different when using a tablet PC as opposed to before you used a tablet PC?**

When you use a tablet PC while doing work at school, you can access the Internet instantly if you don't understand what a teacher is talking about. This helps you to follow along in the classroom if you can't for some reason ask questions. Also, at home the tablet allows you to work on your homework, do research, check your e-mail, and turn in your assignments without leaving your position in front of your computer. Sometimes you can even find books online for research, and you don't even have to leave home to go to the library. All of these things could also be accomplished using a traditional monitor PC, but with a tablet, you also have the option of writing in your own handwriting, and it seems as if you are still using paper to take notes and complete assignments.

2. What advice would you have for other students using a tablet PC for the first time?

Patience is very important when first starting out using a tablet PC. Once you understand how you use the basic programs and functions of the tablet, you are free to explore all the extra perks, features, and unique applications that this computer has to offer. It also gives you a sense of accomplishment when you discover a hidden ability that the tablet PC has to offer in order to help you with your work.

3. What advice would you have for teachers just starting to teach in a tablet PC classroom?

I also believe that patience is key for teachers as well as students. Generally, teachers have a little more trouble learning how to use the computers than the students, so don't get frustrated. Asking the students for help often doesn't hurt either. We are always more than happy to help teachers understand how to use the computers if they can't quite get the hang of it. Therefore, this also helps build a helping relationship between the students and the teacher, because the students feel like they are on a level playing field with the teachers. It's their job to teach us, but why shouldn't we teach them when given the chance?

Case Study

TABLET TAKE THREE: HUNTERDON CENTRAL REGIONAL HIGH SCHOOL

Hunterdon Central Regional High School is a public high school for Grades 9–12. The school enrolls approximately 3,200 students on its college-style campus that is located in Flemington, New Jersey. Hunterdon Central has a long history of technology adoption that has been early and effective. Among the school's many honors, Hunterdon Central was named a National Blue Ribbon School of Excellence and received the United States Department of Education's first "Classrooms: Connections to the Future" grant. Hunterdon Central has also been named one of America's best high schools by both *Redbook* and *Business Week,* in part because of the school's technology initiatives.

THE TABLET TRANSITION

Hunterdon Central differs from the American School of Bombay and St. Ursula Academy in that it is still in the process of transitioning to a 1-to-1 tablet PC program. However,

Expert Advice

Use Teachers as Tablet Trainers

It is no surprise that teachers are effective at teaching, nor is it surprising that teachers like to learn from their peers. These facts were exploited at Hunterdon Central to help the school support a large number of teachers who needed to get up to speed quickly on the use of the tablet PC after the school's successful pilot program. The almost two dozen teachers who had already taught with tablet PCs served as guides for more than a hundred teachers who were new to this technology. The experienced tablet PC teachers worked in pairs, with each pair supporting between 8 and 13 new tablet teachers during formal summer professional development classes. In addition, seven days were set aside at the end of the summer when experienced tablet teachers were available to meet with those who were new to the program. As a result of these teacher-to-teacher professional development programs, new tablet PC teachers started the fall with high confidence that they were ready to leverage the tablet PC.

the school has laid a solid foundation for this journey. As reported by Rob Mancabelli, director of Information Systems at Hunterdon Central, cornerstones of the foundation include a broad and effective deployment of tablet PCs to teachers as well as a pilot program that is providing tablet PC carts for classroom use.

In 1994, Hunterdon introduced a six-computer classroom model supported by a campus network and Internet access. This model has continued, sometimes being supplemented with special laboratories and laptop carts that provide a 1-to-2 or 1-to-1 model for subject areas that need a higher computer to student ratio.

In 2003, the school's educational technology committee established a goal of empowering teachers to embrace and adopt emerging technologies in ways that improve teaching and learning systematically. The committee organized a series of professional development days to help academic departments better understand available technology options. These workshops led to the development of five specific technology pilot programs for which teachers could submit proposals. The pilot that focused on providing tablet PCs to teachers proved to be the most popular; more than half of all the submitted proposals related to this topic.

With participation from 33 volunteer teachers in every academic department, the first year of the tablet PC pilot was judged to be a great success. A graduate student from Columbia Teachers College assisted with an assessment that found that teachers perceived greater flexibility in classroom instruction, more student engagement, increased productivity, better organization, and a feeling of empowerment. As a result of the excitement created by the pilot, more than 170 of the remaining 213 teachers volunteered to use a tablet PC in the program's next phase. The budget allowed the school to provide half of these volunteers with tablet PCs immediately, with the rest of the teachers receiving tablets the following year. As of this writing, 250 teachers (99% of the faculty) are using Dell and Toshiba tablet PCs.

With tablet PC usage well established by teachers at Hunterdon Central, the school is preparing to implement a 1-to-1 student tablet PC program. In order to facilitate this transition, tablet PCs are available on carts as part of a pilot program that is helping teachers to explore 1-to-1 tablet PC teaching in preparation for a broader implementation. This phased approach to a 1-to-1 student tablet PC program parallels Hunterdon's successful phased rollout of tablet PCs for teachers.

KEY TABLET USES

Mancabelli reports that teachers are using tablet PCs across all academic departments. While a large number of standard curricular software tools (including Microsoft Word and Microsoft PowerPoint) are used heavily with tablet PCs at Hunterdon, Mancabelli singles out two tools as being especially effective when used in conjunction with the tablet PC pen. Specifically, teachers across disciplines are using IE Ink to annotate and save webpages, and they are using Microsoft OneNote for taking notes and annotating documents.

Subject-specific applications of the tablet PC pen-input have included annotations of maps in history and English classes, annotation of pictures in world language classes, geometry sketches in mathematics classes, drawing in art and engineering classes, and graphic sketching in science laboratories. In fact, the majority of teachers report that they use the tablet PC for pen-input very frequently.

Figure 10.9
One of the 250 teachers at Hunterdon Central integrating tablet PCs into teaching and learning.

RECOMMENDATIONS

Mancabelli offers the following advice to educators who are considering 1-to-1 tablet PC programs at their home institutions:

▶ Visit schools that are using tablet PCs, and watch how they are used by teachers and students in the classroom.

▶ Begin with a tablet PC pilot involving teachers who participate as volunteers. Ask these teachers to write about what they envision doing with tablet PCs, and share these ideas with the pilot group to promote discussion. After this exchange, require each teacher to redesign one or two lessons to take advantage of the tablet PC inking functionality.

▶ Require ongoing professional development during the pilot phase in order to provide opportunities for teachers to share their uses of tablet PCs with each other. Capture this information on a tablet PC best practice website and share it with all teachers to help generate the teacher buy-in that is needed to move beyond the initial pilot. Remember that teacher support does not end with the pilot—a successful tablet PC program depends on an ongoing professional development program.

▶ Before selecting a tablet PC model, give careful consideration to tablet-specific issues, such as the reliability of the tablet hinge and the feel of the pen on the screen. At the same time, do not fail to overlook standard issues such as battery length, machine weight, and manufacturer support options.

Expert Advice

Offer Continuing Professional Development and Support

Mancabelli believes the success of Hunterdon's tablet PC initiative is due in part to continuous professional development and a high level of technical support. While this is important for any technology initiative, it is crucial when deploying a less-familiar technology such as tablet PCs. Each Hunterdon tablet PC teacher participates in two full days of summer professional development and a once-a-month departmental meeting to learn how to integrate tablet PC use into the curriculum and instruction. Teachers can access technical support easily using classroom telephones and can rely on immediate in-classroom help in case of a technical problem. The combination of ongoing professional development and responsive support was a key enabler of a rapid and broad adoption of tablet PCs at Hunterdon.

PITFALLS AND PROGRESS

The only tablet-PC-specific pitfall reported at Hunterdon Central is pen loss and breakage. With the exception of this minor issue, Hunterdon's tablet PC program has proved successful. This is perhaps best evidenced by the fact that 99% of the teaching staff has volunteered to use a tablet PC. Teachers consistently report, through surveys and focus groups, that they are comfortable with the tool and that they use it broadly. Two-thirds of the teachers report that they use the machine for pen-input (as opposed to keyboard-input) more than 50% of the time. Interestingly, the surveys and focus groups also demonstrate that becoming comfortable with the tablet PC has frequently served as a gateway to the use of non-inking technologies in the classroom, including the district's learning management system and web 2.0 technologies. With all of these positive indicators, Hunterdon Central is well positioned to move to a 1-to-1 student tablet PC program.

Looking to the Future

There was a time when relatively few laptops provided an option to include a color screen, a built-in wireless card, or a USB port. Over time, however, these peripherals became common add-ons and later became standard built-in components. Today, a consumer is hard-pressed to find a laptop that does not come with a color display, a wireless card, and a USB port. If history is a guide, digital pens will follow a similar trajectory. The laptop industry has already moved from a time when it was difficult to find a pen-enabled laptop (tablet PC) to one in which pen-enabled laptops have become a reasonably common option. If this trend continues, it may soon be hard to find a laptop that is not a tablet PC. Schools that are currently exploring 1-to-1 tablet programs will be well prepared for this shift.

There are a number of helpful resources available for educators who want to learn more about tablet PC deployments in K–12 education. An excellent starting point is the book *Tablet PCs in K–12 Education,* edited by van Mantgem, which provides information about tablet PC hardware and software, lesson plans, and case studies.

The annual Workshop on the Impact of Pen-based Technology in Education (WIPTE) is another comprehensive source of information (www.itap.purdue.edu/tlt/conference/wipte/). This event covers both K–12 and higher education deployments of tablet PCs and other pen-based computing approaches and offers an opportunity to gain a broad view of tablet PC deployments across schools, grade-levels, and content areas. The workshop has a video track, a poster track, and a paper track. The latter track focuses on the evaluation of the impact of tablet PC deployments; a monograph containing papers based on this track is published by Purdue University Press.

There are also two well-run K–12-focused tablet PC events that occur several times each year and are run by schools that are already using tablet PCs. The popular Tablets in the Classroom Conference is hosted several times each year by the Cincinnati Country Day School (www.countryday.net/programs/technology.aspx). This event is notable for its exclusive focus on 1-to-1 tablet PC deployments as well as for its thoroughly hands-on nature. Participants are lent a tablet PC at the start of the event. They use the tablet PC to experience firsthand how teachers at the school are using this technology to engage students.

Similarly, Hunterdon Central Regional High School regularly offers a three-day Tablet PC Academy (http://central.hcrhs.k12.nj.us/TabletPCAcademy/) for K–12 teachers, administrators, and technologists who wish to learn more about effective uses of tablet PCs to support teaching and learning. Loaner tablet PCs are available at this event for participants who do not have their own device.

Conclusion

Tablet PCs bring even more possibilities to the 1-to-1 classroom than traditional laptops. When the vehicle for learning allows more fluid use and multiple modes for input and manipulation, it's possible for student thinking to occur more quickly and easily. Imagine the classroom without notebooks; with one digital assistant facilitating multiple learning styles; with the center of the classroom shifting continually as students work in groups, learn as part of the whole class, or project their individual or group work onto the screen for all or a small group to view. Consider students taking notes in a participatory way instead of as a rote activity, with interactive notes and diagrams and drawings and personal reminders—and then later being able to retrieve all these notes based on keywords. These possibilities can be truly empowering, promote self-directed learning, and take teaching and learning to new levels. But remember what Dave Berque says— expect even more use than in laptop classrooms once the potential for these assistants begins being realized.

Technology in near-constant use to deepen learning and to allow thinking to occur more readily—it is possible with tablet PCs.

Much of the material in this chapter was sourced from *Tablet PCs in K–12 Education, van Mantgem, M. (Ed.), (2007)*, and used with permission. See Appendix B for full citation.

Chapter 11

THE SHIFT
(WEB 2.0 AND BEYOND)

Introduction

ABOUT 10 YEARS AGO, I was attending an educational technology conference and decided to spring for a $25 luncheon/talk and forgo a quick sandwich. The speaker's bio included a lengthy list of educational credentials both in the classroom and in the principal's office along with quotes of praise for her inspirational talks. It sounded good to me.

Figure 11.1
Students with laptops help teachers engage in The Shift.

She began by saying she didn't hold too much interest personally in this "technology stuff" (Where were we again?) and that she was going to speak to us as teachers. Okay, I thought, let's hear it; I'm a believer that it shouldn't be about the technology but about the teaching and learning. Plus it was all paid for—and meant eating from ceramic plates and using cloth napkins. The details now escape me save one—her quoting the following line of poetry:

> "Little children looking up, full of wonder, like a cup."

I was horrified. She obviously felt that we teachers were the great and important pourers of knowledge into the faces/cups of the little children, who were looking up at us in awe and anticipation. Lower than us in learning stature as well as physically, these little children needed us to pour the knowledge into them, knowledge they could not obtain on their own. We were the controllers of the knowledge, and all eyes were eagerly upon us in our teacher-centric classrooms. Imagine the power. There was the implication of enjoying this, surely, and the beneficence and vital role of being a teacher. I agree with the importance and the calling of teaching and am not disparaging in any way our profession. No school improvement program of any type, 1-to-1 or not, can succeed without teachers on board, and that fact is a thread throughout this book.

What I am saying is that we need to make "The Shift." The Shift: to classrooms that are not solely teacher-centric, with the teacher as lone disseminator of knowledge and the children in the awe-stricken and lesser role of recipients of the knowledge. The Shift: where the teacher sometimes has the central role when he or she explains and coaches and elaborates on work to be done . . . but not always. The Shift: where the learners sometimes have the central role, either individually or in groups. The Shift: where the roles of teacher and learner are fuzzy; sometimes the teacher learns from the students; sometimes the students learn from one another; and, yes, sometimes the students learn from the teacher. The Shift: where sometimes it's hard to know who has the central role, where activities are buzzing along, learning is happening, dynamics are shifting, and no one is "looking up" to anyone as the sole source of knowledge.

Nothing jumpstarts The Shift quite like 1-to-1. Because when every student in the room has a digital assistant, he or she does not have to look "up" to the teacher for resources or ideas—the student has resources at his or her fingertips. There is no distribution or retrieval of materials, no sole purveyor of information, and no firm start or stop to learning because it can continue beyond the classroom into the library, or home, or anywhere.

It Can Be Dangerous

Some find The Shift dangerous. And in a way, it is. It's dangerous to the educator who controls the classroom with an iron fist and wants all the answers on the test to be things he or she said in class, repeated word-for-word. It's dangerous to educators who have assigned the same report on Gandhi over the past 20 years and haven't started to require synthesis or analysis of information. It's dangerous to teachers who physically stay in one place—the front of the classroom—and move only to write on the chalkboard or whiteboard. It's dangerous to educators who don't want anyone to "read ahead" or to "think ahead."

It's dangerous to educators who view themselves as the most knowledgeable person in the room and are personally invested in staying that way. It's dangerous to teachers who haven't paid attention to their unengaged students and keep covering the material anyway, the way they think it ought to be covered, believing students should adapt to their approach. It's dangerous to educators who refuse to read their e-mail, don't use advanced search techniques, and haven't bothered to consider web 2.0 applications for instruction. Of course, you're reading this book; so none of those categories apply to you!

This chapter takes a look at some of the approaches and pedagogies that can work when 1-to-1 is an integral part of teaching and learning. It's for educators who are bold and reflective and concerned about growing and not about staying put.

WHAT THE SHIFT ISN'T

Let's clarify what The Shift isn't.

▶ It isn't students led to a trough and left alone to drink.

▶ It isn't "if we build it, they will come."

▶ It isn't lower standards and lack of rigor.

▶ It isn't students picking anything and learning about it.

▶ It isn't passive instruction.

▶ It isn't work without assessment.

▶ It isn't exactly the same every time you do it.

▶ It isn't grading tests and homework while students work.

Most of all, it isn't easy.

Instruction Remains Key

While reading studies and articles for this chapter, I came across the work of John Sweller and Paul Kirschner (2006) and have now made a shift of my own. I am no longer completely a believer in the power of constructivism (project-based learning, inquiry-based learning, discovery learning, etc.) solely in and of itself. Because of Sweller's ideas on cognitive load theory, I now understand that when completely new learners are taught in a totally constructivist style without the opportunity of guided instruction, more harm than good can ensue.

Much of this has to do with working memory and how much (or little) it can hold and process—as many as seven things and as few as one or two. These authors define learning as moving information from working memory to long-term memory. Project-based learning (PBL), inquiry-based learning (IBL), and constructivism require much searching for information by learners who do not already have a base of knowledge on the topic, and this search process requires working memory resources that consequently are unavailable for developing knowledge to be stored in long-term memory. PBL, IBL, constructivism, etc. are based on emulating real-world experts but, say the authors of this article, confuse the actual research done by the experts of a field (say science) with the teaching of the discipline of science. So, rather than pulling apart what scientific research is and teaching it discretely, constructivists begin by putting students in the role of scientist and have the students research and do the work of the scientists, largely unguided, so the students can construct their knowledge.

The problem is, students are not scientists and do not have the wealth of knowledge and experience that scientists possess in their long-term memories, and therefore can become confused and unfocused by the requirement to research like scientists. The authors of this article say working closely with students who are new to a concept, pulling apart ideas, working through problems, and designing instruction carefully are the approaches that work best.

As I grappled with these ideas and my own shift, I contacted Dr. Sweller, who helped me clarify ideas, even looking over these paragraphs and offering suggestions. In addition, he offered the following thoughts:

> IBL, PBL, etc. are a disaster for someone entering a new area. We all have a limited working memory when dealing with novel information. It is only with the development of expertise that working memory limitations in a given area begin to fade away due to knowledge held in long-term memory. For novice learners, there is neither a theoretical rationale nor empirical evidence for withholding information. It is only with the development of expertise in a given area that the situation begins to change. For more knowledgeable learners, explicit instruction becomes less important.
>
> —John Sweller, July 28, 2008

My opinion is that PBL, IBL, and constructivism still make a lot of sense, especially for today's learners. I do believe they can help students develop problem-solving and thinking skills. However, these approaches need to be used carefully and phased in when your learners are new to a topic.

WARREN APEL: "IT'S MORE THAN JUST AUTOMATING OLD APPROACHES"

One of the most powerful technology-enhanced lessons I've seen used DyKnow and tablet PCs, and it was a lesson that the instructor had done for years just using handheld dry erase boards. The technology didn't create a new lesson—it allowed him to make his existing lesson more interactive, faster, more efficient, more easily shared, and more easily saved.

I've also seen stoic lecturers turn their old transparency overheads into colorful PowerPoints that were just as stoic. They got a bunch of technology and used the same old pedagogy.

So, I think you can have a learner-centered environment regardless of the presence or absence of technology. But if you have teachers who buy into the learner-centered environment in the first place, then the laptops or tablets make it better.

—Warren Apel is director of technology at the American Embassy School in Delhi, India.

1-to-1: How and Why

This chapter was originally going to be about web 2.0, but I began to wonder how long the term "web 2.0" would be used—might it soon become as passé a term as the "information superhighway"? Has it already tipped in terms of use in classrooms and offices to the point where we no longer discuss its newness but instead automatically integrate its applications in how we teach and learn?

Web 2.0 is important and still requires an explanation in general. Gwen Solomon (coauthor, with Lynne Schrum, of *Web 2.0: New Tools, New Schools*) provides great information later in this chapter. In addition, Appendix C contains a table showing possible uses of web 2.0 tools for different disciplines.

TREVOR SHAW:
THE ROLE OF THE TEACHER IN LEARNER-CENTERED ENVIRONMENTS

One major difference that I have noticed between teachers that embrace student-centered learning and those who struggle with it is that the latter view the primary function of education as the conservation of culture. This view puts the content at the center. There are certain books that must be read, certain historical facts that must be committed to memory, certain mathematical functions that must be understood in order to call oneself an educated person, and if we as teachers don't deliver these particular experiences to students, they will be fundamentally deficient as learners. We, as the stewards of knowledge, will have failed.

The student-centered teacher, on the other hand, believes that the purpose of education is the cultivation of curiosity and the development of skills needed to satisfy that curiosity. This teacher realizes that the content is important, but she or he understands that unless we can create a motivating context and genuine curiosity for that content, it is largely inert and meaningless. She or he understands that the process through which true learning occurs is grounded in context, is social, and is uniquely individual for every child in her or his classroom.

—Trevor Shaw, director of technology at Dwight-Englewood School in Englewood, New Jersey

As important as web 2.0 remains, the idea of how and why 1-to-1 is being used by educators for teaching and learning became the new, broader focus of this chapter. So I now include some ideas on how IBL, PBL, and constructivism can be furthered and deepened by thoughtful use of 1-to-1 (this chapter is not, however, a complete guide to IBL, PBL, or constructivism). Also interspersed are interviews with 1-to-1 educators and leaders in our field, such as Warren Apel, Trevor Shaw, Howard Levin, and Gwen Solomon.

I do believe we need these approaches, mediated by instruction and phased in appropriately. I hope we see a resurgence in educators using inquiry-based learning, because the idea of framing learning around complex, learner-generated questions is one answer to our search-and-run, cut-and-paste, change-a-few-words-and-hand-it-in climate. If we can teach our students to think deeply by formulating complex questions, to examine others' questions and assumptions, and to move forward with this approach, our students will have the cognitive framework for whatever comes next. They will have learned to be analytical, reflective, discerning, creative, and thoughtful. The trick is for meaningful inquiry to be the norm and for teachers to guide students continually to go deeper and always to question the question.

TABLE 1. Inquiry-Based Learning and 1-to-1

COMPONENT	HOW THIS IS A PART OF IBL	HOW 1-TO-1 ENHANCES
Collaboration	Students work in groups to assess artifacts, ideas, and information for subsequent inquiry.	Each student with a digital assistant can analyze and assess ideas, artifacts, and information using software and online tools. Students can divide and conquer, each taking parts of the analysis, equipped with the same resources and analysis and writing tools because of 1-to-1.
Journaling while learning	Students grapple with ever more complex inquiries, coached and guided by their teacher, to come up with questions that become deeper and more complex.	When all students have a digital assistant, they can journal their work to deepen the inquiries. When these inquiries are recorded and saved, the students can go back and see their progress and thinking, understanding more completely the process that unfolded and glimpsing into their own learning.
Researching artifacts and resources	Students examine artifacts (primary sources and other material) and locate resources as part of their inquiries.	Having the ability to research easily from their digital assistants makes the research less a planned event and more a natural flowing element of the work.
Writing and presenting	Students create a closing activity in writing or via a presentation to explain what was learned during the IBL work.	Having 1-to-1 means all students can take parts of their recorded journals, plus resources and other materials from their research, and pull them together for written reports or for presentations. When each student has a digital assistant, there is no need to move to another location for the resource. Plus home to school work is possible, seamlessly.

HOWARD LEVIN: "IT'S ABOUT THE CULTURE"

One strategy in reaching toward a learner-centered environment that is supported by a laptop program has nothing to do with laptops, but rather with the broader school culture and norms established in an institution. I believe it's a big mistake to assume that you can use a tool such as laptops to create a learner-centered environment. Schools need to look deeply at themselves prior to implementing laptops in terms of other structures in the school that may enhance or limit a student-centered focus.

At our school, we emphasize collaborative learning in all aspects of the learning process. Students often work together in teams and rely upon each other to build understanding. For example, a pedagogical foundation of our math department is table-based learning in small teams of problem solvers and supporters. There is no overt sense of direct competition between students that one often sees in more traditional schools that pit students against each other, often resulting in a negative atmosphere. A piece of technology as rich as a laptop—complex, with an unending supply of potential uses—is best used in an environment where students learn to rely on each other, to ask questions, to seek advice from each other, rather than expecting the adults in the school to provide all of the learning and all of the information and skills that students need.

I believe the traditional 45–60-minute class that still pervades our country is perhaps one of the greatest barriers to allowing our schools to embrace more 21st-century notions of collaboration and students as independent learners. At our school, our block schedule—where our "short" classes are 70 minutes and our long classes are 130 minutes—opens up possibilities in the classroom that are literally impossible in the 50-minute classroom. This engenders many more projects—in particular, highly creative and complex projects. This move to longer class periods has been dramatically enhanced since we moved to 1-to-1 seven years ago, given the enormous possibilities of the writing, artistic, and creative tools that exist within the laptop. Students can be creative and productive, either solo or in a team, in a time frame that enables these complex processes.

We've had over 100 schools visit Urban in the last few years, attracted by our laptop program, and more often than not these teams leave the school with a greater appreciation of the importance of revisiting their scheduling before implementing 1-to-1 laptops in their schools.

In sum, my advice to schools considering moving to a 1-to-1 program or schools simply desiring to move to a much more student-centered, project-based curriculum is that they must look at their schedules first and foremost to find ways to carve out longer periods of time when students can actually work together.

—Howard Levin, director of technology at The Urban School in San Francisco, California

Project-Based Learning and Constructivism

When having students work on projects and construct their own knowledge, schools providing a 1-to-1 program will enhance and deepen the work and the possibilities. Compare the classroom without 1-to-1 when projects and constructivism are at work and the bottleneck of resources is evident. True independent work can happen when every student has a digital assistant at his or her fingertips and when he or she does not have to keep returning to the library or finding time in the computer lab. Additionally, writing and presenting can occur fluidly because all the writing and presenting applications are immediately available to every student.

TABLE 2. PBL, Constructivism, and 1-to-1

COMPONENT	HOW THIS IS A PART OF PBL	HOW 1-TO-1 ENHANCES
Collaboration	Students work in groups to research and solve problems and work on projects.	Each student has a digital assistant for journaling, researching, recording, and developing and sharing ideas— no need to move to other locations, as collaboration can happen in any location at any time.
Research	Students use their digital assistants to find resources, primary source material, and other information to support their project and goals.	With his or her own digital assistant, each student can research during school or at home or other locations and have access to the same materials equally.
Writing and presenting	Students describe their work in writing, via audio, as video, as a presentation, or using other media according to the requirement, so they can demonstrate their understanding, growth, learning, and findings.	When each student has a laptop or tablet, he or she has all the tools and resources to create, edit, revise, and present what has been learned to other students, the rest of the class, or any group. Additionally, the laptop or tablet can create an electronic record of the findings or closing presentation or document, which can be shared or become part of a class or school portfolio of completed work.

GWEN SOLOMON ON WEB 2.0:
WHAT'S THE SIGNIFICANCE FOR TEACHING AND LEARNING?

What is web 2.0? On one level, it's about the free new tools like blogs, wikis, photo/video sharing, and social networking that people are talking about and that many are using already. On another level, it's about a real change in what we can do, how we learn and connect with people, and how we keep pace with a globalized world.

What does it mean for education? These tools are changing how people, including our students, interact with information and others. The changing nature of information and the new ways our students understand and make sense of the world signal that we need new strategies and new tools for teaching and learning. The challenges that face them in the future will require them to have skills such as being analytical, adaptable, and able to use the best tools for ever-changing tasks.

Why should we care about these new tools and methods? In spite of all of the hype, technology has not yet changed schools very much. But the world has changed, our students have changed, and traditional tools are no longer enough for the task of educating young people for the future. So we have to find new ways of teaching and learning—and these tools can help.

Students no longer just search for information. Now they provide information, too. They can write in a blog and get immediate feedback. They can create, communicate, and collaborate with peers near and far. They can post photos, videos, podcasts, and other items online. The reality is that students can control the tools of production and publication and avoid gatekeepers. The tools are democratizing.

Using some of these tools, educators are also changing the ways that they learn and prepare, and they create their own models of professional development. For example, they can gain the benefits of a community of practice and on-demand learning, approaches that are respectful of educators' time and learning preferences.

The impact of these changes and the web 2.0 experience can be the catalyst to changing the nature of school so our students are truly prepared to live, work, and learn in the 21st century.

—Gwen Solomon, director of techLEARNING.com,
the award-winning website of *Technology & Learning* magazine

An Overarching Approach: CPCP

One of the things to consider when making The Shift is how to ensure that rigor remains the norm. Even though technology has been a facet in classrooms since the '80s or even before, some educators and administrators do not approach technology use with the same rigor and expectations as they have for other activities, and as a result, technology use becomes about technology and not about learning. While this is changing in many classrooms, it is important to examine technology use carefully to ensure that deep learning based on deep thinking is the norm.

When planning and assessing any technology, there are certain elements to consider. They can be abbreviated as CPCP:

C **CONTENT:** The content to be assessed should be the same for a wiki, blog, podcast, or any other technology as for a paper or other traditional activity done by the student. The bells and whistles of technology must not overshadow the content.

P **PLANNING:** Creating a wiki, blog, podcast, or other technology project takes planning and thought, so evaluation of how the students plan their wiki/blog/podcast should be assessed.

C **COLLABORATION:** How the students work together, how work is shared, how they make decisions, how they deal with conflict, how they become productive, and whether they use their shared time together effectively—all these should be assessed.

P **PRODUCT/PRESENTATION:** The final product or presentation, including how it looks or sounds and whether care was taken to make the product free of most errors, should be assessed.

Starting with CPCP, you can customize a rubric to evaluate most any technology project. This can help set the bar high so that no one element of a project overwhelms another and so that students understand how all the components make up the work. If the teacher and learners consider CPCP, then the amazing video with original music and artwork but irrelevant content does not receive a higher evaluation than the content-rich but plain PowerPoint presentation. The understanding that all elements need to work in concert should be conveyed, and it should be clear that the rigor of assessment when technology is utilized in the classroom is not lower than when technology is not used.

Conclusion

How *you* define a learner-centered environment in your school will likely differ from the school down the road or across the country or across the ocean. But what happens in your classrooms every day determines your success with 1-to-1. Teachers and administrators who want 1-to-1 to work continuously, to provide a movement to improve teaching and learning, and to be a vehicle for 21st-century learning need to address The Shift from pure teacher-centricity. There will be times that the teacher is right at the center, times when the learner holds that spot, times when the center shifts, and times when no one is really performing from the center at all. But for The Shift to occur successfully, there's one role the master teacher must occupy in the classroom—the embracer of possibilities and the role of lifelong learner.

Chapter 12

CLASSROOM MANAGEMENT STRATEGIES FOR 1-TO-1

Introduction

THERE'S NO DOUBT that teaching in a 1-to-1 classroom is different from teaching in a room without laptops. If there's a wireless network available and if students have ready access to the Internet, e-mail, and all sorts of student-installed goodies, teachers are bound to encounter some classroom management challenges. Yet, with a little planning, those challenges can be met, and the payoff can be truly astounding.

As always, the best defense is a good offense: if you can make what's happening in the classroom more interesting than what might be happening on the students' laptops, you'll have few problems keeping the students' attention. And that's what good teaching has always been about, anyway: what's going on in the classroom has to be more engaging and immersive than what's going on outside the window, or what's going on next door, or who just walked into the room, or any number of other interruptions and distractions. Laptops simply raise the ante somewhat. The teacher's task in a 1-to-1 environment is to structure projects and activities so that they're challenging, fun, and social—but not so social that only purposeless surfing and random messaging are taking place.

This chapter will introduce you to a number of management strategies used by laptop-using teachers—optimizing the setup of desks and tables, encouraging student collaboration, monitoring what's on the screens and keeping students on task, to name a few. These techniques and strategies will help you build a classroom environment that will be conducive to learning and social collaboration. As John Seely Brown has written (2001), "Learning is a remarkably social process. In truth, it occurs *not* as a response to teaching, but rather as a result of a social framework that fosters learning." The goal of this chapter is to help you create such a framework in your classroom.

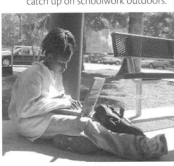

Figure 12.1
Students at Beaufort County School can catch up on schoolwork outdoors.

Before the Students Arrive (P for Planning)

Some classroom management strategies can be put in place before students even take a seat. For instance, you can keep your 1-to-1 classroom running smoothly by

▸ making sure that technical support will be readily available when something goes wrong (and something *always* goes wrong, especially when you least expect it);

▸ placing desks and tables where they'll work best;

▸ determining where laptops will be stored and charged when not in use;

▸ having spare parts available when needed.

At The Peck School, students are told to charge their laptops overnight and bring them to school fully charged. However, Peck keeps spare batteries charged and ready for those students who fail to do this. Spare power adapters are also available in the school's tech support office. Given Peck's school schedule—classes are divided into 40- and 60-minute blocks—most students find they can use their laptops throughout the day on a single charge. If they *do* need a recharge, power outlets in each classroom are designated for that purpose. Some schools find it useful to set up a special charging station area in classrooms, or even incorporate charging outlets into their laptop cubbies or cubicles.

Lessons Learned

Videos from Veterans: Irving ISD

Irving Independent School District has interviewed some of their veteran laptop teachers and asked them to pass on their best classroom management techniques. New 1-to-1 teachers can learn much from these short videotaped interviews at www.irvingisd.net/one2one/classroom_management/cm_interviews.htm.

Just-in-Time Technical Support

I've found that just-in-time technical support is a crucial component of classroom management. When—not if—computers have problems, fixing or replacing them right away can mean the difference between an integrated classroom and a disjointed one.

Peck is small enough that students and teachers are always close to the tech support office. Nevertheless, the school outfits its technicians with walkie-talkies. When called, the network manager and technical support specialists stop whatever they're doing and come right away to fix problems. Teachers and students know they can leave their classrooms anytime and drop by the technical support area and either get a problem resolved quickly or walk back to class with a loaner laptop, battery, or power cord.

Room Setup

Room setup can go a long way toward determining the success of your 1-to-1 implementation. This is hardly news to educators, of course. More than 100 years ago, Dewey (1902, p. 31) pointed out the importance of classroom design when he related his struggle to find desks and chairs conducive to the kinds of learning activities he envisioned for his students:

> We had a great deal of difficulty in finding what we needed, and finally one dealer... made this remark, "I am afraid we [do not have] what you want. You want something at which the children may work; these are all for listening.

Unfortunately, a full century later, we still have many classrooms set up for listening and not working. To get the most out of your laptop program, you need functional desks and seating arrangements that encourage student collaboration as well as teacher monitoring and facilitation.

Most of the laptop classrooms at Peck feature clustered seating and desk arrangements, allowing students to collaborate easily on projects and permitting teachers to circulate freely around the room. The school is also planning a new computer lab for K–5 classes, which do not have their own laptops. Desks are arranged in either a double V or double U pattern, with plenty of space for teacher movement.

Some teachers have found it useful to teach from the back of the classroom, projecting the lesson, assignment, or PowerPoint presentation on the front wall while standing behind their students and monitoring laptop screens. This helps ensure students stay on task and helps the teacher spot difficulties students might be having navigating to a website or using a function of their word processing or spreadsheet program.

Expert Advice

Furniture, A/C wiring, Smart Boards, and so forth are important infrastructure considerations. We've moved toward flat-topped, rectangular desks as a replacement for the all-in-one chair/desk combos we previously had in many classrooms. We're adding SmartBoards to classrooms, and one day we'll probably have mounted projectors and SmartBoards in every classroom.

— Fred Bartels, Rye Country Day School, Rye, New York

Filtering and Logging Internet Use

As Peck is a K–8 school, it filters and logs all Internet use. Filtering keeps students away from questionable sites and provides a teachable moment when students get "locked" from Internet access for repeated attempts to access a prohibited site. Once they're locked down, students have to come to the Technology Department to get unlocked, and we can talk to them about why the sites they tried to visit aren't appropriate. The practice of Internet filtering in schools has provoked a lot of blog traffic and commentary on free speech versus censorship themes. However, at Peck, there's not much controversy; because the school teaches younger age groups, nearly everyone at Peck supports filtering.

Logging Internet use is helpful for determining what a student did to get locked down, and it can also provide a way to see whether students are straying from their appointed project during class time. If students are buying shoes or checking out the latest music video instead of working on a math project, that can be discovered fairly easily if a school or district logs all Internet traffic.

Software Solutions for Classroom Management

A number of new classroom management programs can help you manage your 1-to-1 classroom.

If monitoring every student's screen is important to you, consider the Apple Remote Desktop (ARD) for Apple computers. This program has an easy-to-use interface and allows any user with an administrator's license to view any client's computer on the network. It's even possible to view several client screens at the same time. The ARD can be installed on all student computers; students are told they may *not* delete the software. ARD can be used judiciously, primarily in situations where students are doing independent research online and may be tempted to do a little off-task surfing or shopping.

Similar programs are available for PCs, including Discourse and DyKnow, both of which offer features in addition to remote desktop monitoring. For example, DyKnow Monitor allows administrative users to call up screen snapshots of client computers, lock client keyboards and mice, and black out client screens on command. It can also be used to control access to specific software on client computers, preventing your class of eighth-graders from using their Internet browser when they're supposed to be filling in data on their spreadsheets, for instance.

CLASSROOM MANAGEMENT THROUGH INTEGRATED SOFTWARE AND TEACHER TRAINING MODELS

Bruce Montgomery of Michigan's Freedom to Learn (FTL) laptop program (see Chapter 3) reports that Michigan has contracted with several professional development providers to offer teachers ongoing training in technology integration and classroom management techniques. These programs include the following:

NTeQ Model (www.nteq.com): Integrating Computer Technology into the Classroom. In this program, FTL teachers receive systematic skill development training in specific technology integration techniques. The NTeQ model focuses on student-centered, problem-based teaching and learning. "Supercoaches" serve as statewide trainers of the NTeQ model and share their technology expertise with FTL teachers.

The ATA Technology Academy (www.macul.org/ata/). This team-based program focuses on curriculum integration of technology, especially in individual school buildings. ATA has developed four special workshops to help FTL teachers and media specialists with the integration process.

Bringing the Wandering Sheep Back to the Fold

A typical challenge for 1-to-1 teachers is dealing with Internet "wanderers." No matter how engaging, social, and fun your lessons and projects may be, students with a live Internet connection will still be tempted to drift off to parts unknown. This can be dealt with in several ways.

At the 2004 Lausanne Laptop Institute, I learned a terrific technique called "Stick 'em Up." Dan Hudkins of the Harker School in San Jose, California, told us that whenever Harker teachers begin to suspect that their students' attention (and browsers) are wandering, they simply pull out their five-fingered six-shooter and say, "Stick 'em up!" Students must immediately put their hands in the air, allowing the teacher to walk around and check screens. Students who hesitate to raise their hands are checked more thoroughly. Judiciously used, this can help you identify and deal with those incorrigible Internet free rangers.

A similar and less punitive technique is "lids down," in which the teacher simply tells students to put the lids of their laptops down. Other teachers use the "fist rule." Students are instructed to lower their computer screens to about fist height—too low to look at without a lot of obvious scrunching down, but not totally closed. This method isn't entirely foolproof, as Cheryl Brockman of the St. Paul Academy and Summit School in St. Paul, Minnesota, reports (personal communication, January 21, 2006):

> In the beginning, we would try to be kind and ask the students to 'lower their lids.' Most would, but eventually those little hands were able to sneak back under a fairly low lid and begin typing on something rather 'non-academic.' Now, we say 'lids down and I need to hear the click,' so that we can be sure that all lids are completely closed.

Speak Less, Facilitate More

Active, student-centered teaching and learning offers its own built-in classroom management benefits. When students know what to expect and what's expected of them, more work can be accomplished.

In my tech class at Peck, students knew the structure of every session. We started the day by discussing what we're going to do, I answered any questions, and then I sent students off to do the work. I circulated during the class period, observing and interceding as needed. At the end of class, we usually got back together as a group to discuss what we'd done.

In the lower grades, basic skills are stressed in the beginning. I walked around and viewed students' work and checked that they saved their work to the right location and under the right name. Students knew that if they didn't listen carefully at the start of class, they wouldn't get their hands on their laptops as quickly. So they had a strong incentive to be on task right from the beginning. Taking advantage of students' inherent motivation to use the technology helps to get them to the learning and thinking more quickly.

Training Students on Laptop Care, Procedures, and Expectations

Students need to be given some training on the proper care and feeding of their equipment: how to charge the batteries, how to carry laptops back and forth to school, how to lock them up, what to do when something goes wrong, and so forth. A good laptop orientation session at the beginning of the year, reinforced with a refresher course during the middle of the year, will help ensure the computers are properly maintained.

Lessons Learned

Loaners That Aren't Cool

Every year Peck holds a few "loaner" laptops in reserve just in case students lose or damage the computer they've been issued. These older laptops aren't nearly as cool as the sleek, beautiful iBooks that all seventh- and eighth-grade students get at the start of the year. Instead, they're clunky, heavy clamshells, fully functional but totally lacking the cachet of iBooks. These clunky loaners provide students with a strong incentive to take good care of their laptops.

The Peck School spends a lot of time teaching students how to put laptops into their cases and lock them securely in the cubbies. Students are told to carry their laptops *in their cases* whenever they're walking *anywhere*—between classes, to the bus stop, at home, *anywhere*. Even in the classroom, carrying a laptop for any distance without its case is a recipe for disaster. As we've already noted, many schools have opted to use always-on cases to help prevent damage.

Policies and Consequences

It's the nature of students to test the boundaries that adults set for them. Rules for school computer usage are no exception. Students will push the envelope with their laptops just as they will with respect to the rules governing any other school property or program. It's important to plan for these transgressions and have specific policies and consequences in place.

You should have an Acceptable Use Policy that describes what everyone in your school or district may or may not do with regard to computers. Peck's LARK agreement, which states that all student computer usage must be **L**egal, **A**ppropriate, **R**esponsible, and **K**ind, is covered in Chapter 8. Students are required to sign the LARK agreement as well as a full AUP, which goes into even more depth on these elements of appropriate technology use. The consequences for failure to observe the LARK rules range from a stern warning, to loss of computer privileges, to suspension, to expulsion from school.

The Best Defense...

Designing lessons specifically for the 1-to-1 classroom and making these activities and projects fun, absorbing, and interactive will head off the vast majority of classroom management challenges. Thoughtful curricular design and regular, ongoing reflection on student responses and performance are always the best ways to ensure effective teaching and learning.

Millennials who are interested in the work they're doing and invested in the project at hand are far more likely to stay on task. The wise teacher plans ahead and uses multiple classroom management strategies to keep students engaged. In this regard, teaching in a 1-to-1 classroom is no different from teaching in a non-laptop classroom. Reflective, well-planned teaching always wins out in the end.

Chapter 13

TEACHING WITH LAPTOPS—
A MODEL LESSON

Introduction

STUDENTS WITH 24/7 ACCESS to a digital assistant benefit in many ways. They can complete schoolwork both in class and at home. Their research, writing, calculations, presentations, and problem solving are likely to be better organized, more thorough, and more polished. The work they do is more readily available for timely and useful formative assessment. Given the comfort level with technology that is typical of this multitasking generation of millennials, it makes perfect sense for schools to provide students with the best tools available for the work they need to do.

Figure 13.1
Students work on their laptops at Whitfield School.

Where investment in laptops really pays off is in the daily work of the classroom that teachers and students engage in together. When a teacher embraces 1-to-1 and works it into every aspect of the curriculum, new worlds of learning open up in ways never before imagined. Technology as a means to deepen and enhance every aspect of instruction—the vision that so many of us have had for so many years—is finally within reach. However, integrating laptops into day-to-day schoolwork is neither automatic nor easy. Teachers need both time and guidance to assimilate and experiment with new techniques and approaches before they can become fully competent and confident in a 1-to-1 environment.

Early in my education career, I worked for the Fieldston School in Riverdale, New York. I had no teaching experience then but was hired to run the computer network and provide technical support. One day, an experienced teacher of English invited me to visit her classroom. When I arrived, they were discussing *Huckleberry Finn*. I remember sitting spellbound as she led the discussion, amazed at how many instructional functions she was able to perform and accomplish at the same time: facilitating, coaching, encouraging, restating, energizing, persuading, questioning, summarizing, listening, and leading everyone, myself included, to a greater understanding of the book. It was the first time I was made fully aware of what a master teacher can do in the classroom.

Teachers may worry that this kind of intuitive rapport with their students will only be made more difficult when everything gets mediated through technology. But my experience at Peck, as well as the experience of the other 1-to-1 pioneers interviewed for this book, has proved to me that this kind of teaching is eminently possible in a 1-to-1 classroom. With reflective practice and support, teachers can learn to be more engaging and masterful than ever before.

When I worked at Fieldston, I saw many examples of fine teaching. Even in those class-rooms where the teacher was in front and students faced forward, the learning environment did not *feel* teacher-centered. Every student voice had validity and authority and contributed something to the discussion. Teachers were unafraid to shift roles—from authority, to witness, to facilitator, to learner, and back again—at any point in the discussion. It's this flexibility of approach that's crucial to teaching in a room full of laptops.

We've all heard the "sage on the stage" versus the "guide on the side" debate so many times that it's become an easily ignored cliché. I would argue, however, that in a 1-to-1 classroom, this debate is stood on its head to a considerable degree. In a 1-to-1 class-room, we're all sages because we all have access to every conceivable fact or resource that we'll ever need. They're right at our fingertips. And in a 1-to-1 classroom, we're *all* potentially guides on the side, sharing what we know and learning what we don't in an ongoing collaboration. The teacher who can embrace these possibilities and let go of the fear of not knowing all there is to know about the technology will be the one to succeed in a 1-to-1 environment.

Rethinking Curriculum When Resources Are Distributed

One of the first things teachers realize when planning lessons or projects for a 1-to-1 classroom is that learning resources are now distributed and don't have to be doled out. This can eliminate a whole lot of front-end planning about who uses what, how, and when. Everyone with a laptop has equal access to the Internet, the school's computer network, printers and presentation tools, and online research databases and search engines. It's almost impossible to overemphasize how this changes curricular planning: there's no more "who uses the reference books first?" or "what do the others do while the reference books are being used?" Instead, teachers and students can get right to the more important issues of problem solving, synthesizing, evaluating, and presenting.

My personal approach is to get students' hands on a project as quickly as possible. The students I teach seem to need less "chunking" than students used to; in other words, they don't need me to disassemble an idea or assignment and have them reassemble it later. Instead, they seem to prefer either onscreen highlights or electronic instructions (sent by e-mail) that they can act on right away. This approach supports differentia-tion in a simple but powerful way: students can immediately tackle the assignment in whatever way works best for them rather than following a series of prescribed steps and waiting for others along the way. Easy differentiation is one of the major potential benefits of 1-to-1, as highlighted in the model lesson that follows.

Differentiated Learning with Laptops

Staff members at St. Thomas Episcopal Parish School in Coral Gables, Florida, know a good deal about differentiated learning. They've invested many hours collectively exploring how this approach can help their students. Students come to St. Thomas with varying educational experiences, learning styles, and developmental readiness. How can teachers reach every student in the classroom when students vary so widely in their abilities and inclinations? Where do you place the bar when you want your school to be challenging but not daunting? The teachers at St. Thomas have decided that differentiated learning—enabled and enhanced by technology—can be a key to meeting all of their students' needs. The following lesson demonstrates how laptops can be used to differentiate instruction and support student success.

Model Lesson
THE STUDY OF LIFE IN ANCIENT MESOPOTAMIA

Elizabeth Cohen, Director of Technology
St. Thomas Episcopal Parish School, Coral Gables, Florida

CONTENT AREA: Social Studies

GRADE LEVEL: Sixth Grade

UNIT DESCRIPTION: In this unit, students work in teacher-assigned groups to research and report on all phases of life in ancient Mesopotamia. Within each group, specific research tasks are differentiated by complexity: one student studies irrigation and farming (the least complex area), another student studies occupations, and another studies laws and religion (the most complex area). Each student is given a series of guiding questions to answer, and the group leader must see to it that each member of the group submits a complete set of answers for the group notebook. Once the group has finished with this task, group members work together to construct a model of an ancient Mesopotamian city that physically represents what they've learned through their research.

At intervals during the course of this project, all students who are studying a particular area (such as irrigation and farming) meet to discuss their guiding questions and what they've discovered. Using a projector, students share their answers and compare them for completeness and accuracy. Information, web links, and suggestions for revision can be exchanged by e-mail. In this way, students become "experts" in their particular area and then "jigsaw" back to their original project group to teach the other members about their specialty.

TECHNOLOGY TOOLS: Laptop computers, wireless network with filter, Internet, classroom LCD projector with wireless access, printers.

TECHNOLOGY SKILLS:

▶ Students are expected to do Internet searches independently, authenticate information, and cite sources properly.

▶ Students must demonstrate independent use of applications such as e-mail, Word, Word tables, and spell checker.

▶ Students must demonstrate that they're able to connect, through the wireless device in their room, to the classroom projector.

▶ Students must demonstrate use of print screen, copy and paste, formatting tools, and draw and paint tools.

WEB-BASED AND PRINTED RESOURCES: All instructions and guiding questions are posted on the school's website along with a few web links to jump-start the students' research.

Figure 13.2
The main page for this project.

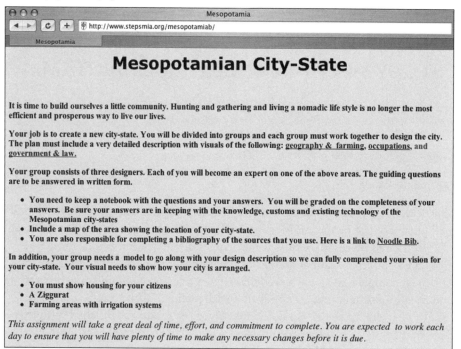

Students are encouraged to use Google's highlighter tool to assist their search. They are also directed to look at other classroom materials, magazines, maps, and books from the library about ancient Mesopotamia.

Figure 13.3
Guiding questions for the "Irrigation and Farming" research area.

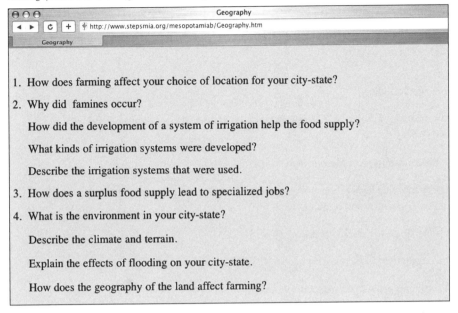

Geography

http://www.stepsmia.org/mesopotamiab/Geography.htm

Geography

1. How does farming affect your choice of location for your city-state?

2. Why did famines occur?

   How did the development of a system of irrigation help the food supply?

   What kinds of irrigation systems were developed?

   Describe the irrigation systems that were used.

3. How does a surplus food supply lead to specialized jobs?

4. What is the environment in your city-state?

   Describe the climate and terrain.

   Explain the effects of flooding on your city-state.

   How does the geography of the land affect farming?

ACTIVITY SEQUENCE

The teacher begins this unit with a series of direct instruction classes about ancient Mesopotamia and the Fertile Crescent, after which students take an open book test assessing their general knowledge (see Figure 13.4). Some of the questions are factual, while others are open-ended; this is another way to differentiate the lesson. While the rest of the unit is almost entirely collaborative, no collaboration is allowed during tests.

As students learn about this topic and discuss the project with their group, they should keep a digital notebook to record their guiding questions and answers. During the project, task groups should periodically come together to discuss these questions. All resources must be cited correctly using NoodleTools' NoodleBib. Sources that cannot be authenticated or are not cited may not be used.

After the notebook is completed, students use found materials to create a model of an ancient Mesopotamian city. Each group presents its model and findings to other faculty and administrators on a scheduled "Ancient Mesopotamia" day.

At the end of the lesson unit, students take a final test on the core curriculum. The test is used as a summative assessment and is generally very similar to the quiz taken earlier (see Figure 13.4), but it's taken with books closed rather than open.

Lessons Learned

NoodleBib

NoodleTools' NoodleBib is an example of online technology that has made much simpler an activity that used to be far more complicated and troublesome for students—creating accurate bibliographical citations. While accurate citation is still crucially important and something that students need to learn and understand, with resources such as NoodleTools they no longer have to type in the references themselves and follow all the arcane rules specified by the various stylesheets. This saves them time and energy and results in more accurate citations.

Figure 13.4
The Fertile Crescent Quiz.

THE FERTILE CRESCENT QUIZ

Name

Open Homework/Outline

Explain the meaning of the name "Fertile Crescent." What does each word mean in describing this region? (8 pts.)

What are the 2 major rivers in Mesopotamia? (8 pts.)

Explain the relationship between the following words: farming, drought, famine, flood, irrigation, surplus, and specialization and trade. (27 pts.)

Why are Sumerian cities called "city-states"? (4 pts.)

What was a ziggurat and what was its purpose? (8 pts.)

Why did Sumerians begin to use cuneiform? (4 pts.)

What was the Code of Hammurabi and why is it important to history? (8 pts.)

What religion did the ancient Hebrews begin to develop? (4 pts.)

What 3 major religions come from the family of Abraham? (9 pts.)

Describe 2 things that Moses did. (8 pts.)

What is the difference between polytheism and monotheism? (8 pts.)

For what was Solomon known? (4 pts.)

Why Laptops Enhance This Lesson

1-to-1 laptops allow all students in the classroom to research, communicate, write, draw, plan, and present their findings simultaneously, using the same set of tools at the same time—no waiting or sharing.

Laptops support differentiated learning because students can be grouped in a variety of ways and can work at their own pace, using their own learning styles. The project is challenging, fun, and collaborative, and laptops are the perfect vehicle for connecting and combining all the individual pieces of work being done by each student.

This constructivist project gets students engaged and excited about customizing their own end product, giving them ample opportunity to exercise higher-order thinking and problem-solving skills. In the end, every member of each group has a chance to be an expert, and presenting to and learning from the other members, leading to greater learning for all.

Assessment Rubrics

Provided here are three rubrics. The first assesses student progress as the member of a group, the second evaluates the student's project notebook, and the third assesses the student's city-state model.

\multicolumn{5}{c}{SKILLS RUBRIC—GROUP PROJECT}
GRADE	A	B	C	D
Working with others	Almost always listens to, shares with, and supports the efforts of others. Tries to keep people working well together.	Usually listens to, shares with, and supports the efforts of others. Does not cause waves in the group.	Often listens to, shares with, and supports the efforts of others, but sometimes is not a good team member.	Rarely listens to, shares with, or supports the efforts of others. Often is not a good team player.
Contributions	Routinely provides useful ideas when participating in the group and in classroom discussion. A definite leader who contributes a lot of effort.	Usually provides useful ideas when participating in the group and in classroom discussion. A strong group member who tries hard.	Sometimes provides useful ideas when participating in the group and in classroom discussion. A satisfactory group member who does what is required.	Rarely provides useful ideas when participating in the group and in classroom discussion. May refuse to participate.
Focus on the task	Consistently stays focused on the task and what needs to be done. Very self-directed.	Focuses on the task and what needs to be done most of the time. Other group members can count on this person.	Focuses on the task and what needs to be done some of the time. Other group members must sometimes nag, prod, and remind to keep this person on task.	Rarely focuses on the task and what needs to be done. Lets others do the work.
Effort	Work reflects this student's best efforts.	Work reflects a strong effort from this student.	Work reflects some effort from this student.	Work reflects very little effort on the part of this student.

SKILLS RUBRIC—NOTEBOOK

GRADE	A	B	C	D
Notebook	Notebook has been completed and shows clear, logical relationships among all topics and subtopics.	Notebook has been completed and shows clear, logical relationships among most topics and subtopics.	Notebook has been started and includes some topics and subtopics.	Notebook has not been attempted.
Quality of information	Information clearly relates to the main topic and provides several supporting details and/or examples.	Information clearly relates to the main topic and provides 1–2 supporting details and/or examples.	Information clearly relates to the main topic, but no details and/or examples are given.	Information has little or nothing to do with the main topic.
Organization	Information is very organized, with well-constructed paragraphs and subheadings.	Information is organized, with well-constructed paragraphs.	Information is organized, but paragraphs are not well-constructed.	The information appears to be disorganized.
Mechanics	No grammatical, spelling, or punctuation errors.	Almost no grammatical, spelling, or punctuation errors.	A few grammatical, spelling, and punctuation errors.	Many grammatical, spelling, and punctuation errors.

SKILLS RUBRIC—CITY-STATE MODEL

GRADE	A	B	C	D
Model construction	Model is constructed of appropriate materials and demonstrates the students' pride in construction. Construction problems are solved. Model is completed on time.	Good choices are made in choosing material and display the students' creativity. Persistence is shown while problem solving. Model is turned in on time.	Model looks similar to descriptions; however, some features are not supported by the research.	The materials are poorly chosen. When troubles occur, problem solving is absent. Model is not turned in on time.
Accuracy	Model is created accurately. It shows many added details that make it come to life.	Model is created to look similar to the descriptions found during research. Imaginative details are added.	Information clearly relates to the main topic, but no details and/or examples are given.	Model has little or nothing to do with the topic.
Research	Bibliography shows many research references used in planning the model.	Bibliography shows some of the references used in planning the model.	Bibliography shows a few of the references used in planning the model.	No bibliography is included.

Conclusion

LOOKING TO THE FUTURE OF UBIQUITOUS COMPUTING

HERE IS A SHORT TRANSCRIPT of an IM chat between two Peck School seventh-graders discussing the question, "What is the future of laptops in schools?"

Student A: watches

Student B: watches?

Student A: that have pop up holographic screens

Student A: touch screens

Student B: oh come on…seriously…like in the near future, do you think that all schools will have laptops and they'll become something like textbooks, or what do you think?

Student A: hmmmm…

Student A: i think that by the time every student in every school has an iBook, we'll have the watches

Student A: i wonder if they'll make edible electronics?

This somewhat funny exchange is included here for several reasons. First, it's to show that instant messaging, despite its rather free and easy approach to grammar and spelling, is certainly not the "bane of the English language" that it's sometimes reported to be. Instead, it's a natural forum of communication for the millennial generation, where children feel empowered to discuss and debate ideas both big and small.

More important, though, it's to demonstrate that the future is forming right now in the dreams and ideas and expectations of our students and that we as adults need to listen to what they're saying and thinking, or we'll be left far behind. This is the reality we're tacitly acknowledging when we speak of "digital natives" and "digital immigrants": children growing up in today's digital, networked environment are different from us. They've grown up in a different place and culture. They think differently, learn differently, and communicate in a technology-mediated "creole" that doesn't easily translate into the language of their digital immigrant parents and teachers. If we hope to understand what the future of ubiquitous computing might look like, the best place to start might be to ask our children.

With that in mind, here are some more interesting and thoughtful responses to the same question:

Student A: what do you think the future of laptops in schools is?

Student B: umm…laptops that have unlimited memory and wireless is available everywhere

Student A: cool

Student A: so pretty much, not having the limits that restrain our use of laptops today

Student B: yeah

Student A: awesome idea

Student B: like all memory could be shared on the Internet, so there's this huge amount of memory that everyone has access to. So if one person has more memory than they need, their computer will give the memory out to the worldwide server and someone else who needs it can have it

Student A: that would be cool…but then i guess you'd pay for the memory you got off the Internet

Student A: and there would be a very delicate balance of worldwide memory…

Student B: well, yeah but 1) we would all pay an up-front premium price for sharing memory and 2) the system would be so tested and perfected that the balance would be preplanned

Student A: wow

Student A: huge project

Student B: also, the system would be broken up into several divisions so that the entire thing was never down

Expert Advice

There is a great need for software that allows students creatively to explore and play with the various knowledge domains taught in schools. We need a Physics Sketchpad, a Chemistry Sketchpad, a Biology Sketchpad. In other words, we need computer-based manipulatives for *all* subjects taught in school. When they've finally been created and embraced by teachers, school will become a much more enjoyable and humane environment for all.

— Fred Bartels, Rye Country Day School, Rye, New York

It's fascinating to see how these seventh-graders are exploring the possibilities of our interconnected, digital world—sharing limited resources and learning to work together with people all over the world. Clearly, for these seventh-graders, the world is already *flat*.

No doubt about it, planning for this new, flat world at the school or district level is a difficult challenge. Schools are goal-oriented, consensus-driven, thoughtful, and cautious institutions not given to rapid change. Technology, on the other hand, is constantly changing, interactive, and prone to 180-degree shifts and early obsolescence. Technology planning, therefore, is an extremely tricky and complex process: the technology has often moved on before the ink on the latest five-year plan is dry. In response, many schools are now going to two- or three-year technology plans so that they can react faster to the latest technology innovations.

While no one can say with any certainty what education technology will look like five or ten years from now, we can still hazard some guesses, based on what's already happening in the field. From this digital immigrant's perspective, these are the trends that seem most likely to continue:

▶ Tablet PCs will continue to proliferate, and other major hardware vendors will enter the fray, bringing prices down. Tablet PCs will become smaller and more durable for the educational market. The number of specialized programs designed for tablet PCs will increase, supporting constructivist teaching practices and hands-on applications.

▶ Handhelds will get larger while laptops and tablet PCs get smaller. A form factor will emerge somewhere in the middle that will offer the ideal weight, configuration, durability, and price to make mobile computing accessible to every school and household.

▶ Broadband Internet access will become available and affordable for nearly all households, eliminating much of the current digital divide. Wireless and satellite-based Internet service will fill in access gaps in rural areas. Some schools today are already broadcasting Internet signals to their entire school district by means of wireless towers.

▶ Instant messaging will continue to grow, and savvy teachers will discover how to integrate these communication tools in educationally useful ways. Network managers will get better at eliminating their noneducational uses.

▶ Streaming audio and video, web-based videoconferencing, podcasting, and other web-based applications and technologies will proliferate in a web 2.0 world.

▶ Textbook publishers will fully embrace e-book distribution models, making back-breaking book bags a thing of the past. Books will still be available in classrooms and school libraries for those who prefer to read from paper.

▶ Eventually, all networking will be outsourced. A utility bill will be paid every month for access to the Internet, as well as shared, off-site databases and large-scale server farms. Pricing will be based on the services requested, including Internet screening and filtering. There will still be a need for school-based tech support people, but only for the desktop hardware, not for the network.

This just scratches the surface of what may be possible in the coming few years, but what a different educational landscape these changes portend!

Expert Advice

We're coming to a time—probably sooner than later—when students will carry their own laptops or portable computers wherever they go. They'll probably be something like today's Palm or PocketPC, but far more capable. They'll carry them like they now carry cell phones and use them just as regularly. Schools will provide network infrastructure—servers, printers, etc.—but not basic equipment. I think our days of providing machines are numbered.

I believe we should be very careful about extending out complex tech plans that require funding for machinery. We should instead put that funding into providing wireless access. Even faculty and staff will soon prefer their own portable machines to the hardware that schools provide.

— Catherine Meany, Boston Latin School, Boston, Massachusetts

1-to-1, Nationwide

To anticipate the future, it's important to have a solid sense of what's happening in the present. The groundbreaking survey *America's Digital School 2006* (www.ads2006. org/main/pdf/ADS2006KF.PDF), by Greaves and Hayes, shed new light on the 1-to-1 movement. This extensive survey targeted key individuals in ubiquitous technology programs around the country. It covered both existing 1-to-1 programs and those schools and districts planning to start similar programs in the next five years. The survey was conducted by Jeanne Hayes of the Hayes Connection and Tom Greaves of the Greaves Group and was sponsored by current partners Pearson Education and Discovery Education. I spoke with Dr. Greaves as the survey was just getting underway and asked him to give a preview of his research approach and focus.

Greaves began by noting the lack of data on laptop programs at that time in the United States (personal communication, January 30, 2006):

> There is no repository of everything that is being done.... Nationally, there are many unanswered questions. Even those in the best position to name laptop programs seem to be aware of only a handful of the one-to-one programs.

Greaves spoke about a ubiquitous computing committee in California that he had recently served on that included public school personnel as well as several major hardware vendors. While each vendor was able to name its own programs, no one had any real awareness of other programs, nor was anyone trying to learn from others' successes and failures. Moreover, no broad-based study of 1-to-1 laptop schools existed for this group to review. This lack of information was the driving force behind the first and subsequent studies that Greaves and Hayes have undertaken.

Even within a state or district, the ways that 1-to-1 can be delivered and used often differ from school to school and classroom to classroom (Greaves, 2006):

> The actual implementation of 1-to-1 schools is highly variable. I went to one Maine school where the English teacher handed out printed assignments, asked students to go to a single website to do research, and then write up a report and hand it in on paper. This, to me, is not a particularly effective use of the tremendous resources that 1-to-1 can offer. The math teachers at this school hardly used the laptops at all. Even in a "state of the art" 1-to-1 program like Maine's, then, it seems that very few people have put together the "people" side of it all.

Another interesting thing Greaves noted in the 2006 survey's early returns are the different ways that schools and districts have started their 1-to-1 initiatives (2006):

> A lot of people want to start their 1-to-1 programs with a full-building implementation, but others have started with just one grade. Unfortunately, if you limit it to just one grade, the school administration often seems reluctant to buy in.

This tends to support his view that the single biggest factor in a successful laptop implementation is administrative support and leadership.

Most of the district leaders and policy makers he had spoken to are focused on the future and where education technology is going in the next five to ten years (2006):

> School districts and states are getting ready to spend large amounts of money—millions, perhaps even billions for a statewide program—so they want to know where the world is going.

He also heard this refrain from hardware vendors. While school leaders and legislatures are asking vendors to ramp up production so that they can take advantage of the economies of scale, vendors are coming back with the question "How do we know you will really buy a million of them?" They point to examples like that of Cobb County (Georgia), where a large district order for laptops was pulled at the last minute because of a legal challenge to the program's funding formula.

Capturing these intersecting interests and perspectives is a major goal of this survey, which asks pointed questions about how much districts plan to spend on 1-to-1 technology in the next five years and what their timeframe for purchase and adoption is (Greaves, 2006):

> We have included items on where districts might start, at which grade levels, what platforms they are considering, what changes they plan in the curriculum, what types of professional development will be included, etc. Altogether, we came up with 238 questions.

The survey was sent out at the end of January 2006, first to the 500 largest school districts in the country, then to 2,000 smaller districts. While the survey was designed to target public school districts, private and independent schools were also welcome to participate (2006).

> At the end of the study, we will be providing every respondent with a comprehensive set of results. They can then do a comparison of their own district with others in their state and around the country.

The researchers also plan to make the report available to state-level policy makers and commercial vendors. A major presentation on the survey results took place in summer 2006. A presentation to the Chief State Officers organization was also planned. Data analysis will be crucial to making sense of all the different responses from all the different parties (2006):

> Once we have analyzed the data, there will be things that pop out. Half will probably reinforce what we know, half will probably be surprises. As we go through and note the surprises, we need to dig in and say, "Why are we getting this?"

For example, on questions regarding the purchase of curriculum content, researchers will need to delve into the reasons behind these purchases: Is it because of increased demand for math, science, and technology jobs? Is it because teachers are asking for more electronic media? Is this demand coming from parents and students, or are test scores behind the push?

The results of this survey have informed our planning for the future of 1-to-1 in many powerful ways. See more recent data in the ADS 2008 report (www.ads2008.org).

So, Why Laptops?

We return again to the questions we started with—why laptops, and why 1-to-1? Why restructure our schools and districts, plan and develop wireless networks, purchase hardware and software, invest in professional development for teachers, hire technology leaders and technicians, and heap yet another huge initiative onto the overloaded plates of our teachers and administrators by introducing a 1-to-1 laptop program?

While every school, district, and state will need to answer this question on its own based on its overall educational mission or philosophy, the most important rationale is true for them all: the digitally enhanced, comprehensively networked world our students are entering demands it. It's a world that demands instant access to information, higher-order thinking skills, and the ability to collaborate over distance. 1-to-1 provides them all—in spades. It's not easy, it's not straightforward, it's time-consuming and expensive, yet it's the most important thing we can do for our children to prepare them for the world to come.

Appendix A

SUPPORT DOCUMENTS FROM THE PECK SCHOOL'S 1-TO-1 PROGRAM

Acceptable Use Policy
for the Use of Computers and Telecommunications

THE PECK SCHOOL PROVIDES computing and network resources for students, employees, and others affiliated with The Peck School for school communication and educational use. Members of The Peck School community are encouraged to use the computers, peripheral hardware (digital cameras, scanners, DVD players, Smart Boards), software packages, electronic mail (e-mail), and software installed by Peck's technology department for educational or school related activities and for the exchange of useful information. However, the equipment, software, and network capacities provided through The Peck School computer services remain the property of The Peck School.

Appropriate or acceptable educational uses of these resources include:

▶ The use of Peck-owned software, hardware, and the Peck intranet for scholastic endeavor.

▶ Accessing the Internet to retrieve information from libraries, databases, and websites to enrich and expand curriculum.

▶ E-mail capabilities to facilitate communication and distance-learning projects.

All users are expected to conduct their online activities in an ethical and legal fashion. The use of these resources is a privilege, not a right. Misuse of these resources will result in the suspension or loss of these privileges, as well as possible disciplinary, legal, and/or monetary consequences.

Examples of inappropriate or unacceptable use(s) of these resources include, but are not limited to, those uses that violate the law, the rules of network etiquette, that are used in a manner disruptive to the work or educational environment or that hamper the integrity or security of any network connected to the Internet. Some unacceptable practices include:

▶ The use of AOL IM, iChat, Yahoo Messenger or other Instant Messaging programs while at Peck.

▶ Transmission of any material in violation of any U.S. or state law, including but not limited to: copyrighted material; threatening, harassing, pornographic, or obscene material; or material protected by trade secret. The transmission of copyrighted materials without the written permission of the author or creator through The Peck School e-mail or other network resources in violation of U.S. copyright law is prohibited.

▶ As with all forms of communications, e-mail or other network resources may not be used in a manner that is disruptive to the work or educational environment. The display or transmission of messages, images, cartoons or the transmission or use of e-mail or other computer messages that are sexually explicit constitute harassment, which is prohibited by The Peck School. It is also illegal for anyone to knowingly allow any telecommunications facility under his/her control to be used for the transmission of illegal material.

▶ The use for personal financial or commercial gain, product advertisement, or the sending of unsolicited junk mail or chain letters is prohibited.

▶ The forgery, reading, deleting, copying, or modifying of electronic mail messages of other users is prohibited.

▶ The creation, propagation, and/or use of computer viruses are prohibited.

▶ Deleting, examining, copying, or modifying files and/or data belonging to other users are prohibited.

▶ Unauthorized copying/installation of software programs belonging to the school is prohibited.

▶ Intentional destruction, deletion, or disablement of Peck installed software on any computer is prohibited.

▶ Vandalism is prohibited. This includes, but is not limited to, any attempt to harm or destroy the data of another user, the network/Internet, or any networks or sites connected to the network/Internet. Attempts to breach security codes and/or passwords will also be considered a form of vandalism.

▶ Destruction of hardware or software or attempts to exceed or modify the parameters of the system is prohibited.

▶ Nothing in this policy shall prohibit The Peck School operator from intercepting and stopping e-mail messages that have the capacity to overload the computer resources.

▶ Discipline may be imposed for intentional overloading of The Peck School computer resources.

Access to The Peck School e-mail and similar electronic communication systems is a privilege, and certain responsibilities accompany that privilege. The Peck School users are expected to demonstrate the same level of ethical and professional manner as is required in face-to-face or written communications. All users are required to maintain and safeguard password protected access to both personal and confidential Peck files and folders.

▶ Unauthorized attempts to access another person's e-mail or similar electronic communications or to use another's name, e-mail, or computer address or workstation to send e-mail or similar electronic communications are prohibited and may subject the individual to disciplinary action. Anonymous or forged messages will be treated as violations of this policy.

▶ All users must understand that The Peck School cannot guarantee the privacy or confidentiality of electronic documents, and any messages that are confidential as a matter of law should not be communicated over e-mail.

▶ The Peck School reserves the right to access e-mail to retrieve The Peck School information and records, to engage in routine computer maintenance and housekeeping, to carry out internal investigations, to check Internet access history, or to disclose messages, data, or files to law enforcement authorities.

▶ Any information contained on any Peck School computer's hard drive or computer disks that were purchased by The Peck School are considered the property of The Peck School.

This agreement applies to stand-alone computers as well as computers connected to the network or Internet. Any attempt to violate the provisions of this agreement will result in revocation of the user's privileges, regardless of the success or failure of the attempt. In addition, school disciplinary action, and/or appropriate legal action may be taken. The decision of The Peck School regarding inappropriate use of the technology or telecommunication resources is final. Monetary remuneration may be sought for damage necessitating repair or replacement of equipment.

_____   _____
Peck Student Signature   Peck Parent or Guardian Signature

Acceptable Use Policy—Student Summary

Note: Students need to know and follow the entire AUP. This section is an overview and a summary; all students must follow the entirety of the AUP.

Use of Peck computers, software, the network, e-mail, the Internet, and any component of information technology installed or in use at The Peck School must be:

LARK: Legal, Appropriate, Responsible, and Kind

▶ Legal: illegally copied or downloaded software, music, or games may not be used on any computer at Peck _including laptops issued to Peck students_.

▶ Appropriate: only appropriate words and images are used and viewed—if inappropriate materials are viewed or received, it is the responsibility of the recipient to see that an adult is informed.

▶ Responsible: meaning that diligent care is taken with all hardware, systems settings (including shared computer screensavers or systems files), and software, so as to prevent damage, changing, or misuse, whether intentional or not.

▶ Kind: computer use does not in any way tread on the rights or feelings of others in the Peck community.

Peck's Laptop Policy from the Parent Handbook

THE PECK SCHOOL STUDENT LAPTOP PROGRAM
LAPTOP GUIDELINES AND POLICY

Loan Period

The computers will be issued to students at the distribution/orientation session at the beginning of the school year. The computers must be returned, with all accompanying cables, drives, and other items no later than the Wednesday before commencement.

Distribution and Orientation

The distribution of laptops to students takes place at the beginning of the school year, followed by orientation sessions explaining proper care of the laptops. A parent or guardian is required to sign for the laptop and other items.

Additional instruction in the maintenance, care, transportation and proper handling of the laptops will be held in classes at the beginning of the school year.

Liability

The laptop is issued to the student who, with his or her parents or legal guardians, is the only authorized user of that computer. Although each student accepts responsibility for the care and use of the laptop, the laptop remains the sole property of the Peck School.

The Peck School owns licenses for the software installed on the laptop. Under no circumstances may any of this software be transferred to any other computer except under the direction of the Technology Department.

The Peck School purchases an extended warranty contract on all laptops. However, in the event of damage or negligence to the laptop determined by our Apple warranty provider to not be due to normal wear and tear, parents will be charged a portion of the required repair.

Case

The laptop must always be transported in a case approved by the Technology Department. It must be purchased from or issued by the Tech Department, and students must keep the original luggage tag on the case. Students may personalize this bag any way they wish.

Daily Use

Students are expected to arrive at school every day with their laptop fully charged.

Network Access

Use of the Peck network is governed by the Peck School Acceptable Use Policy.

Students have a personal folder on the server accessible only to them and the Technology Department. They also have access to group folders shared by other students or teachers.

Web Access—E-mail Access

Homework assignments are located on Peck's e-mail system. FirstClass e-mail software is installed on student laptop computers.

There is also a web version of e-mail, which should be used only when the laptop or home computer is not available, and is accessed by clicking on PeckNet.

Sports policy

A student may not take his or her laptop to away games. The student or his/her parents must make plans to transport it home.

Batteries, power adapters

Loaner batteries and power adapters will be available in the CT lab help desk. A student may borrow a battery during the day at any time by signing it out. It must be returned at the end of the day. No one may take a battery from the charger without signing it out first.

A student may sign out a power adapter to borrow from the CT lab help desk.

Any batteries or power adapters not returned will be charged to parents.

Care

Laptops should not be left in temperatures below 35 degrees or above 90 degrees.

Food, drinks, or pets should not be near the laptop to avoid damage.

Rain, wet hands, and high humidity are risky to laptops and should be avoided.

Security

The laptop should be with the student or locked in his or her locker in the CT building at all times. Unattended laptops will be "kidnapped" by faculty and taken to the Upper School Office.

Students should always guard their laptop closely. It must not be left on car seats, on benches, or anywhere that might be tempting to others.

Students who use public transportation will transport the computer inside the school-provided backpack. The computer must stay in the backpack until the student arrives home safely.

Internet and Printer Use at Home

The Technology Department will help you get your laptop to work from home to access the Internet and/or your home printer. See the Technology Department if you need this assistance and be sure to bring in any CDs or any other materials from your printer or Internet provider.

Flashcards

Parents may purchase USB flashcards which fit into the port of any newer computer, and which allow saving of files, through CDW-G. The cost for a 256 MB flashcard is $27.99; a 512 MB flashcard is $49.99. There is also a shipping cost of $5.30.

Loaner Laptops

Should the laptop become inoperable, students may come to the CT Computer Lab and borrow a loaner while their laptops are being repaired.

Backing Up

Students are responsible for backing up their personal files to Peck's computer network. Server files are backed up and saved on tape every night.

Troubleshooting

Students should report any laptop problems right away to the teacher in the class or to the Technology Department.

Damage

All physical damage to the laptop must be reported immediately to a responsible adult—either at home or at school. It then must be reported to the Technology Department as soon as possible. The Technology Department will arrange for repair and a loaner as needed.

Damages not covered by our Apple warranty will be partly charged to parents.

Software/Printing Problems

Students should see the Technology Department with any software, printing, or other problems.

TO ACCESS PECK SCHOOL E-MAIL FOR 5–8 HOMEWORK ASSIGNMENTS AND THE TESTS AND MAJOR WORKS CALENDARS

All homework for Grade 5 through Grade 8 students is accessible from student e-mail. Students do the following:

1. Doubleclick to access e-mail. Type your ID and password.

2. Doubleclick on the folder for the subject, e.g., math.

3. Doubleclick to see homework assignments.

There is also a calendar for tests and major work, which students may view from their e-mail desktops by doubleclicking on the calendar.

Parents may access the same class assignments and tests and major work calendars from The Peck School website.

Seventh-Grade Laptop Program—FAQ (Frequently Asked Questions)

Note: This FAQ form is for new seventh-graders getting laptops for the first time.

Congratulations. Being given a laptop computer means we think you are ready for this responsibility. We expect using a laptop will be very helpful for studying, organizing, and learning.

Q: When do I receive my Peck Laptop?

A: You will receive your Peck-issued laptop computer on the second day of school, Friday, September 9, for use in school. We'll also have sessions about using and caring for your laptop.

Q: What do my parents have to do in order for me to get my laptop?

A: Your parents need to provide you with a check for $165 for the first day of school. They (and you) also have to sign the green assessment sheet and the Peck Acceptable Use Policy for you to return the next day.

Q: What if I can't purchase the case the first day?

A: You need to purchase the case to get your laptop, so you won't have a laptop right away. Once you can purchase the case, you will get your laptop. It's really important the laptop be transported in the proper case.

Q: May I use my own case?

A: No, you have to use the case your parents will purchase for you. We have investigated cases and have found that the one you are purchasing is the best and minimizes possible damage.

Q: May I use the case from my brother/sister/friend who graduated from Peck and had a Peck-issued case?

A: Yes, you may use that case if you have it. You must bring it to Peck the first day of school.

Q: May I decorate my case?

A: Yes, it's yours, go ahead and decorate it. Of course, be sure there is nothing inappropriate or offensive about how you decorate the case.

Q: Who owns the laptop?

A: Peck School owns the laptop computer, not you and not your parents. It is therefore very important that you take good care of it, leave the tags in place, don't damage it or write on it, as it doesn't actually belong to you.

Q: May I take the laptop home?

A: Yes, once the two forms (green assessment sheet and Peck Acceptable Use Policy) are signed, you will be able to take your laptop home. It's important that you have these forms signed first, however, so until the forms are signed, your laptop will stay at Peck.

Q: May I access the Internet and my printer at home with my laptop?

A: If you want to use the computer for the Internet and your printer at home, try first to install the correct software and see if you can make it work. If you have any problems with this, come to Mrs. Livingston and Mrs. Maguire's office for help. Be sure to bring any CDs, manuals, and the name and model of your printer, or the name of your Internet provider.

Q: What do I do if my laptop doesn't work or is damaged?

A: See the Tech Department as soon as possible. It's important not to delay as one problem can lead to another if not solved right away. If your computer is damaged, we will try to fix it or send it out for repair. If it needs to be repaired, we will loan you a computer to use until it's returned.

Q: May I put games or software on the laptop?

A: Any games, software, or music that you have legally purchased may be put on your laptop. However, if anything you install causes the computer to not function, your computer may have to be reformatted. This means all files will be lost. So take care that you don't install too many files or software programs, as you could fill up the hard drive or cause problems.

Q: How do I carry my laptop?

A: Always carry your laptop in its case, even when at home. The hinge on the laptop can become damaged if you carry it open, and the risk of tripping or dropping the computer exists if you don't have it in the case.

Q: Where do I keep my laptop at school?

A: At school, you will use your laptop for nearly all your classes. For any classes not requiring your laptop, or during lunch, you must store your laptop in your cubby and thread the cable/lock we will give you through the handle of your laptop case and through the loop affixed to your cubby, and lock the lock. If you do not do this, you run the risk of having your laptop *"kidnapped"* by Peck faculty or administrators. We do this to make the point that you must be responsible for the laptop and never leave it unattended or unlocked.

Q: Is there anything special I should do with my laptop at home?

A: Just be sure you plug it in overnight so you come to Peck with a fully charged battery. Also, you should always print your papers from home to eliminate the early morning "bottleneck" at Peck printers.

Q: **What else should I know or read?**

A: You and your parents should thoroughly read the Technology Appendix that will be given to you the first day of school. There is an entire section about the laptop program. This appendix also contains the Peck Acceptable Use Policy, which you and your parents must sign and understand.

Q: **How long do I have my laptop?**

A: The laptop is yours to use during seventh and eighth grade at Peck. Over the summer, we collect the computers and reformat them. Once school starts up again, you will get your laptop back.

Q: **What if I have any other questions or problems with my laptop?**

A: Come by the office where Mrs. Maguire and Mrs. Livingston are in the lower floor of CT. We are there every recess and somewhere around the school (fixing computers) every day. You can also send an e-mail to Tech Support or to Mrs. Livingston.

THE PECK SCHOOL LAPTOP PROGRAM—ASSESSMENT

SCHOOL YEAR: 2005–2006

Inventory Info			Student Info	
iBook #	701		Student Last Name	sample
serial #	UV32204DNDF		Student First Name	sample
			Lock #	26
security #	USF81113		Lock Combination	xxx-xxx
			Cubby #	28

Items and Condition (Please Circle)

Top Case: Excellent   OK   Poor/Explain: _____

Bottom Case: Excellent   OK   Poor/Explain: _____

Screen: Excellent   OK   Poor/Explain: _____

Keyboard: Excellent   OK   Poor/Explain: _____

Power Port: Excellent   OK   Poor/Explain: _____

Trackpad: Excellent   OK   Poor/Explain: _____

Other: Excellent   OK   Poor/Explain: _____

I hereby accept responsibility for the care of this laptop computer. If it is damaged or lost while in my care, I understand that I may be charged for its repair or replacement.

Student Signature: _____   Date: _____

Parent Signature: _____   Date: _____

Tech Dept. Signature: _____   Date: _____

JUMP TO INVENTORY

Appendix B
REFERENCES AND RESOURCES

Literature

Apple Learning Interchange, and the George Lucas Educational Foundation. (n.d.). The Maine Learning Technology Initiative: www.state.me.us/mlte/ *The Maine idea: A computer for every lap*. Retrieved January 15, 2005, from http://ali.apple.com/ali_sites/glefli/exhibits/1001165/

Barrios, T. (2004, March 22). *Laptops for learning: Final report and recommendations of the Laptops for Learning Task Force*. Retrieved December 21, 2005, from University of South Florida, Educational Technology Clearing House website: http://etc.usf.edu/L4L/Cover.pdf

Bransford, J., Brown, A., & Cocking, R. (2000). *How people learn: Brain, mind, experience, and school. Committee on Developments in the Science of Learning*. Washington, DC: National Academy Press.

Bransford, J. D., Sherwood, R. D., Hasselbring, T. S., Kinzer, C. K., & Williams, S. M. (1990). Anchored instruction: Why we need it and how technology can help. In Nix, D., and Spiro, R. (Eds.), *Cognition, education, and multimedia*. Hillsdale, NY: Lawrence Erlbaum.

Britto, J., Fish, T., & Throckmorton, A. (2002). *Leadership and technology at independent schools: A handbook for school leaders in administration, technology, and academics*. Washington, DC: National Association of Independent Schools.

Brown, J. S., Collins, A., & Duguid, P. (1989). Situated cognition and the culture of learning. *Educational Researcher, 18* (1), pp. 32–41.

Brown, J. S. (2001). *Learning in the digital age*. Paper presented at the Forum for the Future of Higher Education, Aspen, CO. Retrieved January 21, 2006, from www.educause.edu/ir/library/pdf/ffpiu015.pdf

Cloutier, M. & Gomes, E. *Maine IS Technology. Leading to Change: Technology as a Tool for 21st Century Learning*. Retrieved January 2, 2006: www.state.me.us/newsletter/backissues/nov2000/leading_to_change.htm

Cognition and Technology Group at Vanderbilt. (1990). Anchored instruction and its relationship to situated cognition. *Educational Researcher, 19* (5), pp. 2–10.

Collins, J. (2001). *Good to great: Why some companies make the leap . . . and others don't.* pp. 152–3. New York: Harper Collins.

Cuban, L. (2001). *Oversold and underused: Computers in the classroom.* Cambridge, MA: Harvard University Press.

Darling-Hammond, L., & Bransford, J. (2005). *Preparing teachers for a changing world: What teachers should learn and be able to do.* San Francisco, CA: John Wiley & Sons.

Dewey, J. (1902). *The school and society and the child and the curriculum.* Chicago and London: University of Chicago Press.

Dickard, N. (Ed.). (2003). *The sustainability challenge: Taking edtech to the next level* (Benton Foundation and the Education Development Center's Center for Children and Technology, Internet document). Retrieved January 4, 2005, from www.Benton. org/publibrary/sustainability/sus_challenge.html

Edwards, M. A. (2004, February 1). Fulfilling the promise of ed tech: Laptops spur learning. *eSchool news.* Retrieved January 2, 2006, from www.eschoolnews.com/ resources/mobile-computing/mobile-computing-articles/index.cfm?rc=1&i=35556

Fairman, J. (2004, May). *Trading roles: Teachers and students learn with technology* (Maine Learning Technology Initiative Research Report #3). Retrieved November 27, 2004, from www.state.me.us/mlte/

Fodeman, D., & Monroe, M. www.childrenonline.org

Fullan, M. (2001). *Leading in a culture of change.* San Francisco: Jossey-Bass.

Garthwait, A., & Weller, H. (2004, July). *Two teachers implement one-to-one computing: A case study* (Maine Learning Technology Initiative Research Report #5). Retrieved November 30, 2004, from www.state.me.us/mlte/

Gladwell, M. (2000). *The tipping point: How little things can make a big difference.* Boston: Bay Back Books.

Goldberg, A., Russell, M., & Cook, A. (2002). *Meta-analysis: Writing with computers 1992–2002.* Retrieved June 23, 2006, from inTASC website: http://www.bc.edu/ research/intasc/PDF/Meta_WritingComputers.pdf

Greaves, T., & Hayes, J. *America's Digital Schools 2006.* Available from www.ads2006. org/ads/Report06

Greaves, T & Hayes, J. *America's Digital Schools 2008.* Available from www.ads2008.org

Gulek, J. C., & Demirtas, H. (2005). Learning with technology: The impact of laptop use on student achievement. *Journal of Technology, Learning, and Assessment, 3*(2). Available from www.jtla.org

Hill, J., & Reeves, T. (2004). *Change takes time: The promise of ubiquitous computing in schools* (Athens Academy, Athens, Georgia, 4-year evaluation report). Retrieved December 10, 2004, from http://lpsl.coe.uga.edu/projects/aalaptop/pdf/finalreport. pdf

Johnstone, B. (2003). *Never mind the laptops: Kids, computers, and the transformation of learning.* iUniverse.com.

Jonassen, D., Peck, K., & Wilson, B. (1999). *Learning with technology: A constructivist perspective*. Upper Saddle River, NJ: Merrill Prentice Hall.

Karten, N. (2001) *Managing expectations: Working with people who want more, better, faster, sooner, NOW!* New York, NY: Dorset House Publishing Company, Incorporated.

Kearsley, G. (2005). *Explorations in learning and instruction: The theory into practice database*. Retrieved September 29, 2005, from http://tip.psychology.org

Kim, A. S. (2002, September 6). The whole world is watching you. *Maine Today*. Retrieved January 2, 2006, from http://news.mainetoday.com/indepth/laptops/020906laptops.shtml

Kirschner, P. A., Sweller, J., and Clark, R. E. (2006). "Why minimal guidance during instruction does not work: An analysis of the failure of constructivist, discovery, problem-based, experiential, and inquiry-based teaching." *Educational Psychologist* 41(2), 75–86. Available from www.cogtech.usc.edu/publications/kirschner_Sweller_Clark.pdf

Knowles, M. S. (1975). *Self-directed learning: A guide for learners and teachers*. Englewood Cliffs, NJ: Prentice Hall/Cambridge.

Knowles, M. S. (1984). *Andragogy in action: Applying modern principles of adult education*. San Francisco: Jossey-Bass.

Kousez, J., Posner, B. (1995). *The leadership challenge: How to keep getting extraordinary things done in organizations*. San Francisco: Jossey-Bass.

Kulik, J. (2003). *Effects of using instructional technology in elementary and secondary schools: What controlled evaluation studies say*. Arlington, VA: SRI International. Retrieved March 30, 2005, from www.sri.com/policy/csted/reports/sandt/it/Kulik_ITinK–12_Main_Report.pdf

Lane, D. M. (2003, April). *Early evidence from the field: Impact on students and learning* (Maine Learning Technology Initiative Occasional Paper #1). Retrieved November 15, 2004, from www.state.me.us/mlte/

Lenhart, A., Madden, M., Hitlin, P. (2005). *Teens and technology: Youth are leading the transition to a fully wired and mobile nation*. Washington, DC: Pew Internet & American Life Project. Available from www.pewinternet.org/pdfs/PIP_Teens_Tech_July2005web.pdf

Lenhart, A., Simon, M., & Graziano, M. (2001, September). *The Internet and education*. Retrieved December 23, 2004, from the Pew Internet & American Life Project website: www.pewinternet.org/pdfs/PIP_Schools_Report.pdf

Levin, D., & Arafe, S. (2002, August 14). *The digital disconnect: The widening gap between Internet-savvy students and their schools*. Retrieved December 19, 2004, from the Pew Internet & American Life Project website: www.pewInternet.org

Levin, H. (2005, December/January). Reflections on the effects of one-to-one computing in a high school. *Learning and Leading with Technology, 33*(4), 17–20.

Levine, M. (2002). *A mind at a time*. New York: Simon & Shuster.

Light, D., McDermott, M., & Honey, M. (2002, May). *Project Hiller: The impact of ubiquitous portable technology on an urban school*. Retrieved June 23, 2006, from the Center for Children and Technology website: http://cct.edc.org/admin/publications/report/Hiller.pdf

Livingston, P. (2004). *7th graders and 24/7.* Unpublished master's thesis, Chestnut Hill College, Philadelphia.

Lowther, D. L., & Morrison, G.R. *NTeQ Model: Integrating Computer Technology into the Classroom.* Available from www.nteq.com

MacDonald, J. (2005, November). *School effectiveness: Leadership styles used for change.* Retrieved February 4, 2009, from the Associated Content website: www.associated-content.com/article/14376/school_effectiveness_leadership_styles_pg2.html?cat=4

Macworld. *Cobb County iBook program halted.* Retrieved July 29, 2005: www.macworld.com/news/2005/07/29/cobbcounty/index.php

Montgomery, B. (2006). Personal correspondence, January 4, 2006.

Morrison, E. D. (1992). *Because they cared.* Morristown, NJ: The Peck School.

Muir, M., Manchester, B., & Moulton, J. (2004, July). Maine learns: The four keys to success of the first statewide learning with laptops initiative. *T. H. E. Journal.* Available online at http://thejournal.com

Muir, M., Manchester, B., & Moulton, J. (2005, Summer). Special topic: Learning with laptops. *Educational Leadership, 62.* Available online at www.ascd.org

Nair, P. (2000). *The student laptop computer in classrooms: Not just a tool.* Retrieved January 2, 2005, from www.designshare.com/Research/Nair/Laptop_Classrooms.htm

One-to-One Institute. *Michigan Freedom to Learn.* www.one-to-oneinstitute.org

Papert, S. (2003, July/August). Creativity can be hard fun *Frames.* Retrieved June 23, 2006, from www.papert.org/articles/HardFun.html

Papert, S., & Harel, I. (1991). *Situating constructionism.* Retrieved September 29, 2005, from www.papert.org/articles/SituatingConstructionism.html

Parsad, B., & Jones, J. (2005). *Internet access in U.S. public schools and classrooms: 1994–2003* (NCES 2005015). Washington, DC: National Center for Educational Statistics.

Peterson, S. (2000, January 15). *King of Maine.* Retrieved December 23, 2005, from www.govtech.com/gt/3194

Restak, R. (2001). *Mozart's brain and the fighter pilot: Unleashing your brain's potential.* New York: Harmony.

Rockman, S. (2003, Fall). *Learning from laptops. Threshold.* Retrieved November 29, 2004, from Cable in the Classroom website: www.ciconline.org

Rockman et al. (2000). *A more complex picture: Laptop use and impact in the context of changing home and school access.* Retrieved March 15, 2005, from http://rockman.com/projects/projectDetail.php?id=126

Rockman et al. (2004, April 14). *Year three: Students at center of learning.* Retrieved December 30, 2004, from www.microsoft.com/education/AALResearch3.aspx

Sargent, K. (2003, April). *What is the impact on teacher beliefs and instructional practices?* (Maine Learning Technology Initiative Occasional Paper #3). Retrieved November 14, 2004, from www.state.me.us/mlte/

Schank, R. C. (1991). *Case-based teaching: Four experiences in educational software design* (Tech. Rep. No. 7). Chicago, IL: Northwestern University, The Institute for the Learning Sciences. See www.engines4ed.org/hyperbook/misc/rcs.html

Schrum, L., & Solomon, G. (2007). *Web 2.0: New tools, new schools.* Washington, DC: International Society for Technology in Education.

Silvernail, D. L., & Harris, W. J. (2003, March). *Teacher, student, and school perspectives* (Maine Learning Technology Initiative Mid-Year Evaluation Report). Retrieved December 15, 2004, from http://mainegov-images.informe.org/mlte/articles/research/Mid-Year%20Evaluation2003.pdf

Silvernail, D. L., & Lane, D. M. M. (2004, February). *The impact of Maine's one-to-one laptop program on middle school teachers and students: Phase one summary evidence* (Maine Education Policy Research Institute Research Report #1). Retrieved November 15, 2004, from www.state.me.us/mlte/

Solomon, G. (Ed.). (2005). 1:1 computing: A guidebook to help you make the right decisions [Special section]. *Technology & Learning.* Retrieved from http://download.microsoft.com/download/8/d/c/8dc3ebfe-6849-4534-a4b7-846a8c327874/HP1to1Guide.pdf

Stevenson, K. R. (1999, November). *Evaluation report—Year 3, Middle School Laptop Program* (Executive Summary, Beaufort County School District, Beaufort, South Carolina). Retrieved December 15, 2004, from www.beaufort.k12.sc.us/district/evalreport3.htm

Urban School, The. *Telling their stories: An oral history archive.* Available at www.tellingstories.org

U.S. Department of Education. (2004). *Toward a new golden age in American education: How the Internet, the law and today's students are revolutionizing expectations* (National Educational Technology Plan). Washington, DC: Author, Office of Educational Technology. Available at www.ed.gov/about/offices/list/os/technology/plan/2004/plan.pdf

van Mantgem, M. (Ed.) (2007, 2008). *Tablet PCs in K–12 education.* Washington, DC: International Society for Technology in Education.

Vygotsky, L. (1978). *Mind in society: The development of higher psychological processes.* Cambridge, MA: Harvard University Press.

Waters, T. (2003). *School leadership that works: What we can learn from 25 years of research.* (Paper presented, CCSSO Fall Policy Conference, Indianapolis, Indiana.) Retrieved February 4, 2009, from the Council of Chief State School Officers website: www.ccsso.org/content/pdfs/APF03SchoolLeadershipMcREL.pdf

Weiser, M.(1993). *Some computer science issues in ubiquitous computing.* Retrieved December 22, 2004, from www.ubiq.com/hypertext/weiser/UbiCACM.html

Wenglinsky, H. (1998). *Does it compute? The relationship between educational technology and student achievement in mathematics.* Princeton, NJ: ETS Policy Information Center.

WestEd. (2002, August). *Investing in technology: The learning return.* Retrieved November 9, 2004, from www.wested.org

Wireless Developer Network. *Michigan Department of Education and Michigan Virtual University launch $9.5 million grant program for wireless learning technology.* Retrieved January 2, 2006: www.wirelessdevnet.com/newswire-less/aug392992.html

Zucker, A. A., & McGhee, R. (2005, February). *A study of one-to-one computer use in mathematics and science instruction at the secondary level in Henrico County public schools.* Retrieved March 10, 2005, from http://ubiqcomputing.org/FinalReport.pdf

Web

1-to-1 Blogs: www.technorati.com/tags/1to1

Anytime Anywhere Learning Foundation: www.aalf.org

ATA Technology Academy: www.macul.org/ata/

Case Study Teaching in Science: http://ublib.buffalo.edu/libraries/projects/cases/case.html

Classroom 2.0: www.classroom20.com

Concepts to Classroom: www.thirteen.org/edonline/concept2class/inquiry/

Delicious: http://delicious.com

Denver School of Science & Technology. *Results:* http://scienceandtech.org/results/results.php

Diigo: www.diigo.com

Edelson, D. The Case-Based Teaching Architecture: www.engines4ed.org/hyperbook/nodes/NODE-196-pg.html

eSchool News: Technology News for Today's K–20 Educator: www.eschoolnews.com

Family Educational Rights and Privacy Act (FERPA): www.ed.gov/policy/gen/guid/fpco/ferpa/index.html

Irving Independent School District: www.irvingisd.net/one2one/classroom_management/cm_interviews.htm

Learning in Informal and Formal Environments (LIFE): http://life-slc.org

Maine Center for Meaningful Engaged Learning: www.mcmel.org

Maine Education Policy Research Institute: www2.umaine.edu/mepri/

Maine International Center for Digital Learning: http://www.micdl.org. Formerly: www.mainelearns.org. Now available from: www.state.me.us/mlti/

Maine Learning Technology Initiative: The Maine Learning with Laptop Studies. www.mcmel.org/MLLS/

Oliver, K. (2002). Teaching Models: www.edtech.vt.edu/edtech/id/models/

One-to-One Institute: www.one-to-oneinstitute.org

Plurk: www.plurk.com

Schank, R. The Institute of the Learning Sciences: creANIMate: www.engines4ed.org/hyperbook/movies/crean.mov (imovie)

Twitter: www.twitter.com/plivingst

University of Southern Maine: www.usm.maine.edu/cepare/mlti.htm

Using Cases in Teaching: http://tlt.its.psu.edu/suggestions/cases/

Professional Development Conferences

Building Learning Communities. Alan November. July, Boston. www.novemberlearning.com/Default.aspx?tabid=29

Christa McAuliffe Technology Conference. www.nhcmtc.org

Connecticut Association of Independent Schools (CAIS). Holds a summer technology conference at a Connecticut boarding school. Excellent sessions and opportunities for sharing and networking. www.cais.org

Consortium for School Networking (CosN). www.cosn.org

EdACCESS. Technical conference for small independent K–12 schools and small colleges. Moves every 2 years to a different boarding school. Not about laptops in schools but provides lots of great technical information for participants. Small and grass roots in nature. www.edaccess.org

Florida Educational Technology Conference (FETC). www.fetc.org

Lausanne Collegiate Laptop Institute. Laptops in schools conference for public, private, and parochial schools. Has keynote speakers, panels, and concurrent sessions. Has grown every year. Highly recommended. http://laptopinstitute.com

National Association of Independent Schools (NAIS). Yearly conference. Independent school organization geared toward school heads, but if you are a head and already attending, there are also technology vendors and some sessions that deal with school technology issues. www.nais.org

National Educational Computing Conference (NECC). Sponsored by ISTE (International Society for Technology in Education) and moves to different locales every year. Very extensive conference that has lately held a laptop track. Highly recommended. www.neccsite.org

National School Board's Technology + Learning + Leadership Conference. www.nsba.org/t+l/

New Jersey Educational Computing Consortium (NJECC). Regular workshops and meetings and a yearly conference for New Jersey public, private, and parochial schools. www.njecc.org

New York Association of Independent Schools (NYSAIS). Yearly technology in schools conference. November, at Mohonk in New York. Well-attended and positively recommended. www.nysais.org

One-to-One, One for All Symposium. By invitation only. For existing one-to-one schools and districts. www.irvingisd.net/symposium2005/about.htm (This site requires a user name and password.).

Tablet PC Academy. Hunterdon Central Regional High School: http://central.hcrhs.k12. nj.us?TabletPCAcademy/

TCEA—TX. Computer Education Association. February, Austin, Texas. www.tcea.org

Tablets in the Classroom Conference. Cincinnati Country Day School: www.countryday.net/programs/technology.aspx

TIES Conference. www.ties.k12.mn.us/Conferences.html

WEMA (Wisconsin Educational Media Association) and Brainstorm Conference. www.wemtaonline.org/se3bin/clientgenie.cgi

Workshop on the Impact of Pen-based Technology in Education (WIPTE). www.itap.purdue.edu/tlt/conferences/wipte/

Appendix C

WEB 2.0 FOR
AUTHENTIC LEARNING

Pamela Livingston for Learning Sciences

AUTHENTIC LEARNING TAKES CONCEPTS and real-world examples and allows students to develop higher order thinking and analysis, because learning is no longer about memorization and repetition but about exploration, analysis, thinking, and discovery. Web 2.0, the "read/write" web, takes the Internet from a viewable, passive medium to one that is collaborative and participatory. Web 2.0 is authentic in that it brings learners into the real world in a collaborative way, facilitating involvement, participation, analysis, creativity, publication, presentation, evaluation, and problem-solving in ways never before possible. Students work together, share together, see one another's ideas, and deepen their thinking as they extend their conversations online. Additionally, research on the benefits of students producing work for a larger audience is clear—students work harder, write more, and write better when their work is published and viewed by others.

Along with collaboration, an important 21st-century skill developed with web 2.0 tools is adaptability—as web 2.0 allows editing and feedback and is an iterative and adaptable medium.

An additional web 2.0 possibility not listed below is the use of GPS maps online, which can deepen history and English understandings because actual maps of areas being studied can be viewed interactively. For instance, looking at the Globe Theatre and the proximity of various other London landmarks can help students visualize Shakespeare's times. Mapping Jerusalem and the proximity of holy sites for world religions can deepen understanding of Middle East conflicts. Specific web 2.0 tools are listed with examples of how teachers can enhance and deepen learning with these rich learning vehicles for English, history, math, and science.

STRUCTURE NOTE: There are one or two possibilities for each web 2.0 vehicle and one global outreach possibility. Some also have a notes section of how web 2.0 content that exists online can be used by students.

INTERNET SAFETY NOTE: The teacher will want to monitor work continually that is published on the Internet to ensure that students do not post their full names, provide personal information, or engage with others on the Internet except under teacher supervision.

Web 2.0 for Authentic Learning (by Subject)

ENGLISH

Podcasting

▶ Students create and distribute podcasts in character from novels or plays (e.g., *Boo Radley Tells His Story* from *To Kill a Mockingbird*). This could involve students writing a script in character, acting out scenes, choosing sounds and music and other audio elements, and editing/producing/distributing the podcast.

▶ Students write, perform, produce, edit, and distribute scenes from novels or plays. Students create the scripts; perform the scenes; choose audio elements, including sound and music; and edit and distribute the podcast.

▶ **Global Possibilities:** Students search podcasts from other students, collaborate or share ideas, and reference other podcasts. **Note:** In addition to creating podcasts, students may search and listen to podcasts on the work being studied. This can deepen the learning, offer new insights, and provide collaboration possibilities.

Wikis

▶ Students critique novels and plays on wikis, citing work, and referencing other material. Students view and edit one another's wikis, similar to peer editing but more immediate and far-reaching. Ideal for a wiki as anyone can edit entries. Students will likely want to set up the ability to check whenever their entries are updated.

▶ Students create comparative wikis on works read in class or within a genre, describing approaches and ideas, citing specific passages and ideas from the work, and referencing other material.

▶ **Global Possibilities:** Students partner with another classroom in school, in the U.S., or internationally and write and revise a wiki together.

Blogs

▶ Students create blog entries as they are reading a novel or play, describing the work, elements and importance of the writing, and their reactions and feelings as they read the material. The teacher may start the process by asking specific questions (e.g., why did this character leave town at this point?). Students comment on one another's blog entries.

▶ Students are assigned characters either with the knowledge of all students or without others knowing. Students blog in character, and others comment on the blogs, also in character. **Note:** If identity of character is not known, part of the work is to guess which characters they are portraying in their blog entries.

▶ **Global Possibilities:** Students partner with others in their school, perhaps across disciplines (e.g., a history class studying American history and an English class reading *Huckleberry Finn*) or on the same genre or work—or students partner with other schools in the United States or internationally. The ease of commenting on the blog makes this collaboration ideal.

Video Sharing

▶ Students produce short videos on an aspect of the work being read or studied—a character, a plot element, or changing the outcome of the play or novel and how this would work. Students write the script, produce the video, choose visual and audio elements and props, edit the work, and then distribute it to others.

▶ Students create a commercial for the work being read or just finished, describing what is of interest and why someone might want to read this work. Students write the script; produce the video; choose visual and audio elements and props, etc.; edit the work; and then distribute to others.

▶ **Global Possibilities:** Students ask for feedback on their video from others in their school, around the United States, or internationally. Partnerships or collaborations may result from this outreach. **Note:** There may be videos to find created by teachers or students on the work being read, the era in which the writing is set, or other elements of the novel or play.

RSS Feeds

▶ Students set up feeds on items relating to the novel, play, or stories being read, the author, or the setting (e.g., Shakespeare's *Midsummer Night's Dream*) and then read references to the work by others. This allows reading ideas from other classes and information about performances of the play around the world. The RSS feed may result in a collaboration, discussion of a different element of the work, or question that all may discuss.

▶ **Global Possibilities:** Find out what others around the world are thinking about the work being studied or references to the work in book reviews, magazines, or articles internationally. Compare and contrast with how the students view the work.

HISTORY

Podcasting

▶ Students immerse themselves in the topic or time being studied by taking an aspect of the era and turning it into a podcast. For instance, there might be a podcast of communiqués from the Oregon Trail with different students taking different roles—a child, a mother, a stage coach leader, a Native American—and describing different stops and challenges along the way. Students would write, perform, edit, and produce the podcasts.

▶ Students produce podcast broadcasts on "this day in history," taking an aspect of what they are learning and turning it into a news show similar to what might be shown on a cable news channel. Students would write, perform, edit, and produce the podcasts.

▶ **Global Possibilities:** Students search for podcasts on the topic studied and see if other classes may want to collaborate. They also may comment on podcasts done by others and invite comments on their own podcasts.

Wikis

▶ Students evaluate different historical perspectives and material on what is being learned and create wiki pages. This may be an analysis of immigration from the 1800s to 1850s, for example, with references to websites (Ellis Island, history from different countries), synthesis of the importance of the topic, and a bibliography. Because it is a wiki, students in the class as well as others may comment and contribute.

▶ Students contribute to wikis that already exist on the topic being studied—adding to, expanding, or correcting information from previous wikis.

▶ **Global Possibilities:** Students review wikis by others studying their topic, post on those wikis, and invite posting to their own wiki.

Blogs

▶ Students create a blog about an aspect of what is being studied (e.g., the rise of the global economy), and different students take turns posting comments. This would provide an opportunity for students to interject their own opinions, thoughts, and questions and to comment on others' thinking on the topic.

▶ Students find blogs related to the topic being studied, post comments, ask questions, and invite comments on their own blogs.

▶ **Global Possibilities:** Students interact with other classes or nationalities to discuss the historical significance of what is being studied. Finding different viewpoints from those in other countries would be important to deepen understanding and challenge ideas.

Video Sharing

▶ Students interview one another as historical characters, creating scenes and using props, researching clothing, and including maps to deepen the understanding of the history being studied. The questions may relate to the history being studied (e.g., "Why did you take the side of the northerners during the Civil War?") and may allow the students to explore other aspects and ask "what if" questions—What if you were unable to camp through the winter at Valley Forge, how might the war have changed? Students write the scripts, produce and edit the movies, and share online.

▶ Students act out examples from the history being studied, as everyday citizens with different roles. Students write the scripts, produce and edit the movies, and share the videos online.

▶ **Global Possibilities:** Videos related to the topic from around the United States and around the world may be viewed, comparing and contrasting their approaches and ideas with those of other students.

RSS Feeds

▶ Students set up RSS feeds related to the history being studied or a projection of an aspect of the history being studied. If students were studying the Middle East, they could set up RSS feeds for mentions of Gaza, Israel, Egypt, etc. One aspect of such an RSS feed is that postings from news and other sources around the world can be viewed, offering differing viewpoints and ideas.

▶ **Global Possibilities:** Students track opinions and ideas from various RSS sites. Students may set up a database to record the demographic and economic information about the country where the poster resides. Students then analyze why the person or newspaper or organization states particular views and what demographic, social, cultural, and economic factors could contribute to various viewpoints.

MATH

Podcasting

▶ Students create podcasts describing how to solve mathematical problems or how to understand a mathematical concept or theory. As the podcast is an auditory tool, students would have to describe in words or sounds the problem or concept, requiring the use of verbal counsel and not visual imagery. Teachers know that the value of having students teach others and having only the verbal element will stretch the students to communicate only with speech.

▶ Students create a real-world example of the mathematical concept being studied—for instance, they can design a structure using geometric models and then describe the model as a podcast. The auditory component requires that they use language and not pictures to describe the resulting model.

▶ **Global Possibilities:** Students create podcasts with other students at their school, in the United States, or internationally to see how the same underlying concept is communicated and understood by different people.

Wikis

▶ Students solve problems and explain math theories in wiki postings, scanning in and including mathematical notations.

▶ Students create a project based on a mathematical theory and use words and pictures through a wiki to describe how the project operates. Students encourage participation from other students. Additionally, students reach out to mathematicians through university and math sites to ask for critiques and feedback on their projects.

▶ **Global Possibilities:** Students track visits to their wiki and, using online tools, map which states and which countries are represented by visitors.

Blogs

▶ Students post problems and ask posters to solve the problems.

▶ Students act as historical mathematicians, explaining their theories: why and how they formulated the theories and what influenced their thinking and lives.

▶ **Global Possibilities:** Students find university mathematicians online and ask for professor and student feedback on their blogs.

Video Sharing

▸ Students describe how to solve a problem or demonstrate a mathematical concept (e.g., the Pythagorean theory), making the concepts as real as possible, videotaping the lesson, and distributing the video online.

▸ Students are assigned a mathematical concept and told to demonstrate how this concept works in the real world and to create videos demonstrating the concept. For instance, how maps conform to the earth's contours and how slope can be calculated based on maps. Students may video different hills around their homes from different angles and calculate and explain the slope. They may incorporate online GPS tools to add to their understanding and demonstrate their knowledge.

▸ **Global Possibilities:** Students post their videos online and ask for feedback, including locations of viewers and what math courses the viewers have taken.

RSS Feeds

▸ Students consider real-world examples of math concepts and then receive feeds on these examples (e.g., architecture, the stock market, economic trends, etc.). They then read and analyze the postings, considering how math is an element in the topic and how the article or information used math to inform the reader or to draw conclusions.

▸ **Global Possibilities:** RSS feeds from various locations on topics related to the math project created are compared in light of what underlying assumptions are the same and what ideas vary according to the location. For instance, how is currency valued in various countries, and what other factors are part of how currency is valued?

SCIENCE

Podcasting

▸ Students create podcasts on global warming around the world—researching, writing, editing, and recording podcasts. Students include their own thoughts, opinions, concerns, and ideas on solving ecological issues and global warming.

▸ Students create podcasts in the role of historical or contemporary scientists, describing their theories and interjecting opinions on future uses of these theories.

▸ **Global Possibilities:** The student podcasts are published online, and comments from students around the world are encouraged and tracked.

Wikis

▸ Students create wikis with words and images on solving a major problem through science. Students are encouraged to think deeply, interject their personal ideas and opinions, and include solid research and citations.

▸ Students create a current science times wiki, which comments on current events and the science behind these events. Students include interviews with scientists when possible and offer opinions on what will happen next.

▸ **Global Possibilities:** The wikis are published online, and the students reach out to scientific universities around the world to ask for comments and ideas.

Blogs

▶ Students describe a scientific theory and how it impacts the world today. Students research the theory completely and offer links to other resources online. Students comment on one another's blogs.

▶ Students interview other students, their parents, their friends, and others on current scientific topics and post the interviews online along with their opinions and ideas. Students encourage others to comment.

▶ **Global Possibilities:** Students and teachers from around the world are encouraged to comment on the blogs, and their comments and home states or countries are tracked. Students consider whether there are regional, cultural, or national factors that impact poster opinions.

Video Sharing

▶ Students videotape a park over the entire school year, recording the foliage, rainfall, and other factors that affect the plants and ecosystem. Students theorize what will happen to the plants and why and research what plants exist and factors that can affect the health of the plants.

▶ Students videotape science experiments in their classroom instead of creating a traditional lab report. Students include titles and words to explain their experiment, record their initial opinions on what the experiment will produce, and then describe in the conclusion whether the experiment turned out as they thought and why. Students are encouraged to be creative and thoughtful when making the videos.

▶ **Global Possibilities:** Students participate in an online global science project, video-taping their contribution.

RSS Feeds

▶ Students set up RSS feeds based on concepts from their science classes. For example, for a unit on weather and natural disasters students might set up an RSS feed on earthquakes and get information on earthquakes from around the world. They could then examine the data received and compare it to earthquakes from the past and track current and historical earthquake activity. They might theorize how earthquakes happen over time around the world and whether other factors impact the severity of earthquakes.

▶ **Global Possibilities:** Students track reactions of the scientific community around the world to major weather events and compare how different countries support science. Students may also consider how scientific ideas are portrayed in the news. Students may compare these international reactions to their own ideas and the ideas of their classmates to weather events.

Appendix D
NATIONAL EDUCATIONAL TECHNOLOGY STANDARDS

National Educational Technology Standards for Students (NETS•S)

All K–12 students should be prepared to meet the following standards and performance indicators.

1. **Creativity and Innovation**

   Students demonstrate creative thinking, construct knowledge, and develop innovative products and processes using technology. Students:

   a. apply existing knowledge to generate new ideas, products, or processes

   b. create original works as a means of personal or group expression

   c. use models and simulations to explore complex systems and issues

   d. identify trends and forecast possibilities

2. **Communication and Collaboration**

   Students use digital media and environments to communicate and work collaboratively, including at a distance, to support individual learning and contribute to the learning of others. Students:

   a. interact, collaborate, and publish with peers, experts, or others employing a variety of digital environments and media

   b. communicate information and ideas effectively to multiple audiences using a variety of media and formats

   c. develop cultural understanding and global awareness by engaging with learners of other cultures

   d. contribute to project teams to produce original works or solve problems

3. Research and Information Fluency

Students apply digital tools to gather, evaluate, and use information. Students:

    a. plan strategies to guide inquiry

    b. locate, organize, analyze, evaluate, synthesize, and ethically use information from a variety of sources and media

    c. evaluate and select information sources and digital tools based on the appropriateness to specific tasks

    d. process data and report results

4. Critical Thinking, Problem Solving, and Decision Making

Students use critical-thinking skills to plan and conduct research, manage projects, solve problems, and make informed decisions using appropriate digital tools and resources. Students:

    a. identify and define authentic problems and significant questions for investigation

    b. plan and manage activities to develop a solution or complete a project

    c. collect and analyze data to identify solutions and make informed decisions

    d. use multiple processes and diverse perspectives to explore alternative solutions

5. Digital Citizenship

Students understand human, cultural, and societal issues related to technology and practice legal and ethical behavior. Students:

    a. advocate and practice the safe, legal, and responsible use of information and technology

    b. exhibit a positive attitude toward using technology that supports collaboration, learning, and productivity

    c. demonstrate personal responsibility for lifelong learning

    d. exhibit leadership for digital citizenship

6. Technology Operations and Concepts

Students demonstrate a sound understanding of technology concepts, systems, and operations. Students:

    a. understand and use technology systems

    b. select and use applications effectively and productively

    c. troubleshoot systems and applications

    d. transfer current knowledge to the learning of new technologies

National Educational Technology Standards for Teachers (NETS•T)

All classroom teachers should be prepared to meet the following standards and performance indicators.

1. **Facilitate and Inspire Student Learning and Creativity**

   Teachers use their knowledge of subject matter, teaching and learning, and technology to facilitate experiences that advance student learning, creativity, and innovation in both face-to-face and virtual environments. Teachers:

   a. promote, support, and model creative and innovative thinking and inventiveness

   b. engage students in exploring real-world issues and solving authentic problems using digital tools and resources

   c. promote student reflection using collaborative tools to reveal and clarify students' conceptual understanding and thinking, planning, and creative processes

   d. model collaborative knowledge construction by engaging in learning with students, colleagues, and others in face-to-face and virtual environments

2. **Design and Develop Digital-Age Learning Experiences and Assessments**

   Teachers design, develop, and evaluate authentic learning experiences and assessments incorporating contemporary tools and resources to maximize content learning in context and to develop the knowledge, skills, and attitudes identified in the NETS•S. Teachers:

   a. design or adapt relevant learning experiences that incorporate digital tools and resources to promote student learning and creativity

   b. develop technology-enriched learning environments that enable all students to pursue their individual curiosities and become active participants in setting their own educational goals, managing their own learning, and assessing their own progress

   c. customize and personalize learning activities to address students' diverse learning styles, working strategies, and abilities using digital tools and resources

   d. provide students with multiple and varied formative and summative assessments aligned with content and technology standards and use resulting data to inform learning and teaching

3. **Model Digital-Age Work and Learning**

   Teachers exhibit knowledge, skills, and work processes representative of an innovative professional in a global and digital society. Teachers:

   a. demonstrate fluency in technology systems and the transfer of current knowledge to new technologies and situations

   b. collaborate with students, peers, parents, and community members using digital tools and resources to support student success and innovation

    c.   communicate relevant information and ideas effectively to students, parents, and peers using a variety of digital-age media and formats

    d.   model and facilitate effective use of current and emerging digital tools to locate, analyze, evaluate, and use information resources to support research and learning

4. Promote and Model Digital Citizenship and Responsibility

Teachers understand local and global societal issues and responsibilities in an evolving digital culture and exhibit legal and ethical behavior in their professional practices. Teachers:

    a.   advocate, model, and teach safe, legal, and ethical use of digital information and technology, including respect for copyright, intellectual property, and the appropriate documentation of sources

    b.   address the diverse needs of all learners by using learner-centered strategies and providing equitable access to appropriate digital tools and resources

    c.   promote and model digital etiquette and responsible social interactions related to the use of technology and information

    d.   develop and model cultural understanding and global awareness by engaging with colleagues and students of other cultures using digital-age communication and collaboration tools

5. Engage in Professional Growth and Leadership

Teachers continuously improve their professional practice, model lifelong learning, and exhibit leadership in their school and professional community by promoting and demonstrating the effective use of digital tools and resources. Teachers:

    a.   participate in local and global learning communities to explore creative applications of technology to improve student learning

    b.   exhibit leadership by demonstrating a vision of technology infusion, participating in shared decision making and community building, and developing the leadership and technology skills of others

    c.   evaluate and reflect on current research and professional practice on a regular basis to make effective use of existing and emerging digital tools and resources in support of student learning

    d.   contribute to the effectiveness, vitality, and self-renewal of the teaching profession and of their school and community

National Educational Technology Standards for Administrators (NETS•A, 2002)

All school administrators should be prepared to meet the following standards and performance indicators.

I. Leadership and Vision

Educational leaders inspire a shared vision for comprehensive integration of technology and foster an environment and culture conducive to the realization of that vision. Educational leaders:

- A. facilitate the shared development by all stakeholders of a vision for technology use and widely communicate that vision

- B. maintain an inclusive and cohesive process to develop, implement, and monitor a dynamic, long-range, and systemic technology plan to achieve the vision

- C. foster and nurture a culture of responsible risk taking and advocate policies promoting continuous innovation with technology

- D. use data in making leadership decisions

- E. advocate for research-based effective practices in use of technology

- F. advocate, on the state and national levels, for policies, programs, and funding opportunities that support implementation of the district technology plan

II. Learning and Teaching

Educational leaders ensure that curricular design, instructional strategies, and learning environments integrate appropriate technologies to maximize learning and teaching. Educational leaders:

- A. identify, use, evaluate, and promote appropriate technologies to enhance and support instruction and standards-based curriculum leading to high levels of student achievement

- B. facilitate and support collaborative technology-enriched learning environments conducive to innovation for improved learning

- C. provide for learner-centered environments that use technology to meet the individual and diverse needs of learners

- D. facilitate the use of technologies to support and enhance instructional methods that develop higher-level thinking, decision-making, and problem-solving skills

- E. provide for and ensure that faculty and staff take advantage of quality professional learning opportunities for improved learning and teaching with technology

III. Productivity and Professional Practice

Educational leaders apply technology to enhance their professional practice and to increase their own productivity and that of others.
Educational leaders:

- **A.** model the routine, intentional, and effective use of technology

- **B.** employ technology for communication and collaboration among colleagues, staff, parents, students, and the larger community

- **C.** create and participate in learning communities that stimulate, nurture, and support faculty and staff in using technology for improved productivity

- **D.** engage in sustained, job-related professional learning using technology resources

- **E.** maintain awareness of emerging technologies and their potential uses in education

- **F.** use technology to advance organizational improvement

IV. Support, Management, and Operations

Educational leaders ensure the integration of technology to support productive systems for learning and administration. Educational leaders:

- **A.** develop, implement, and monitor policies and guidelines to ensure compatibility of technologies

- **B.** implement and use integrated technology-based management and operations systems

- **C.** allocate financial and human resources to ensure complete and sustained implementation of the technology plan

- **D.** integrate strategic plans, technology plans, and other improvement plans and policies to align efforts and leverage resources

- **E.** implement procedures to drive continuous improvements of technology systems and to support technology replacement cycles

V. Assessment and Evaluation

Educational leaders use technology to plan and implement comprehensive systems of effective assessment and evaluation. Educational leaders:

- **A.** use multiple methods to assess and evaluate appropriate uses of technology resources for learning, communication, and productivity

- **B.** use technology to collect and analyze data, interpret results, and communicate findings to improve instructional practice and student learning

- **C.** assess staff knowledge, skills, and performance in using technology and use results to facilitate quality professional development and to inform personnel decisions

- **D.** use technology to assess, evaluate, and manage administrative and operational systems

VI. Social, Legal, and Ethical Issues

Educational leaders understand the social, legal, and ethical issues related to technology and model responsible decision-making related to these issues. Educational leaders:

    A. ensure equity of access to technology resources that enable and empower all learners and educators

    B. identify, communicate, model, and enforce social, legal, and ethical practices to promote responsible use of technology

    C. promote and enforce privacy, security, and online safety related to the use of technology

    D. promote and enforce environmentally safe and healthy practices in the use of technology

    E. participate in the development of policies that clearly enforce copyright law and assign ownership of intellectual property developed with district resources

This material was originally produced as a project of the Technology Standards for School Administrators Collaborative.

DATE DUE